SIGNS OF AGNI YOGA
SUPERMUNDANE
Vol. I

SUPERMUNDANE

THE INNER LIFE

I

1938

Agni Yoga Society
319 West 107th Street
New York NY 10025
www.agniyoga.org

© 1994 by the Agni Yoga Society.
Published 1994.

Reprinted 2017. Updated July 2020.
Translated from Russian by the Agni Yoga Society.

Friend, how can we discuss the Supermundane if energy is not yet realized as the foundation of Existence? Many will not understand at all what is meant by this, while others may think that they understand the significance of fundamental energy, but cannot think about it with clarity. It is necessary to train one's thought upon the idea of energy until the feeling of it becomes as real as the feeling about any solid object. We speak about feeling, because knowledge alone cannot provide an understanding of energy.

Even if man accepts the truth that fundamentally there is only one energy, this alone will not be enough for progress—one must also learn to picture to oneself its innumerable qualities. Man's customary narrowness of thought limits his perception of the properties of this energy, and thus limits his understanding. Lofty thinking helps one avoid harmful limitation, but it is not easy to establish an appropriate level of beautiful and lofty thought amidst life's misfortunes, and very few are prepared to understand that it is life's difficulties themselves that can assist lofty thinking. Goalfitness will help one's thinking when the properties of the fundamental energy appear to be contradictory. A blind man may be unable to perceive an event visible to others, but everyone can realize the Supermundane by learning to understand the many properties of the fundamental energy.

Those who think of the Supermundane as the very Highest are correct. "As below, so above." Let this ancient saying serve as a guide to cognition of the forces of the Supermundane.

SUPERMUNDANE
The Inner Life

1. Urusvati knows the Tower of Chun, and remembers how the exterior of the Tower resembles a natural cliff. It is not difficult to prevent access to this Tower. A small landslide can conceal the structure from those below. A small dam can change a mountain stream into a lake, and in time of dire need the entire district can be immediately transformed. People may smile, thinking that organized expeditions could sooner or later penetrate into all the passes. But even before the physical transformation of the area, the power of thought would already have diverted the caravan! In addition, chemical effects can be utilized to prevent the approach of the curious. Thus do We guard the Brotherhood.

Even the most advanced aircraft cannot discover Our Abode. Hermits living in nearby caves are watchful guards. Travelers sometimes speak of having met a sadhu who persistently advised them to follow a specified path and warned them of the danger of proceeding into certain other areas. The sadhu himself had never gone farther, and had been instructed not to provide directions. The sadhus know about the Forbidden Place and know how to guard the secret. Sometimes they may be highwaymen, yet even highwaymen can be trusted guards of a sacred mystery. One should not doubt the existence of an inviolable Abode.

Urusvati remembers the appearance of the passages that lead to Us, and also remembers the light from Our Tower. Many details of these paths are remembered by Our Sister Urusvati. These landmarks are unforgettable and give courage to all, on all paths. She has seen Our co-workers gathering useful plants, and has also seen Our repositories, buried deep. One should see these archives of knowledge to comprehend the work of Our Abode. One should hear Our singing in order to understand the life of Our Ashram.

Thus, We shall speak about Our life and labors.

2. Urusvati has seen many of Our apparatuses. In appearance they do not differ much from those in use elsewhere. However, the way they are used is different, for psychic energy is applied. It has long been known that some apparatuses will operate only in the presence of a particular person, and now there are even people whose organisms can substitute for entire complicated apparatuses. Man is growing accustomed to his inner forces.

We long ago accepted the principle that each apparatus can be made more powerful by man himself. One can achieve a transformation of one's entire life simply by the realization of the Primary Energy. Over the centuries We have become accustomed to the idea that a concentration of energy can be directed to any domain. Energy, like lightning, unites accumulated forces in its discharge. So-called magical phenomena are based on the same principle. In reality, the term "magical" can only mislead. Any electrical apparatus can be called magical. When Urusvati performed levitation or the moving of objects, it was done not through magic but simply by not impeding the energy. The manifested energy was accepted and then projected. It was united with the cosmic energy, and thus could act.

Our mirrors cannot be called magical. They simply increase the effectiveness of Our energy. Many appliances can be found that make energy more effective. Strong magnets could hardly be called magical, even though their action is remarkable. The subtle body and all experiments connected with it belong to science, not to magic. Thus, one should abolish the superstitious use of the confusing term "magical."

Man has always been afraid of anything mysterious, forgetting that the key to the mystery is within himself. One must free oneself from all impeding conditions or circumstances, which are different for everyone. Progress depends upon free will that is directed toward good. The power of good compels even machines to act not for themselves, but for humanity. Thus, Our apparatuses function with Our collaboration.

People may laugh, but ideas do rule the world. These words are entered into the Statutes of the Brotherhood.

3. Urusvati has seen some of Our repositories. Objects of art are collected according to eras, but the collections do not constitute a museum as it is usually understood. These objects serve as a reservoir of accumulated auras, and the creative emanations of their former owners remain in them much longer than one might suppose. If one could gather a collection of objects created at the same time and with the same striving, one would truly see the radiations of their eras. We can study in this way the true meaning of a particular era. Such a possibility is exceedingly important for the psychic sciences. Some of Our Brothers are the former owners of objects in Our repository. Sometimes an object is sent into the world to carry out a certain task. For example, it may be buried in some place as a magnet.

Let the ignorant deride the repositories of the Brotherhood. Let the egoism of ignorance regard Our repositories as the treasures of misers. In truth, each object is for Us a useful apparatus, and can be used for important observations. It is especially valuable to observe the relationship of ancient auras to later emanations. Sometimes a total opposition between objects, or a mutual sympathy between them, can be observed. In Our many experiments with ancient objects, We observe not only with spiritual vision but also verify by the use of Our apparatuses. This is not so-called psychometry, but a science of radiations. Just as you can observe the usefulness of fruits and plants, We can study the language of objects by their radiations. One can thus observe that few religious artifacts have beautiful radiations, for they were too often created with self-interest, and then fell into even more mercenary hands.

Equally instructive is Our collection of inventions. The psychic energy with which an invention is invested puts its seal upon it; it permeates all inventions with harmful or beneficial effects. Let the hands of inventors be pure!

We watch inventors with great attention. We sometimes rejoice, but more often grieve. Our Tower is open to all that is new, and it is a special joy when the thought that is sent by Us has been accepted by a worthy worker.

4. Urusvati knows how difficult is the transference of thought over a distance. Many conditions may affect it. Man is either like a boiling kettle or a radiant discus thrower, propelling thought into space. One should not only control oneself, but should also foresee the chemical reactions that in their contradiction may interfere with a strong will.

We are often reproached about why at times We interrupt Our sendings of thought. Our earthly friends do not realize that during such intervals We guard not Ourselves, but them. We know how to sense spatial tension and protect Our friends who are in an earthly state.

Do not think that superficial methods will produce complete results. The most essential is in the depths of one's consciousness. An impure servitor cannot perform a pure action, and the most sanctioned ritual cannot free him from impure thinking. Thus, many err, supposing that outward rituals will compensate for inner abominations.

The thoughts of the Teacher must overcome many hindrances in space. I affirm that each action must be coordinated with the thoughts of the Teacher; such help is true collaboration.

We have apparatuses that assist the transference of thought over a distance. People would be astonished to see that certain apparatuses that are familiar to them are here applied quite differently. The application of psychic energy can transform the simplest of motors.

5. Urusvati has seen Us in both the dense and the subtle bodies. Only those few who have had this experience can know the tension that accompanies it. Often We make it possible to see only Our faces or hands, in order to prevent shock. Thus you may remember the Writing Hand, but even this manifestation was too strong, because the vibrations could not be restrained. One must be all the more cautious.

Not without reason do We speak constantly about caution. People simply do not understand the significance of this attitude. How many perilous illnesses are caused by the lack of reciprocal caution between individuals! It is most necessary when there is a great disparity of vibrations. Vigilance and mutual care are then required in order not to cause harm.

During Our earthly trips We sometimes transmit Our instructions through a third person who does not know the true meaning of the commission and is only performing his duty.

The manifestation of Our Shield also requires precautionary measures. It is difficult to understand the need for such care. People cannot take into account all the reasons that compel Us to be so cautious, and in their ignorance they wish to experience the strongest manifestations without thinking of the consequences.

Likewise, people do not want to understand the difference between the power of Our vibrations and those of an ordinary subtle body. Sometimes they have seen materializations without experiencing strong shocks, but Our vibrations are of a different intensity. All is relative, and one should give serious attention to rhythm and vibration.

Today you spoke about the fear experienced by plants. If sensitivity to vibrations is strongly developed in plants, it must be immeasurably stronger in people.

Let us bear in mind that Our vibrations will never be forgotten by those who have experienced them, for in them there is joy, but also an intensity that not every heart can endure.

6. Urusvati has witnessed the healing vibrations sent by Us. Their rhythms are varied and not everyone can recognize them. Some may suppose them to be the effect of an earthquake, others may assume that they are an attack of fever, and still others may attribute them to their own nervousness. But the majority will think them to be merely imagined. However, on all continents Our healing solicitude is often felt. People receive help and sense a sudden recovery but do not understand whence came the help. We are not speaking about gratitude, for We do not need it, but a conscious acceptance of Our help increases the beneficial effect. Each negative reaction or mockery paralyzes even the strongest vibrations. We hasten to help, We hasten to bring good, yet how often are We accepted?

The ignorant assert that We provoke revolutions and sedition, but actually We have tried many times to prevent murder and destruction. Brother Rakoczy himself fulfilled the highest measure of love for humanity and was rejected by those whom He tried to save. His actions were recorded in well-known extant memoirs, but still certain liars call him the father of the French Revolution.

People likewise do not understand Our appeal to Queen Victoria, yet history has shown how right We were. Our warning was rejected; nevertheless, it is Our duty to warn the nations. Similarly, Our warning to the northern country was not understood. Eventually, people will recall and compare the facts. One can mention events from the history of various countries—recall Napoleon, the appearance of the Advisor to the American Constitutional Convention, the manifestation in Sweden, and the Indication given to Spain.

Remember that ten years ago the ruin of Spain was foretold. The sign of salvation had been given, but, as usual, it was not accepted. We hasten to send help everywhere and rejoice when it is accepted. We sorrow to see what destiny nations prepare for themselves.

7. Urusvati knows Our Voices, both spoken and silent. One may wonder about the differences in transmission; there are many reasons, beyond earthly conditions, for these differences.

We often instruct that unity be preserved. Such an Indication is not merely a simple moral teaching— disunity is the most abhorrent dissonance. Nothing strikes space as sharply as dissonance. When people are filled with malicious discord, damaging disruptions in space result immediately. Such people not only harm themselves they also create a spatial karma involving others like them. It is dreadful to battle with such newly-generated chaos.

People who bring discord are truly creators of chaos and the consequences of their malicious abuse are grievous. We are constantly forced to battle with them, and it is not surprising that this battle is often more difficult than a collision of spatial currents. Wherever one must deal with the free will of man a great waste of energy should be expected. The power of free will is great, equivalent to the most powerful energies, and in their malice, people can bring about the destruction of strata of the Subtle World. How much the efforts of experienced Physicians are needed to close these spatial wounds!

We must work for unity, not by hymns and harps, but by labor and struggle. Few will strive to Our Brotherhood when they learn about the sweat of Our labor.

8. Urusvati has seen the drops of Our sweat, and knows how painful is the condition caused by spatial tension, without which the work over great distances would not be possible. Every act of cooperation helps. We speak about cooperation not only as a moral precept, but also as a formula that will provide new possibilities for successful labor.

If people only realized in what visible and invisible ways they can collaborate! If people only realized how much they can increase their strength by cooperating with the Brotherhood! If they at least thought about cooperation, which can be manifested in every moment! But people not only do not approach the Brotherhood in thought, they even consider thought about the Brotherhood foolish. Everyone can apply his strength at each moment; one need only understand that in Our mountains ceaseless labor continues for help to humanity. One such thought alone creates a flow of energy, and advances the consciousness toward service for humanity. It whispers that love for humanity is possible, but earthly conditions often make it difficult to imagine the possibility of such love. Let thought about the existence of the Brotherhood help to open hearts. Then cooperation will be revealed, not as a duty, but as joy, and the drops of sweat and sacred pains will bring the Crown of Enlightenment. Let us not take these words as an abstraction, for such denial will close the best receptacle—the heart. Each drop of sweat from labor, each pain for humanity, lives in the heart.

Glory to the all-embracing heart.

9. Urusvati has been in Our laboratories, and has seen one of the formulas for atomic energy. Her physical memory could not retain it, but the inner receptacle absorbed it. "Atomic atoms!" exclaimed Our Brother during the splitting of the atom. Just as ears of wheat ripen in time for the harvest, so will these possibilities and achievements be preserved until that hour when they are to be given to humanity. It is difficult to make discoveries and then preserve the disclosure until the pre-ordained date. In his madness man would scatter knowledge like hail upon the fields, not caring about the monsters that grow from unbridled passion. Understanding the dates is a great step toward Brotherhood.

The northern tundra and the Gobi desert guard treasures; should one hasten to reveal them? Only a high level of consciousness can deal with such valuable treasures; and with knowledge of the spiral of evolution, diamonds will not be cast under the wheels of chariots. Even for a proven patience it may be hard at times to await the approach of a caravan that brings joy. "Perhaps the date has already passed," pulsates the heart. But wise experience whispers, "It is still too early." The struggle between the heart and reason is an amazing spectacle. Happy is the one who can understand the command of the heart.

We have many formulas ready to be revealed. The Ray from the Tower of Chun shines when the discoveries of scientists coincide with the dates. In their simplicity people do not understand the harmony of dates, and seek to impose their own disorderliness and irresponsibility in all matters. It is of no importance to them that, when certain requirements have not yet been met, a great idea is lost. In addition, they insist that everything be done by their own measures, they regard success as misfortune and rejoice at calamity. The small seems great to them, and the great, insignificant.

The exact knowledge sent out from Our laboratories often cannot be understood because the formulas are given in unusual symbols. But why should We distort ancient formulas that would otherwise have been forgotten? If some formulas survive from Atlantis, they should not be limited by today's scientific concepts. The science that synthesizes and the science that analyzes are worlds apart. Thus it is so difficult to find the harmony that flourishes in the Brotherhood.

10. Urusvati knows Our language, but We must know the speech of all nations. Questions constantly arise regarding the language in which thoughts are best transmitted. Each one should send thoughts in his own language, the language in which he thinks. It is a mistake to send thoughts in a foreign language, supposing that it is more convenient for the person to whom the thought is sent. This can only weaken the power of the sending. Forcing oneself to think in a foreign language calls forth inner images connected with the culture of those who use that language, and disturbs the clarity of one's thinking. I advise the sending of thoughts in one's native language and in the most simple and familiar surroundings. Familiar objects divert the attention less, do not complicate the thoughts, and their emanations cause no irritation.

We arrange for thought transference in an almost empty room whose walls are painted blue or green. Green can be very harmonious for many individuals. We also prefer a comfortable armchair, so that the spinal column is aligned. The chair should in no way discomfort the body. The light should not irritate the eyes, and it is better if it comes from behind. No forced tension is needed, only complete concentration. Sometimes one may place before oneself the image of the person to whom the thoughts are being sent, but it is even better to hold this image in one's mind. Calmness is necessary, and harmonious music may accompany the sending of thoughts.

Remember these conditions as you visualize Us when sending thoughts to Us.

11. Urusvati would like to provide more knowledge to people, but straight-knowledge indicates to her the limits of what is possible. The discovery of these limits is a stumbling block for many, and great misfortune results from overlooking them. It is impossible to indicate in earthly terms the hidden, co-measured boundary, but a broadened consciousness can suggest where the possibility of harm begins. You yourself know how often people demand an answer that they then cannot accept. They say, "Tell us quickly, and we will decide what to accept and what to reject." They like to play jackstraws, pulling out only that which is most attractive to them. They do not care if it all falls to pieces, although even children know that the whole should not be disrupted. Grown-ups throw bombs and are astonished when they are maimed by them. They love to repeat Our analogy of a boomerang but do not see the consequences of their own blows.

People often accuse Us of denying much of what exists, and even reach such a state of falsehood and blasphemy as to say that We reject Christ. Can one believe this blasphemy? Yet many servants of darkness are ready to spread even this slander in order to bring disunity. Everyone who knows the structure of Our Brotherhood will be appalled at the ignorance of such slander. Slander is usually the result of ignorance, and people do not hesitate to repeat lies. One can cite many falsehoods about the Brotherhood. One can point out how the Brothers were thought to be dark forces, and can enumerate the many terrible calamities attributed to Them. We have been accused of using threats and violence. Especially insistent were those who chose not to heed Our Words. Shame upon the unbelievers! Shame upon the ignorant ones! And shame upon those who cause disunity! Let them occasionally ask themselves if they are not in the wrong. But the ignorant cannot *become* wrong, for they already live in error. Let this page about the Brotherhood be remembered by those whose hearts are aflame. Indeed, everyone can affirm at least a grain of Truth.

12. Urusvati can tell about the particular sensations that are experienced in the subtle body during flights to the far-off worlds. It is difficult to describe in earthly words these subtle sensations beyond the limits of the earthly sphere. One must experience such flights in order for the consciousness to accommodate these supermundane sensations. Among the Brothers such distant flights are taken with regularity. People also strive to the higher spheres, but unfortunately do not yet fully accept the mobility of the subtle body. Many experiments succeed, but only with great difficulty.

Much is said about the rays that make one invisible. The next step will be the invention of a small portable apparatus that will make the one who carries it invisible. We gain invisibility by attracting from space the rays needed for it. This is somewhat analogous to the dematerialization of parts of the body, which you recently heard about. Thus, for many manifestations one must have a mobile subtle body. Flights to the far-off worlds definitely require this mobility of the subtle body, which, in its tension, attains fieriness. This ability can be attained through many incarnations and ceaseless striving. Mobility cannot be acquired by force.

Our Sisters are especially successful in these flights, because the synthesis of the feminine nature is helpful. The flights are sometimes of long duration, but the Brotherhood knows how to safeguard the bodies that have been left behind.

What seems like physical torpor is often nothing but the effect of a distant flight. People often do not know how to care for someone in such a condition. In ancient times they would have been thought to have a "sacred" ailment, and people knew how to recognize the symptoms. We have many records of such experiences; in the infinitude of time and space such observations are without number. We record diligently each sensation, although radio waves and electric charges often impede Our observations.

13. Urusvati could reveal the names of members of the Brotherhood, but will not do so because she weighs the commensurability of such information. There are already seven Names upon the lips of the world, and where is the benefit? Deeds are needed, not names. Therefore, when We speak about the personal lives of the Brothers We describe deeds without mentioning names. People do not quarrel about deeds, but about names. When the name of one of Our Brothers who was in the world was revealed, it became necessary to declare Him dead in order to preserve His freedom of action. We have had to change Our names repeatedly in order not to arouse curiosity. We have been compelled to hastily hide Ourselves in order that a good work might not suffer harm. One of the first conditions of the Brotherhood is to put the essence of the action above all.

There are two kinds of thinking. One is born from feeling, in other words, from the heart, and the other from the mind, which is akin to intellect. Self-sacrifice is born from the heart, and the Brotherhood is built upon this. Our cooperation lives by the heart.

When We speak about unity, We assume that the heart is alive. The most repulsive sight is hypocritical unity. Many have dreamed of approaching the Brotherhood, but precisely because of their hypocrisy they have failed. Hypocrisy cannot enter into Our Abode. Participation in the Great Service cannot be feigned.

People find it difficult to become accustomed to the idea of a mental interchange of thought. But among Us such a state is absolutely natural, and serves to simplify Our relations. One thought can often replace an entire exchange of words. Even in daily life, those who have lived together for a long time understand the thoughts of their companions. Certain exercises can, without apparatuses, enable one to understand the thoughts of co-workers. We speak only about what We apply in Our lives.

Let those who strive to Us understand that the quality of labor grows through a feeling heart.

14. Urusvati, can you name even one Sister or Brother who was not subjected to tortures and persecutions in earthly life? Truly, none can be named. Each heroic act invites persecution. Combat with darkness is unavoidable, and the waves of chaos will engulf bold fighters. Yet such touchstones only testify to the invincibility of the spirit. There were Those who were burned at the stake, crucified, beheaded, strangled, killed by beasts, sold into slavery, poisoned, or cast into prison; in short, They endured all tortures so that Their strength could be tested.

It should not be thought that a broadened consciousness is achieved without struggle. Each one who wishes to serve with Us knows that he will have to endure the assaults of darkness. In words everyone is ready to do this, but in deeds will try to avoid it. Does no one realize that every deviation lengthens his path?

Earthly blessings are evident, but the supermundane worlds are invisible, as if in the clouds. Each experiment in approaching the Subtle World can help to clarify the concept of Infinity. Even an ordinary person can be dreamed about simultaneously in various parts of the world. There is nothing impossible in the subtle body manifesting simultaneously in distant places. The study of man's nature will provide direction and broaden the consciousness, and people will sail to Our shores in natural ways, with no need for their former vessels. Let *Santana*, the current of life, carry the expectant travelers to the new shore.

There are many waiting. Let them learn first about

the difficulties of the journey, and clearly understand the fight with darkness. Let them not hope to avoid it. The path to joy cannot be easy.

There will be joy. We shall speak more about joy, but first let us forge the armor of the spirit.

15. Urusvati was amazed to see Our tension when sending ideas to remote distances. We are actually charged with electricity in order to increase the Primary Energy, and use unusual electrical apparatuses to create the special environment needed for the sending of thought. It can be seen that psychic receptivity may be increased in electric power plants, but such a saturation of the environment with electricity can also cause fiery sicknesses. Everywhere harmony is needed.

Pay attention to what I said about tension when sending ideas. A thought sent to a particular place, or to a certain person, does not require as much tension as the sending out of thought into space, where much opposition is encountered. A fierce battle surrounds such sendings, therefore an electric vortex is needed as armor. Such vortices attract to their orbit certain refined souls, who will then feel a great fatigue, for their energy has been magnetically joined to the general current. Thus, if you feel an unexplainable tension and exhaustion of strength, you may be involved in such spatial sendings.

At the time of the world's greatest disturbances We sometimes send thoughts that clash with the desires of most of humanity. People do not understand that madness cannot be cured by madness and try to repeat destructions that have been visited upon Earth more than once. We try to preserve balance as much as possible, but the total effect of free will can overcome Our benevolent advice.

Urusvati will not forget how We are transformed

at times of tension. Let humanity ask to be healed, for without their consent they cannot be healed.

16. Urusvati knows the three states of Our bodies. Each state has its own distinguishing characteristic, and even the dense state is so refined that it cannot be compared to the earthly. The subtle state has become adapted to the conditions of the earthly atmosphere to such a degree that it differs substantially from the usual sheaths of the Subtle World. Finally, the third state, which is between the dense and the subtle states, is a unique phenomenon. All three states are unusual, and their atmosphere is not easy for earthly lungs and hearts to withstand. An earthly person would have to grow accustomed to it, or he would at the very least suffer palpitations. This is not magic, but the natural tension of the atmosphere of Our Abode.

Each earthly house has its own atmosphere, and one can observe that where more labor is performed, the atmosphere is more saturated. In the Brotherhood, where everyone manifests the greatest tension, where there are so many powerful apparatuses, and where so many different experiments take place at the same time, the atmosphere is most saturated. Do not forget about the stores of chemical substances and about the healing plants, both of which have exceedingly powerful emanations. One can avoid aromas, but emanations are unavoidable. Great harmony must prevail in any place from which ideas are sent into space.

Lamas speak about the Abode of the Great Rishis. Each one describes Shambhala according to his own understanding. The mention of treasures is correct, but they are described in different ways. Legends about Our Warriors exist all over the world and are not without foundation. There are also described many gates and mirrors. The legend about the Tashi

Lama granting passports to Shambhala is symbolic. The appearance of similar symbols in various parts of the world proves how much Truth has spread. Even ancient Mexico knew about the Sacred Mountain where the Chosen People live. It is not surprising that all Asian nations preserve legends about the Sacred Mountain. It is described almost correctly, but he who is not called will not reach it.

Many strive to find Us, but it is right to hold back these travelers. We must be found not geographically, but first of all in spirit. You know what is expected of Us—not only expected, but demanded—and complaints tear the last threads. People do not realize that their complaints densify an already-saturated atmosphere. Of course, mistakes are attributed to Us according to the understanding of the one who complains: We do not know how to speak, We do not know how to write! People do not realize the lack of co-measurement in these claims. Do not think that We are displeased; We simply feel regret when We see that energy is not directed to full benefit. Discussion is preferable to complaints. A heartfelt talk is more in accord with the harmony of Our Abode. If help can be given it is not delayed. In this lies the beauty of thought-creativeness.

Obviously, We serve to help those who suffer, but one should not beat down the Gates with one's fists. It is said, "The Kingdom of God is taken by force," but by force of the spirit and not by fists. Thus, let people think about the Brotherhood, and let them not forget where the true Gates are.

17. Urusvati has not forgotten that in Our repositories are models of many cities and historical places, which have a particular inner meaning. They serve as teraphim to establish a link between the ancient places

and new tasks. Also preserved in Our repositories are important objects that are sometimes sent into the world as magnets for planned actions.

It has great significance when Our messengers travel through designated places. In some they bury certain objects, in others they simply pass by, thus strengthening the aura of those places. People do not pay attention to these pilgrimages, but a historian's eye could perceive the periodic nature of such travels. It could then be seen that the consecrated places proved to be especially important in the history of nations.

In addition to the inhabitants of the Stronghold of the Brotherhood, there are others living on Earth who carry out Our missions. One can trace how in different countries, throughout history, people appeared whose tasks and methods of accomplishing them had much in common. Usually these people were regarded with suspicion and hostility because something was sensed in them that could not be expressed in words.

In Our archives maps can be seen on which boundaries are traced that do not conform to the present-day ones. The buried magnets are indicated by stars. Sometimes the significance of these deposited magnets is revealed in just a few years.

18. Urusvati, in her subtle body, continuously participates in Our help to humanity. Through their flights in the subtle body Our co-workers render so much help to people that no records are sufficient to contain it. It should be remembered that We rarely appear at so-called spiritualistic seances, and We consider such gatherings harmful because of the discordant auras of those who attend. Hardly any circle is ever assembled with due consideration of the auras of the participants. One can imagine what kind of entities project and materialize in response to the discordant mental states at these gatherings, and attention has already been directed to the stupidity of answers received in response to questions put by these equally stupid circles!

Our manifestations and help are different. We save worthy people at moments of danger. By gentle contact We draw the attention of seekers, whom We forewarn about their harmful decisions. We help to create and assist the Good. Our Work is dedicated to knowledge. We help each useful worker, unhindered by conventional distinctions of race and class. We watch diligently to discover where the ray of self-sacrificing achievement will flash. Our Temple is the Temple of Knowledge. We bring to it all the highest and We guard there all the affirmations of the future.

Do not lose direct communion with Us. Let it be the highest expression of your being. Do not permit such communion to become a formal performance of duty. Forced effort will never produce a firm step, for the work in the Subtle World must be a natural expression of free will. Do not try to force anyone to such labor, for desire must first be generated in the consciousness. It is difficult to judge when the desire to work for humanity will be ignited. Each one can find his path, and We will help those on that path.

19. Urusvati is grateful to India and Tibet for their protection of the Brotherhood. One can be truly grateful that the concept of the Brotherhood is so carefully guarded. Usually, even talk about the Brotherhood is discouraged and names are not mentioned, for it is better even to deny the existence of the Brotherhood than to betray it. The legends about the Brotherhood are safeguarded, together with the sacred books.

The curiosity of the Western world is not understood in the East. Let us examine why the West wants to know about the Brotherhood. Does the West wish to emulate the Brotherhood in daily life? Does the West wish to preserve the Ordainments of the Brotherhood? Does the West wish to deepen its knowledge? So far they show only idle curiosity and look for reason to criticize and blame. We shall not help them on this path.

Let us imagine a military expedition that discovers the Brotherhood. One can easily imagine the outcome of such a discovery, and the curses and anathemas that would follow! Crucifixions take place even today. Thus the West has never understood the essence of Our Hierarchy. The concept of dictatorship does not fit Our Hierarchy. We have established as law the idea that power lies in sacrifice. Who among today's leaders will accept this Ordainment?

We well understand the nature of the East, and because of its nature one should all the more note its reverence for Our Abode. Many Ashrams were transferred to the Himalayas because the atmosphere of other locations had become intolerable. The last Egyptian Ashram was transferred to the Himalayas because of the well-known events in Egypt and the adjoining regions. At the beginning of Armageddon all the Ashrams had to be gathered together in the Abode in the Himalayas. It should be known that at present We do not leave Our Abode, and We go to distant places only in Our subtle bodies. Thus the records about the inner life of Our Abode are being revealed.

20. Urusvati distinguishes the currents that are favorable from those that hinder. One can imagine the reactions of crowds that are seized by one emotion. At some time We will reveal experiments that were carried out in the midst of crowds, and the results will show over what great distances the energy of crowds

has its effect. The mood of distant crowds is also felt acutely in Our Abode. Not without reason do We insist upon the necessity of maintaining a friendly unity. Even purely physiological experiments produce varying results because of the chemistry of the participants, and sensitive apparatuses will change their vibrations at the approach of even one person. This means that the confused and angry aura of crowds can disrupt the most important experiments, and this causes Our blood-tinged sweat.

We try to modify the psychology of distant crowds in order to protect Our scientific investigations. Archimedes protected his formulas from visible barbarians, but how much more difficult it is to guard scientific treasures against invisible, violent destroyers! And it is not only destroyers and enemies who threaten, but also sympathizers who create discordant conditions. We are ready to beseech them not to destroy Our formulas. There are many such transgressions, but at the root lies doubt in all its forms.

Imagine Our Abode in which every sound disrupts the harmony of the vibrations. We have sufficiently insulated Our laboratories against sound, but psychic energy cannot be stopped. Our co-workers, near and far, must understand what state of mind is of help to Us. Great Service is always co-service. Each person who has approached Us even once has already accepted the responsibility not to impede Our labors.

Our Towers are many-storied, and research is constantly taking place. Who then will be so light-minded as to dare to obscure the accumulated energies? The rebounding blow may be terrible, and no one can avert it once the fundamental energies are set into action. Therefore, We solicitously warn against provoking unpleasant shocks.

21. Urusvati has kept in her heart from early childhood the revelation that the Teacher of Light lives "somewhere." Only memories of reality could call forth in a child's consciousness such a vivid image. We rejoice to see that Our co-workers, from their first conscious hours, bear within themselves an image of what they have previously seen. A confused spirit sees everything in confusion, but a spirit illumined through many achievements will preserve a clear recollection.

Even vivid instructions are not so often retained in one's new bodily sheath, but when a pilgrim is sent out on Our mission, having already been in contact with the Brotherhood in the past, illumination is received even in infancy. He sees the Banners of Light. We come to him in various Images. He hears Our silvery bells, and his silver thread is stretched tautly to Us.

This small girl, even without encouragement from others, was directed by her own consciousness to predestined achievements. This pilgrim of Light proceeded untiringly, in spite of the unsuitable surroundings of her childhood. After inward strengthening, she finally received a vision of Our bidding for achievement. We rejoice when such a mission is accepted, not in words, but by the flame of the heart. Such burning is a harbinger of illumination and of sacred pains. For only in the acceptance of suffering can the embryo of the joy of wisdom be born. It cannot be achieved without suffering. Only with Us is this joy born.

Urusvati came into the world voluntarily. The Word about Fire had been determined already in her previous contact with the Brotherhood. The Word was to be proclaimed in the days of Armageddon. Not an easy time! Not an easy Word, not an easy affirmation of the existence of the Brotherhood when all the powers of darkness are against it. But We welcome and rejoice when achievement is ascendant.

Do not think that Our Inner Life is dominant. On the contrary, the image of man is forged by man himself. Each silver cord resounds as a string in Infinity.

22. Urusvati can affirm the great significance of the heart. Above and beyond the actions of all the centers the significance of the heart is evident. Even *Kundalini* would seem earthly in comparison with the heart, whose significance is little understood. It is regarded as the focal point of physical life, but this view is inadequate. The heart is the bridge between the worlds. Where the meeting-point of the three worlds is especially manifested, the significance of the heart is felt deeply. In Our Abode the heart is especially revered.

There are Those in Our Abode whose incarnations have been separated by many centuries. It would seem that Their mentality would be very different, because after three generations one's thought processes change completely, but in Our collaboration this is not noticed. One of the main reasons is the broadened consciousness, but this alone is not enough. What is required is the cooperation of the heart center. Only the heart can unite consciousnesses separated by many centuries. The heart quality is required for all subtle actions.

After thought-transmission to a distance has been accepted by people, the conditions that guide these subtle activities will be understood. It will be said that harmony is needed, but harmony does not determine which center will be involved. In thought-transference the heart is the prime mover.

You who send thoughts, attune your hearts, but remember that tension of the heart carries the threat of fiery conflagration. Only one who has experienced such a conflagration, inexpressible in words, can know the extreme danger. This suffering is the highest sacred pain, and is caused by the imbalance of the worlds. Various heart ailments come about from the same cause. Man does not wish to take care of his stronghold, the heart, which throughout all the worlds preserves its fiery seed.

You may have heard that this inner fire can be evoked by forcible means. Such a procedure is possible but very dangerous, for the fire can come into contact with the Fire of Space, with destructive results.

The significance of the heart is great; in the future it will replace the most complex apparatuses. Verily, in the New Era people will appear whose organisms accomplish this. At present, people invent robots, but after this mechanical fever has abated man's attention will turn to the powers within himself.

In Our Abode all research is directed toward the freeing of man from the machine. In this process one must educate the heart. One must learn to listen to its voice. Those who accuse Us of egoism should remember Our anonymous Labors.

23. Urusvati has many times experienced Our way of healing through vibrations. There will come a time when medical science will change. Vibrations and hypnotic suggestion will be utilized together with medicines, and the large doses that are usually given will be reduced. Only a small medicinal impulse will be needed, and the rest of the recovery will depend upon vibrations and suggestions. Homeopathy, to a certain extent, foresaw the course of this medicine of the future, but at this time only those homeopathic physicians who possess strong psychic energy can succeed. Perhaps they are unaware of the source of their successful healing, but gradually they will learn about the harmony of the inner and outer influences, and the new methods of healing will then begin. At present, because of unenlightened conditions physicians hesitate to recognize that to a great extent it is their own psychic energy that is acting. They are ready to attribute their success to even the weakest medicines, unaware of their own powerful influence.

Few people pay any attention to the vibrations that develop during certain pains. If they did, they would notice that after the cessation of the pains the vibrations that had shaken their beds stop completely. We develop at Our Abode ways of healing with vibrations that can be effective even at great distances if the patients accept their subtle influence. Voluntary and absolute acceptance is necessary, otherwise the currents are broken and calamity is inevitable.

In Our Abode We too must sometimes make use of vibrations, which are especially needed by those who are between the dense and subtle states. It is not accidental that We are so concerned about this subtle-dense state. This problem was foreseen ages ago and requires special care.

24. Urusvati understands the correlation between the sleeping and waking states. For some, sleep is the opposite of the waking state, but for Us sleep is a continuation of labor, although in a different state. Sleep should not be understood otherwise. That it is a necessity cannot be denied. Some conditions may reduce the need for sleep, but do not remove the need for it. On the heights four hours of sleep may suffice, but this is only possible at a certain altitude.

Do not believe it when someone tries to persuade you that he needs no sleep. Despite the terrible illness of insomnia, sleep must be accepted by people as a necessary part of their existence. Any degree of sleep brings man closer to the Subtle World. There are different degrees of consciousness in sleep, and clarity of consciousness must be cultivated. A man must repeat to himself as he sinks into sleep that he is going to a new work. If his free will accepts this, it will be easier for him to apply his forces in the Subtle World. Let people not worry that they will thus deprive themselves of rest. They will have rest in full measure, for in the Subtle World subtle qualities are used which do not result in fatigue.

It is worse when one goes to sleep, overcome by earthly desires, never thinking about the Higher World. Then, instead of being immersed in illumined labor and knowledge, one wanders in the dark strata, where one's exhausting encounters can be well imagined. Falling asleep should be a conscious transition into the Higher World. The free will, like wings, will carry you up. I speak about sleep in order to show you that in Our Abode We are not strangers to that particular kind of sleep that is a transference of consciousness into the Higher Worlds.

Urusvati understands correctly that We do not oppose the expression of free will. In this expression of free will lies Our Power.

25. Urusvati has explained to many why We are called "The Invisible Government." Truly, everyone to some degree feels that there is somewhere a focus of knowledge. Where there is knowledge there is also power. Not without reason do some people dream about Us, although others hate Us and want to destroy Our Abode.

Those who observe world events may perceive something higher than human logic. Even some who are devoted to Us have accused Us many times of delay and indifference, but that is because these hasty accusers have seen only part of the events. They could not possibly know their causes or effects, or be able to compare the attendant circumstances. They could not foresee exactly when decisive blows had to be struck. Who, then, can know the Plan and the steps leading to it?

Because of their partial understanding, people insist upon their own ways, but Our disciples will never forcibly hinder the decision of their Teacher. They understand how to harmonize their free will with Our decisions. One must possess great equilibrium to understand the wisdom of Our Guidance without crippling his own free will. We care a great deal about such balance. The best leaders of nations had this balance, and it was therefore easier to send them Our decisions.

The "Green Laurel"[1] about whom you have often spoken could combine leadership with sensitivity to the Counsels of the Brotherhood. He accepted the directions of Saint Germain with full confidence. In this lay his success. Perhaps Saint Germain came especially to prepare this future leader.

All over the world one can find established landmarks of Our Guidance. Some enlightened people accepted it, but some poor parodies of monarchs rejected Our Counsel and thereby plunged their countries into calamity. But even these situations We turned to good. You are acquainted with *Tactica Adversa*.

One may recall an arrogant monarch who, before the Great War[2], received Our warnings, but preferred to lose his throne by rejecting Our Advice. Likewise,

---

[1] Mikhail Ilarionovich Kutuzov (1745–1813), Field Marshal of the Russian Empire.— Ed.

[2] World War I.— Ed.

another head of state did not want to listen to Our Ambassador and preferred to plunge his country into confusion.

It cannot be said that in ancient times Indications were given more often. Now also many such Counsels are given, but as usual the ear of humanity is deaf.

We stand vigil the world over.

26. Urusvati has often forewarned her friends about attacks of the dark forces. Such forewarning is needed everywhere. It should not be thought that the dark ones will cease their destructive attacks. Decay is their nourishment, murder their profession. Encroachment upon the spirit and body is their joy. One should not assume that they will not try to penetrate behind even the most protected boundaries. They would rather perish than abandon their demoralizing work of corruption.

Some light-minded people think that a mechanical utterance of the Highest Names will protect them immediately from dark assaults. However, it is not a mechanical repetition but the pure fire of the heart that creates a firm shield.

The cunning ways of the dark ones are multiform. In addition to their crudest attempts, there may be subtle approaches that influence one's weaker side. Creating doubt is one of the favorite methods used by the dark ones, and he who doubts is already defenseless. One would think that this axiom is sufficiently known, yet how many perish from this poison! I consider that a great many enemies of Truth are created by whisperers of doubt. Obvious fools are not as dangerous as petty hypocrites. If new kinds of poisons are invented, why should not new kinds of hypocrisy appear? These descriptions of the attacks of the dark ones must be remembered when you picture the Inner Life of the Brotherhood.

We are always on guard. Not an hour passes without the need to stop somewhere the vicious attacks of the dark ones. Do not think that they attack only Our followers. They try to destroy all constructive work, and because of the law of vibrations, they are able to find the seed of good so hated by them. One should not ascribe omniscience to them, but they do sense their opposites. Our Work is made difficult by the expenditure of energy needed to counter the attacks of the dark ones. They know that ultimately they cannot overcome Us, but they absorb the energy that is being sent into space. When We ask for unity and trust We are calling for help for a speedy victory.

Many signs are flying to Us. No one can imagine how much confusion there is in this world! People have forgotten that each country contains many hearts. Their pain is Our pain!

27. Urusvati has heard the legend about the building of the temples by the jinn. Every legend contains an element of truth, and also the historical data about the many kinds of betrayals that have accompanied each construction are true. It is said that betrayal is like the shadow of a building that indicates the height of a structure. We have been tested by all kinds of betrayals, and have been tempted by all kinds of cunning. It is also said that in order to heighten one's love for humanity one must know all its depths. But who will find the patience within himself to look into all the abysses without losing faith in humanity? Our Abode is the bulwark of such patience, and it is those who have been with Us, and those who have heard about Us, who carry the contact with Us in their hearts, and

wear this armor of patience. We value this quality, for it belongs to Infinity.

People must find the realization of Infinity in themselves, otherwise Our Towers will remain inaccessible to them. People should turn to Us in times of suffering and calamity. They will receive Our Help if their hearts have not yet turned to stone. Even those who are inexperienced will be admitted for constructive work if they preserve a lion's courage and recognize Hierarchy. Let these co-workers be assured that an invisible thread is stretched from their worktable to Us. Let them draw strength from their realization of the existence of the Brotherhood. We shall help them invisibly; We shall find books needed by them; We shall unite them in hope about the far-off worlds; We shall strengthen their confidence, and, provided that they have driven out their snakes and scorpions, We shall find a loving heart for them. Thus, you are becoming acquainted with a very important part of Our Life.

You can imagine Our joy in finding workers worthy of Our trust. Their striving spirits do not fear being tested. Only hypocrites fear that the Ray of Light might penetrate into the depths of their being. Open hearts form a beautiful necklace for the Higher Worlds.

The Teacher does not renounce His obligations. His entire day is filled with carrying out His duties. He who is afraid of these words, let him not think about the Brotherhood.

28. Urusvati has admired Our flowers, in some species of which We have indeed achieved perfection. Of first importance is the use of psychic energy because it helps vegetable growth. We also irrigate with soda and in this way act from both the outer and inner side. One can experiment widely with psychic energy, but it must be done systematically, not forgetting that much time and patience are needed. Many experiments successfully started have been ruined by lack of patience. Moreover, Our radiations are harmonized, and because of the equality of Our psychic energy, each One of the Masters can substitute for another.

People fail to understand to what extent these investigations are of use to them. Psychic energy must be interchanged. The sending of this energy to people may be fatiguing, but with vegetation there is no rebounding blow. Likewise, let us not forget that We maintain close cooperation with the Subtle World, and this reservoir can easily replenish Our energy.

It is difficult for many to imagine how cooperation can proceed between entities in three different states of consciousness, but in reality it is not so complicated. Co-workers in the subtle body are often visible. For this no ectoplasm is required, but certain chemical compounds are used that aid in the densification of the subtle body. During the last war many people had visions, but no one realized that the cause of this lay in particular chemical agents. The conditions differ to such an extent that often something causing decomposition in the physical world can serve quite the opposite purpose in the Subtle World.

Urusvati was surprised to see that flowers from the plains could survive on Our heights. It must not be thought that such acclimatization can take place quickly. Urusvati has met with her Tibetan Friend in Our flower garden. We also have many plants inside Our buildings. For many experiments it is necessary to use the vital substance of living flowers. We advise conversing with flowers more often, for these currents are very close to the Subtle World. I affirm that We apply Our Power to all that exists. Thus We have the organic unity on which I so often insist.

29. Urusvati values Our Help. He who values also safeguards. Each true cooperation requires first of all a cautious attitude. One should not abuse Hierarchic cooperation by a casual state of mind, and must attend respectfully to the Voice of the Elders. Even those who, because of their ignorance, cannot conceive of the existence of Our Brotherhood can still recognize the existence of super-earthly voices. But those who can realize Our Brotherhood within themselves should understand that each light-minded wavering disturbs the flow of the Teacher's thought. Each unfitting word distorts something. Each broken thread can coil into a noose. This is not meant as a threat, but comes only from a desire to bring forth better achievements.

It is right to remember the wisdom of ancient India, when duty was integral to the very designation of the life of man. At its root the concept of duty is one, and it acts accordingly in its ramifications. The concept of The Teacher is sacred to Us. Each one of Us has had His Teacher, and the steps of this ladder are countless. Even standing at the head of a planet is not a consummation, for there can never be a final consummation. In this lies the joy. Great harm would result if the unutterable names of the Higher Lords were pronounced. Such betrayal might have enormous consequences. There could be visible or invisible explosions. One should become more accustomed to a solicitous attitude toward Hierarchy.

There were times when people knew how to express the concept of the Highest in the finest way, but now the Great Service is not understood. One would think that this could not be so, with the Subtle World coming closer, and We being spoken of so often. Yet the abyss of darkness has not diminished when the concept of the Teacher is doubted. You have heard many times that it is those who know about the Brotherhood who still speak of it with irreverence, and such utterances contain ruination.

People thrust upon Us their own ways of helping, but such forcing creates a refraction of the currents. A thrifty head of the household regrets all waste. Great joy will result if those who know about Hierarchy voluntarily bring their own lamps.

Free will is Our motive force.

30. Urusvati is familiar with the varied ways in which light is manifested. Seeing flashes of light is an indication of a spiritual keenness of eye. In themselves these lights do not mean anything special, but they are like banners on the way to Us. The Northern lights, in their lowest degree, are not noticed by people. Similarly, the earliest flashes of the spirit are not evident to many. One can observe that small bright sparks will burst into flame and produce a rainbow-like illumination. Thus a beautiful aura is kindled around people. Note that these lights are especially visible in Our Abode. From ancient times they have been accumulated, and, if desired, can be made to blaze radiantly. In legends people are mentioned who could evoke around themselves a dazzling light. Thus, if one wishes one can be surrounded by a fiery force.

People must become used to the possibility of such manifestations. Even now some people can discern auras, while others rub their eyes, thinking that something has happened to their sight. Often, such luminosity at midday seems like a kind of mist. The perceptions of this luminosity are diverse. Among Us this capacity is so intensified that We can read in Our own light.

One must understand that the concept of darkness gradually vanishes, because one is surrounded by fires, rays, pillars of light, and brilliant sparks beyond counting, all visible with the eyes open or closed. Precisely, darkness vanishes. Twilight reigns only in the lower strata of the Subtle World, for its inhabitants do not know how to evoke Light. This ability depends upon thought, and thought gives birth to Light. Verily, a thinker sends the order, "Let there be Light!" Thus are the great truths taught, although people consider them to be fairy tales.

Only in the spirit and in personal experience can the most natural laws be assimilated. It is not easy to overcome all the surrounding counteractions. Our Abode is so strong because there is no corruption in it. The will of all of Us is merged into one powerful current. The dynamo of unity increases all energies. Not magic, but purified will sends into the world the command, "Let there be Light!"

Our Abode should be considered the triumph of Unity.

31. Urusvati understands correctly the reason for Our long-unchanging features. Relations with the Subtle World impose a special quality that belongs to the Subtle World. There one's appearance does not change except when there is a special desire for it. Thought creates form in the Subtle World. One can call forth any image chosen from the depths of centuries and fix it in the imagination, if the imagination is developed enough. Added to these conditions of the Subtle World is the unity that is strongly manifested in Our Abode. This helps in all details of daily life. It creates a salutary atmosphere and forges a fiery consciousness.

You have heard that Our Brothers became ill from

contact with earthly disharmony, and often suffered from prolonged human discord. This is why We seldom visit your cities, and stay in them for only a short time. Our appearances are prompted by particular circumstances and are not of long duration. Places can be found in nature where the currents of decay are not as strong. In France and in England there are forests near the cities in which there is enough of the pure air that is indispensable to Us. You must not be surprised that even Our concentrated energy needs pure air. However, you must not think that We are not strong enough to withstand the emanations of crowds. Truly, We can concentrate Our energy to a tremendous degree, but co-measurement and caution must be maintained in everything.

You have read how oppressive the aura of some landholders was for Our Brother. Of course, He had the ability to repel them with one discharge of His energy, but such murder was not part of His task. Thus, in many cases, We must co-measure in directing the Ray for the highest benefit. Such co-measurement will define the purpose of Our Brotherhood. To hold back the onslaught of darkness, to protect those who have exhausted their strength, and to apply all possible remedies for the General Good will be the fulfillment of Our Statutes.

32. Urusvati has recognized the existence of a certain substance that preserves equilibrium and provides longevity to the organism. I shall not reveal the complete composition of this substance, for it can be destructive to the physical state. Strong radioactivity is allowable in the subtle state, but can destroy the physical body. In earthly conditions even valerian can be too strong; therefore one must know how to discern the relationships between different substances.

For example, during a certain experiment carried out by My Brother the strongest poison was taken, which would have been deadly for an ordinary man. But since My Brother's body was already close to the subtle state, the action of the poison was beneficial. Many instances can be cited when a lethal poison did not cause death. The reason for this can be found in the special condition of the organism.

A particular physical condition can be observed in people when they unknowingly contact the Subtle World. Indeed, it is remarkable that such people often know nothing about the different worlds; however, somewhere in the depths of their consciousness lies an idea that cannot be formulated. In such cases, We often use *Tactica Adversa* to arouse the consciousness. It becomes necessary to undertake actions to the point of absurdity, otherwise the slumberers will not be awakened. The same tactic is necessary in dealing with world events.

You yourself deplore the loss of the strength of character that existed in past eras. This is true, and We can see to what extent psychic energy is degenerating. It is not brought into action, and therefore slumbers, and since there is no friction to call forth the fire it loses its fieriness. Therefore, Our Abode remains remote and all mention of it sounds abstract. Do not regret this. I affirm that the Battle itself is evidence of the strength of the Brotherhood. Great is the Battle in these days of Armageddon.

Let us listen, and put our ears to the ground, where a great tension is growing.

33. Urusvati rejoices when she observes a person's broadening of consciousness. Verily, one can rejoice when such an offering to the world is accomplished. The broadening of consciousness cannot be considered personal gain, for in every such purification is contained the General Good. The world welcomes each flash of the broadening of consciousness. It is a true festival.

In certain mysteries the broadening of consciousness was likened to the awakening of spring. No one can follow the entire process of the growth of grass, but every heart rejoices on seeing the first flowers of spring. It is likewise impossible to perceive the details of the broadening of consciousness, but a person's transformation is quite evident. He who has become transformed does not know when and how his renewal began, and cannot say how his consciousness was broadened. Frequently, he will cite insignificant events but omit the most important event that influenced him.

Not by chance have the periods of three or seven years been mentioned, for only over such periods can one notice changes in the consciousness. But We and Our near Ones, while carrying out Our missions, can notice shorter periods of growth of consciousness. The gardener knows his own flowers best. We, too, follow the growth of consciousness of those who are close to Us. There are many reasons for such observation.

We can affirm that each one's successful approaches to Us over the course of centuries bears results. We know how to be grateful; this quality of gratitude is indispensable in Our Abode. Each affirmation of Brotherhood brings its good harvest. All assistance to Our Work is appreciated, and each well-intentioned mention of the Brotherhood is remembered. In Our Ashrams records of such good deeds are kept. We like to record each kind smile, and Our disciples know how to rejoice at each kind word about the Brotherhood. No one can forcibly teach such radiant joy. No one can order gratitude. Only a broadened consciousness can indicate where more good can be done.

People generally do not like to speak about consciousness, for improvement is difficult for them, and there are not many who continue to gain knowledge after their school years. One's entire life should be transformed so that learning becomes a relentless necessity. We rejoice at each awakening of consciousness and We record as a sign of success each desire to think about the Brotherhood, even if it is only a thought about how to apply oneself or how to become united.

34. Urusvati strives to apply every hour for the General Good; such resolve is born in the Abode, where hours are not counted. During such a long life, can one think of hours? We do not have earthly hours, for there are so many needs and appeals for help from all parts of the world that it is impossible to divide Our Labor according to such relative measurements. We must keep Our Consciousness in great tension in order to be ready at each moment to send Our Will to that place where it is most needed. Undoubtedly, We shall be accused of sending too much help to the unworthy, and insufficiently to the deserving.

Those who judge by ordinary relative measures cannot discern causes and effects. I speak not only about the tension of labor but also about the vigilance that enables one instantly to weigh and decide what moment and which action are the most necessary. Each plea for help brings with it the emanations of the past and the aroma of the future. One should blend these harmonies in the consciousness and understand the meaning of disharmony. We should not help a man who is ready for evil, and must help one who is suffering. Contradictions often conflict, and only knowledge of the past will provide the balance. Nevertheless, no plea to Us is rejected, for by making such a request a person expresses his recognition of the Higher World, and the fact that such a Reality lives in space. We will not ignore a pleading voice. We will not reject any prayer, but will gather all salutary substances in order to offer goal-fitting help. In this is contained a special vigilance.

We labor constantly, and must determine Our responsibility and where help is most urgently needed. Our Sister from time immemorial has had the ability to strive constantly to the most needed labor. Such a capacity cannot be acquired quickly, but must be affirmed in many situations in order to become a source of joy. This source will provide freedom from irritation, for thought about infinite labor will produce striving without expectation of results. There will be no thought about the past, and in the flight forward the effects of the past will be erased. Thus, the interplanetary whirl will stimulate vigilance and will not disturb the joy of the broadened consciousness.

35. Urusvati remembers the many changes in the long progression of her lives. These memories do not burden her, but only enrich her consciousness. A right attitude toward past lives is very rare. As a rule, remembering past lives does not inspire one toward the future, but chains one to the outlived remnants of the past. Therefore, people can seldom be allowed knowledge of their past lives. Today's consciousness cannot absorb much. People simply cannot understand why distinguished incarnations alternate with ones of hard labor. The illusion of having been a king or a queen impedes one's discernment even though perfectment is still needed. The earthly consciousness does not realize how much an incarnation of hard labor can raise the consciousness above that of many sovereigns of this world. It is even more valuable when an understanding of the ascent of the spirit grows while in the earthly state.

Many learn about one of their distinguished incarnations and fall into pride. It is even worse when people glean from false accounts certain fantastic traits of character, and begin to emulate them, thus obscuring their path. Every old spirit has had some distinguished incarnations, and gained knowledge of leadership. However, of the many needed qualities this ability is not of primary importance. The persecuted learn more than the persecutors, and all domains of hard labor are rife with discoveries. Tests are strewn at every crossroad. I speak of this because We, too, have encountered all tests. We have forgotten the pain, and the suffering has turned into joy. Our tormentors are themselves struggling somewhere and ascending through labor. Our Abode could not exist if We thought of threatening Our tormentors. The Law of Karma flows immutably.

We remember Our incarnations. We must remember them, not for Ourselves, but for the sake of all those whom We have met and whom We have resolved not to forget. The encounters of travelers on earthly paths bring close the most varied people. The expectation of dates, the joy of meeting, the sorrow of parting—none of these human feelings disappear. Those who rejoiced or sorrowed together do not forget for many centuries.

Urusvati remembers many meetings. The feelings generated by them are alive after thousands of years. Such remembrance of feeling can help the broadening of consciousness. The fires of feeling blaze in full inviolability. Earthly words cannot express them, but the heart will throb exactly as it did thousands of years ago. Thus today the rainbow shines again over Christ just as it did in the desert. Similarly, the joys of Hellas live, and the Great Northern Saint, Sergius, passes nearby. There are many meetings in the Subtle World and also in this country in which We now talk.

In the inner life of the Brotherhood this living feeling is never forgotten, for the Abode of Knowledge cannot live without feeling. Thought about Knowledge will also be thought about the Highest feeling. Without it there would be no martyrs, no heroic saints, no victors.

We have images and teraphim that serve to strengthen Our help.

36. Urusvati understands the significance of the calmness necessary for action. People find many ways to explain this quality. Some think that without an effort of the will there can be no calm. Others see calmness as a true innate characteristic, and still others say that a crooked beginning brings a crooked end, or that calmness depends upon the method of labor. All of these observations have a part of the truth in them, but the most basic one, the quality of experience, is often forgotten. An inexperienced seaman is apprehensive when boarding a ship, but after ten voyages he astonishes those around him by his calmness.

Our actions are full of calmness. Like experienced seafarers We have passed through countless storms and know how to weather them. To overcome chaos and darkness is Our daily task. Not unexpected battle, but continuous action is the order of the day. Action should be followed by a conscious calmness. This is not like a narcotic stupor, but is a sober and experienced use of goal-fitting strength. Much is said about calmness, and it is often described as a frozen condition. What a fallacy! The concept of Nirvana is similarly misrepresented.

Calmness of action is the highest tension, like the flashing of lightning or the protecting sword. Calmness is not sleep or a tomb; in it are born creative ideas. Let us remember that Our Abode is permeated with calmness. This tension is invisible to people, for they do not recognize it. Innumerable experiences reveal that one can smile, one can labor, and one can accumulate energy in such calmness.

37. Urusvati carries fearlessness in her heart. We affirm that this quality is accumulated through faith and lengthy experience. Upâsikâ[3] was an example of complete fearlessness in life. She was courageous in all circumstances, and no fear could intrude. The life of Upâsikâ was filled with occasions for fear. It was sad to see how many persecutions came together, how her name was slandered. She had no means, and accusers threatened her from all sides. Verily, she was a touchstone of fearlessness! One can cite many such examples throughout the ages. Every one of Us has frequently had occasion to show such fearlessness.

It should not be thought that We are protected in Our earthly lives from all onslaughts of darkness. Those who fulfill an earthly mission do so under earthly conditions. People usually think that We dwell in safety, and think of Us as supernatural beings. Relatively speaking, We can overcome much, but this battle is a real one. We remain victorious, because the Hierarchy of Light cannot be conquered by darkness. When one of Our Sisters exclaims "How terrible!"

---

[3] Helena Petrovna Blavatsky (1831–1891), founder of the Theosophical movement.— Ed.

she does not show fear, but simply understands the tension.

We travel on far-off worlds where We gather many lessons in fearlessness. The alien conditions of the planets' unusual atmospheres can affect the heart of the visitor. Our Sister Urusvati knows the sensations of these distant flights. She knows the particularly difficult feeling upon the return of the subtle body. There are always complications and much courage is needed during these experiences. One should consult Our records of these distant flights to recognize the degree of daring they require.

A striving for flight has been awakened in the people of Earth. Some remember their dreams of daring, others now fly like birds, but in itself, the striving into the heights has put its mark upon this era. The Iron Bird was foretold long ago[4]; this prediction defines the New Era.

38. Urusvati treasures thought about the Mother of the World. Women's movements have a special significance for the immediate future. These movements should be understood not as an assertion of supremacy, but as the establishment of justice. Much has been said about co-measurement and equilibrium; precisely for the realization of this principle must the full rights of women be strengthened. One should not think that this will benefit only women; it will promote world equilibrium, and thus is necessary for harmonious evolution.

We labor to introduce measures for the achievement of equilibrium, but much opposition is encountered. Atavistic traits are manifested in all nations. However, one should not judge by nationality, but

---

[4] Described by the Buddha.— Ed.

must immediately delve into the web of intricate personal relationships. It is unfortunate that woman herself does not always help in this situation. Therefore We value the labor of Our Sisters all the more. They give up the distant flights so dear to their hearts, perseveringly visit families, and speak untiringly to people, conducting conversations that are often burdensome and even boring.

Let Our Sister recall how often she has spoken in the subtle body with women completely unknown to her, and how often she has witnessed quarrels and misunderstandings. But the work of enlightenment does not tarry. Entire nations strive for knowledge, and with knowledge full rights will come. We can show Our records of the women's movements, and the results are encouraging. One should not think in a routine way. At present, the world has exceeded its bounds, the ship has lost its course, and the cosmic whirl speeds its movement. We are at the helm, but other sailors should also help. The terror of Armageddon can be transformed into a manifestation of success, but first Armageddon must be discerned and the meaning of Hierarchy understood. The role of woman in the world's economy has been strengthened. Never before have so many women been called to high positions. Our Counsels penetrate into far-off places.

39. Urusvati pities people who reject the Brotherhood. We pity each one who deprives himself of knowledge about the Stronghold of the world. If a man preserves in his heart a strong awareness that somewhere work is being done for humanity, then he is already participating in life-saving thought. Let it at first be like a dream, let it at times flash out like lightning. Each flash bears witness to the sacred energy.

Man should not rebel against the affirmation of this truth.

Each one who pronounces the word "Brotherhood" builds a bridge into the future. People must realize that each acknowledgment and each slander of the Brotherhood reaches Us. Like a wave of a current that encircles the whole world, the sounding of the word "Brotherhood" reaches Our Abode. Do not forget that the word "Brotherhood" is heard by Us. This word attracts its consonance like a magnet. One may deplore the slanderers of the Brotherhood. They do not want to understand what power they have touched. In their malicious disbelief they will say, "The Brotherhood does not exist," and when they are asked to prove their assertion they will insist that they have not seen the Brotherhood. Neither have they seen very much of the world, but does this mean that it also does not exist? Since the detractors cannot prove the non-existence of Our Brotherhood, they are irritated by any mention of Our Abode.

It is better to question detractors than to leave them in a paroxysm of blasphemy. It is truly said, "It will be asked of you, and you will have to account not only for the evil words that were spoken, but also for all the kind words that were left unspoken." Many sayings from antiquity teach humanity the simplest truths, and they are as new even today. Thus let us be cautious with the concept of Brotherhood and not forget that sensitive apparatuses record every word about the Brotherhood.

Let us not be among those who intentionally or unintentionally betray. There is a particular sickness in which one who is in despair evokes the Highest Powers with blasphemy. These ailing ones cannot be put into the same category as the malicious blasphemers, who are not in despair, but delight in the destruction of the best dreams of humanity. They will not receive any signs from the Brotherhood. Their creativity will not be uplifted by beautiful thoughts. We therefore pity all those who reject the Brotherhood.

40. Urusvati takes to heart all that happens in the world. All actions can be divided into the heartfelt and the heartless. Humanity should remember this distinction, especially now. Heartfelt perceptions, even with many differences, can be united, but heartlessness is the unity of the dark forces, and among them you will not find co-workers of the Brotherhood. If We recall all the past lives of Our Brothers, We will not find even one heartless action. The action of the flaming heart led them to the stake, to the cross, and to all the tortures invented by the malicious and the ignorant.

We do not shun life. When We manifest Ourselves We cannot be distinguished from other people. You yourselves can testify that when Djwal Khul came to welcome you He appeared no different from the other Lamas. Urusvati immediately sensed something unusual, but this sensation could have been attributed to the presence of the head of the monastery. Thus, outwardly, all Brothers and co-workers bear the usual earthly appearance. But even with such a conventional appearance their heartfelt warmth will shine in every glance and smile. One can call this quality of heartiness by another, more scientific name, but We wish to affirm the most human aspect of Our Abode.

In books one can find some of Our names. They are very solemn ones. One can read about Manu, or about the Bodhisattvas. Remember that some nations are in need of lofty designations, but We are simply Servitors of Light and We revere Hierarchy. Our first call is for perfectment, not for titles or high rank. As it pertains to Hierarchy, this expression "titles and high rank" should not be understood in the earthly sense, in which people express their love for all kinds of ranks and distinctions. We serve the infinite Hierarchy. We accept leadership, not as a distinction, but as an immutable necessity. Such responsibility should be the foundation of all human communities. We do not attach importance to titles, for during Our many different lives We have had a great number of distinctions and titles in different languages. Many of these titles have been completely erased from human memory. Who can name the resplendent rulers of Atlantis? Only amidst the marshes of Tsaidam can one see the radiant images of former cities. Urusvati remembers the structures there, and the sculpture of the Great Bull.

Remember that during the progression of Our lives We have preserved the memory of the greatest events and recorded them in the repositories of the Brotherhood. Let those who wish to have an idea of Our Inner Life assimilate the many details that form the Statutes of Our Abode.

41. Urusvati knows how to withstand hostile currents. This ability does not come without cause or without former accumulations. One must first know the Supermundane World, but without shunning earthly life. The hostile currents can be manifested in various ways, such as psychic disturbances or unusual sicknesses, and worldly complications may occur that require a wise solution. One thus learns discrimination in all domains.

It should be understood that spatial currents influence the psychology of entire nations and generate new kinds of sicknesses. Unfavorable currents can also cause unfortunate events in daily life. When dealing with the currents one must avoid hypocrisy, superstition, or cowardice. Each hesitation makes one subject to the power of the whirlwind of chaos. We especially welcome the equilibrium that is earned in earthly life by extensive and broad experience. In such a progressive motion even karma will not overtake one. Thought that has known the correlations between the worlds obtains its power from them.

Every co-worker of the Brotherhood comes into close contact with the Subtle World. We have entire Strongholds in that world. You already know their names; you have heard about the wondrous tree and the structures created by thought. One must clearly realize these conditions in order to direct oneself to *Dokyood*. Thought not obscured by doubt will lead to Our supermundane Abodes. The Abode of the Hierarchy in the Himalayas is in constant communication with the Abodes in the Subtle World, and the earthly battle resounds and thunders there. People do not want to understand this correlation, therefore even Armageddon is to them only an earthly conflict between peoples, and the most important aspect of Armageddon remains misunderstood. How can one participate in something when only the smallest part of what is happening is known? We affirm that the battle raging in the Subtle World is far more violent than that which is fought on Earth. Truly, much of the spatial battle resounds on Earth. Often Our World tries to warn people of this terrible danger, but in vain. One of Our Brothers used to say, "Let us tell people once again, but how difficult it is to speak to deaf ears." Their warnings will be words of justice and compassion.

You have frequently noticed an incomprehensible sleepiness, which may mean that you are cooperating with distant worlds, or else is evidence of your cooperation with the powers of the Subtle World. You should vigilantly observe the requirements of the organism. You cannot think about incidental happenings when something of importance is taking place. Only through ignorance can Our Ordainments be ignored. But great is the joy when not only the Brotherhood is realized, but also the link with the Subtle World.

42. Urusvati has developed her musical talent beautifully. This proficiency is achieved as the result of much labor in other lives. According to the Teachings of Plato, music should not be understood in the narrow sense of music alone, but as participation in all the harmonious arts. In singing, in poetry, in painting, in sculpture, in architecture, in speech, and, finally, in all manifestations of sound, musicality is expressed. In Hellas a ceremony to all the Muses was performed. Tragedy, dance, and all rhythmic movement served the harmony of Cosmos. Much is spoken about beauty, but the importance of harmony is little understood. Beauty is an uplifting concept, and each offering to beauty is an offering to the equilibrium of Cosmos. Everyone who expresses music in himself sacrifices, not for himself, but for others, for humanity, for Cosmos.

Perfection of thought is an expression of beautiful musicality. The highest rhythm is the best prophylaxis, a pure bridge to the highest worlds. Thus We affirm Beauty in Our Abode. Urusvati has noted that the music of the spheres is characterized by a harmony of rhythm. It is precisely this quality that brings inspiration to humanity. People usually do not think about the sources of inspiration, but if they did they would help Our work greatly.

You know about the special musical instruments

that are in Our possession. Urusvati has heard them. The refined scale and rhythm of Sister Oriole should be acknowledged as the highest harmony. Often such singing has served to bring peace to the world, and even the servants of darkness have retreated before its harmonies. One should learn how to develop one's own musicality by all possible means.

The heart's feeling is sensed not in the words themselves but in their sound. There can be no irritation in harmony. Malice cannot exist where the spirit ascends. It is not by chance that in antiquity the epic scriptures were sung, not only to facilitate memorizing but also for inspiration. Likewise, it is rhythm and harmony that protect us against fatigue.

The quality of music and rhythm should be developed from infancy.

43. In all her many lives Urusvati strove to the Heights. "A mountain bird," she was called by the physicians, not because of poor health, but because of her innermost quest for the Beautiful Mountains. In these flights of the spirit was shown an unusual devotion to the Brotherhood. Each earthly mountain reminded her of Our Heights. Every achievement indicated the paths to Us.

Mountain air in itself is beneficial for some hearts, and also reminds one about the heights above ten thousand feet, where the elements of fire and air purify space, not only physically but also inwardly. Thus physical and spiritual needs are combined. Hearts that have realized this will strive to the Heights, because their inner knowledge reveals to them the salutary spheres. Everyone, everywhere, who feels love for the Brotherhood will strive to Us.

We also strive to the spheres, where We have been before. We divide Our spirits into many parts. We send Our arrows by messengers and Deputies. There are some Deputies to whom We entrust leadership in the far-off worlds. Such substitution is difficult to explain in earthly words.

Man's knowledge cannot encompass all the attributes of the spirit. Even on Earth one knows about obsession, but usually in an incorrect sense. One knows about twin souls, but this is understood as little as obsession. Yet history is witness to those who have been inseparably linked in all their existences. Let us extend these attributes into Infinity, and much will become intelligible.

Let us not forget how varied are the conditions of the Subtle World and life on the far-off worlds. From an earthly point of view life on some planets can hardly be regarded as life, but thought is already in embryonic form, and We do call such a basis "life." Amidst the first sowing We see the Pillars of Light of the Leader, who may be Our Brother or Our Deputy. And when We proceed to the next sphere, Our Deputy may also precede Us as Our forerunner, just as did John the Baptist. Thus, on the far-off worlds, just as on Earth, Our messengers, forerunners, and Deputies exist. One can sense an entire network of relationships, and Our earthly co-workers should know that their Brothers work too in the far-off worlds.

Sacred is the word "Brotherhood"! May it resound whenever one thinks or sees the mountain heights. We revere Hierarchy in Infinite Space.

Let all earthly wayfarers learn that We await them on all the paths to Us.

44. Urusvati embodies fieriness. Of what, then, does this precious quality consist? Some fieriness exists in everyone, but there are particularly fiery natures that can communicate easily with the far-off worlds. People usually understand fieriness as anger, irritability, and bursts of hot temper, but these are merely earthly qualities, and we should not look for true fieriness in them. True fieriness is demonstrated in communion with the Invisible World and in participation in Our Missions.

Moreover, one should not associate fieriness with mediumism. On the contrary, in fieriness the mucous membranes are dry and ectoplasm is not exuded. The special quality of fieriness stands quite independently. With it, courage is present and fear does not exist. Fiery people do not feel fear, and are not afraid of the manifestations of the Subtle World.

Most people fear such manifestations, and therein lies their isolation from the Subtle World, even though there cannot be any transformation of life without this natural bond. We hasten to inspire people with fearlessness by every means. We try to whisper about the harm of fear and the foolishness of terror. From remote times people have been accustomed to fear so-called death. They were always intimidated by hell, and at the same time were not told about the meaning of perfectment. One cannot ask people to be brave if they do not know why they are on Earth, and where they will be directed when liberated. We entrust Our co-workers to repeat as much as they can to people about the great Eternity and the continuity of life.

We have not left, but have voluntarily remained on Earth. We have consciously accepted earthly life. We could be far away, but choose to remain with the suffering ones. Our Vigil would not be unswerving if We were influenced by fear. As physicians We know what devastation fear produces in the human organism.

Earthly physicians should distinguish a special kind

of sickness caused by fear. Let them experience Our tension. Let them understand how harmful is fear.

Do not think that fieriness comes by itself; it must be cultivated through many lives.

45. Urusvati has overcome all the earthly misconceptions about safety and material security. Neither exists in earthly conditions, yet this dark mirage seduces multitudes of people. They dream of building towers where they might be sheltered in complete safety. They dream of accumulating treasures that would provide security, forgetting that they can reach such a stronghold only beyond earthly conditions. Do We wish to plunge humanity into despair? One must realize that it is only when one is beyond the range of all danger that invulnerability becomes possible. Only by acknowledging the vanity of earthly treasures are we able to receive our heritage of everlasting wealth. Let us not regard these Teachings as abstract moralizing. Only by looking at it from a purely scientific point of view can one be convinced that a true knowledge of earthly reality gives freedom of consciousness and perfectment to humanity.

Do not think that after millions of years of existence humanity has accepted the foundation of Be-ness. No indeed, it is now, with shelves breaking under the weight of masses of books, that greed and illusion ensnare humanity! We are concerned that people should understand the illusion of earthly conditions.

Not one of the Teachers has ever proclaimed egotism and greed for mankind. It is not from Light that such vipers are born. Black brotherhoods exist where the teaching of the infamous processes of destruction, decay, and disunity are propagated.

One should ponder the ceaseless Battle We lead against the dark forces. People do not stop to realize that they are surrounded by experienced destroyers. No one repeats the need to turn to the Stronghold of Good. We may receive communications that a conspiracy against constructiveness has developed and We hasten to prevent it, but you yourself know how few listen to Us. Which means that once again *Tactica Adversa* must be applied.

We rejoice at each understanding of Truth.

46. Urusvati has mastered the power of burning evenly. Long ago We spoke about the uselessness of flickering lamps. Flickering is caused either by a lack of oil or by the poor condition of the lamp. With improvement, lamps will burn steadily and everyone will be grateful for their even light. Likewise, in human perfectment, after sinkings and soarings, a powerful radiance will be achieved and the help to humanity will increase. We welcome the stage of burning evenly because We can cooperate with it.

It is impossible to imagine Our Abode as full of dissonance. Even a crowd is powerful if it blends itself into a mighty consonance. Thus, when cooperating we must discipline our thoughts. But many misunderstandings can arise while sending thoughts. Even those who recognize the creativeness of thought are astonished at not seeing immediate results, forgetting that results can take place invisibly and in unexpected places. Also they fail to see that because thought-energy acts through the least-resistant channels, unexpected results occur constantly. The reason for this lies in undisciplined thinking—people might think that they have sent only one thought, whereas in reality they have contrived to scatter hundreds of the most unexpected sendings. What is received will be just as unexpected. Much harm results from these fleas of thought, which jump about and bite unlikely people.

Little attention is given to channels for the spreading of thought.

We consider it most important to preserve pure thinking. This is possible where burning evenly exists. Thought is sent when there is a developed ability to concentrate. There are special apparatuses that enhance the concentration of thought. They are useful for sending thoughts to great distances. You may be surprised to know that these apparatuses are made by fusing various alloys. This fusion was considered from ancient times to be a special science, and an alloy was called a choir of metals.

47. Urusvati guards co-measurement. From this quality are born discrimination and a reverence of Hierarchy. We guard co-measurement. An ancient proverb says, "An elephant's load will crush an ass." There have been instances when egoism hindered the understanding of co-measurement; yet there can be no justice without comparison. We have pointed out many times how novices in thinking sever the thread of communion because of conceit. Yet everyone should remember that even great leaders had to learn discrimination and co-measurement.

Every Teacher in his past lives had to decide whether he wished to depart to the far-off worlds or remain with long suffering Earth. No little co-measurement was required for this decision, and each chose to remain with those who suffer. We permit Ourselves flights to the far-off worlds only to gain knowledge. Only in rare cases do We permit lengthy stays on other worlds. But even these stays are not a complete separation; on the contrary, they are like a web uniting the threads. Thus is the Brotherhood founded invincibly upon co-measurement and devotion.

People can imitate Us, for each one can apply in

life the principles of Brotherhood. Only dark deniers speak about the absolute irrelevance of Brotherhood on Earth. You have read in books about the Builders of the Planets, about Leaders of Nations. Each one should rejoice that during his lifetime here on Earth the Teacher does exist, and that the path to Him is not forbidden. Each one must find inspiration in knowing that he can be in communication with the Teacher.

Let us again remember about co-measurement. Without it one can become misguided in his concept of the Brotherhood and the relationship between the Teacher and the pupil. Usually people do not like to be called pupils, but We retain this honorable name even for Ourselves. Every Teacher also remains a pupil, and in this idea lies co-measurement of the highest degree.

You are rightly indignant when someone uses inappropriate words in speaking about the Teacher. It indicates that their thinking is far from co-measurement. Do not be surprised at Our frequent repetition of this word, but this concept, in particular, is often distorted by people. We affirm co-measurement as one of the foundations of Our Inner Life.

48. Urusvati is in constant communication with Us. It is not easy to receive the currents of intensified energy while remaining in a physical body amidst daily life. We consider such simultaneity a special achievement. One must be able to adapt oneself to the peculiarities of subtle energies. It can easily be shown that little time is needed for even the most detailed dreams. Complicated actions and lengthy discourses are assimilated instantly. Such features of subtle perception are characteristic of communication with Us. One may understand complicated sendings without knowing in which language they are given. The thought reaches the corresponding centers and reveals the essence of the communication. The communication is through the subtle body. One should become accustomed to this subtle perception. This cannot be understood without the broadening of consciousness. Many problems must be understood without earthly limitations. People often notice only one detail, then elevate it to an immutable law.

Generally, man's centers are understood relatively. Their very names have changed, in different languages, over millenniums. Some call the Chalice "the celestial axis," but this does not change its significance. Others may speak about the influence of the Mother of the World, even though in its essence *Shakti* contains the great meaning of the Primary Energy. Also, people forget about the collective action of the centers, which is quite different for each one. Equally individual is the transmutation of the centers in the subtle and fiery bodies. They preserve their essence in each body, but their development depends upon the progress made in passing through earthly life.

It would seem that the muscles have been sufficiently studied, but their functions depend upon one's character. Each part of the body acts individually. The gait depends on the psychic condition, which causes the muscles to work in a particular correlation.

The relativity of opinion is demonstrated in discussions about subtle energy. It is incorrect to insist on a particular number of petals for the Lotuses. In addition, each petal differs from the others. Let us not limit the multiformity of the structure of the world. The most unexpectedly profuse growth of the tissues and branchings of the nerves enriches the organism. Each observation is valuable, but let us be very careful in generalizing.

We have had time to learn much, but it is precisely

this learning that has taught Us to be cautious in expressing Our knowledge. Neophytes hurry to shout about what they have heard, not thinking of the consequences; but with knowledge comes co-measurement.

We are concerned about how best to explain and make easily accessible the understanding of the Universe. First of all, one should discard antiquated categorizing.

49. Urusvati has observed Our collectors of medicinal plants. Some of them know that they labor for an important purpose, but most of them gather the plants without that understanding. They take the plants to a specified place where someone receives and pays for them. This may sometimes be a Chinese trader, but the arrival of a Sart or a Hindu in no way puzzles these humble workers.

It is impermissible to even hint at the importance of these medicinal plants or rumors will spread, and the danger of invasion will arise. It is easy for Us to protect Ourselves from raids, but more difficult to avoid attracting the attention of the local people. They preserve many traditions and are ready to apply them to real life. Their imagination is so highly developed, and their hearing and sight so acute, that they can notice much that is invisible to others. They know life in the mountains and can find tracks where others would not think of looking.

But the local people also understand the significance of the Forbidden Locality, and protection is thus created. This is necessary because Our apparatuses may require supplies from the cities. Sometimes buyers obtain certain things whose use is unknown even to them, and send such purchases to Us through Nepal. I can tell you this because there is no danger that the route will be discovered. Many fairy tales have been woven about Our Abode.

You may be sure that these many centuries have taught people to harken to Our Advice. Let us not forget that at various times We have appeared in the countries of the West. In addition to Our Eastern Ashrams, We have had Our Abodes in Western cities—in Lyon, in Nuremberg, in places near London, near St. Petersburg, and in Italy. Besides the Oriental and Egyptian Ashrams, it was necessary to have Strongholds in some big cities. Let us not forget that the struggle with the forces of darkness evokes the need for many measures.

One can trace many missions sent to humanity at different times. Homeopathy was sent as a means of safeguarding people from enormous doses of poison. Dreams about the need for a universal world-language have been given. Only in this way can the purity of all languages be preserved. Everyone will then know both his own language and the universal one. Thus may be found the best pattern for human relations. People do not understand that the distortion of a language is a crime, for many word-roots have a deep significance in their rhythm and sound. Thus We pave the way.

50. Urusvati has asked about the means of material support for Our abodes. Remember that many streams are filled with gold, silver and sapphires can be found in Our mountains, and We know about many hidden treasures. Do you remember how a pound note was sent flying to London? Often people need help. Thus the earthly is correlated with the Supermundane. Cooperation with the Subtle World must be continuous. The entire multiformity of the subtlest spheres must be understood in order to realize how complex is the work of Our Abode.

First of all one should help on Earth, but help is equally needed in the Subtle World. Epidemics of horror shake the Subtle World. There are battles, and serious illnesses spread. People on Earth are accustomed to fearing contagion and they bring this fear into the Subtle World, where thought about terror is then created. Is it possible that people do not realize that they bring all their earthly prejudices into the Subtle World? If it is hard to eliminate all kinds of pernicious growth on Earth, it is far more difficult to do so in the Subtle World, where the earthly accumulations are crystallized. I think that the condition of Our planet would be much improved if the load brought into the Subtle World were of better quality. One thought alone can destroy a multitude of microbes.

Let us consider how much opposition is met by everyone who sends useful thoughts. Today Urusvati experienced many of Our intensified currents. Such a change of current indicates the concentration that must be manifested, for each current struggles with its counter-current. Thus, the most urgent decisions require defense against clever destroyers. Urusvati helped Us through the entire night, and even found time to be in her motherland.

51. Urusvati has always endeavored to shorten her time in the Subtle World. Such striving reveals a devotion to the direct work of alleviating the suffering of humanity. If earthly people are divided according to warmth of heart and heartlessness, then there also exists a division between those who strive to stay longer in the Subtle World and those who hasten toward perfectment through reincarnation.

We are in favor of those who hasten, despite the paradox of hastening into Infinity. We encourage all perfectment, because in it is contained the General

Good. We have dedicated Ourselves to the Great Service and We summon to it all those who can help the unknown sufferers.

Our Stronghold is actually built upon this concept of help to unknown ones. Multitudes of these unknown ones who need Our care exist on Earth and in the Subtle World. Let Our Abode be called "The Great Service."

We all, at the right time, have hastened to Earth and chosen the most difficult tasks. Such conditions tempered Us and taught Us to despise persecution. The affirmers of Truth will always be persecuted by the falsifiers. No one should think that such persecutions are meant only for certain people. Every messenger of Truth must experience the onslaught of falsehood. This contact with chaos is inevitable.

You have noticed that people always place the location of Shambhala to the North. Even among the Eskimos and the Kamchatkans there exist legends about a wondrous country beyond the land of the midnight sun. The reasons for this displacement are varied. Some wanted to conceal the location of Our Abode. Some wanted to avoid the responsibility of confronting a difficult idea. Some think of their neighbors to the North as being especially fortunate. In reality it seems that all nations know about the Forbidden Country but consider themselves unworthy to have it within their boundaries!

We have a vast collection of literature on this subject. It is impossible to count the legendary heroes who are linked with Our Abode. You know about Gessar Khan and about Prester John. Everyone should understand the boundary between Truth and the popular imagination. The Abode could not have existed for so many centuries without impressing its emanations upon the people's collective memory. One should also remember that We are better known in the Subtle World than on Earth. Thence come faint recollections which inspire haste in those who have understood the significance of Great Service.

52. Urusvati has been able to preserve a true contact with the Subtle World. Let Us explain why We call this contact a true one. There are some people who deny completely the existence of the Subtle World, and in such negation they blaspheme. Others, although they acknowledge the Subtle World, are prejudiced against it, and their misguided attitude often differs little from blasphemy. One can easily appreciate in a cosmic sense the harm of such attitudes that poison the atmosphere and deny the very existence of that realm which should exist in cooperation with earthly life.

One cannot expect the approach of the Subtle World if it is rejected, cursed, and feared on Earth. A correct attitude will accept the Subtle World calmly, honestly, and kindly. The magnet of kindness acts in all worlds. How can one deny that which exists, just as we all exist!

One should not just acknowledge the immortality of the spirit but should also learn how to approach all the manifestations of Infinity. The Subtle World can approach us vitally if it is not rejected. There are two kinds of courage. There are those who are most daring from an earthly point of view, yet tremble when they hear about ghosts! But those who are truly courageous do not fear phantoms, which can appear in the most horrible forms. An experienced observer knows that these phantoms cannot exist where there is courage.

During many incarnations, a correct attitude toward all astral manifestations is developed. You may wonder if all these various subtle entities are able to approach Our Abode. Of course, they can approach but they have no influence. Every place on Earth is filled with subtle entities, and one must discern the extent to which they infringe upon earthly life.

The teacher must, first of all, explain the cooperation between the worlds. Mankind should not be allowed to remain under the illusion that they are isolated from the other worlds. Before it is too late one must provide all that is known about the close cooperation between the worlds. Let us not insist upon the names given to the inhabitants of the Subtle World. In different teachings, different names, some even solemn or threatening, are given to Supermundane Messengers.

We do not argue about names, and We do not waste energy discussing the many strata of the Subtle World. Variety seems to be needed for human imagination. If only this would develop humanity! Thus, We welcome a correct attitude toward the Subtle World. Its reflection will then be found all over the world. Our Abode will be nearer for those who are able to find a right attitude toward the manifestations of the Subtle World.

53. Urusvati is deeply aware of the significance of the creativity in people. We direct Our thought along the lines of cooperation and nationwide creativeness. It is time to realize that people's creativity is an inspired affirmation of their value. In all Our labor We allow time to inspire multiform creativity. Not only those who have dedicated themselves to art, but the entire nation should direct its thoughts to creativeness. Let daily life be created by the hands of the family. Let leisure time be filled with creativeness and let people sing, for the great power of harmony is contained in choirs.

All the arts should be taught in schools. They should not be instilled forcibly, for every beginner can feel beauty in the manifestation of art. In addition, it would be wrong if only a small group of artists were to create and the fruits of their talents be mass-produced. Such mechanization would not help people. Everyone must try to serve creativeness. Let people love the sport of creativeness; a marathon of creativeness is immeasurably more lofty than a marathon of runners!

It will be asked how We adorn Our Abode. Indeed, We do adorn it. Each one of Us was at some time an artist. One can draw from one's Chalice of accumulations and attainments many treasures of creativeness and express them in the various realms of art. If people would learn to know and to understand their former lives, they could draw much benefit from past experiences. But people do not know how to use their former achievements wisely. This simple truth requires an excruciating process of assimilation.

It is almost impossible to tell people how to create by thought. They do not believe that strings can resound in response to the currents of thought. They do not believe that dry pigment can be gathered into harmonious images under the pressure of thought. And yet, people do know about the designs created in sand by rhythm. They admire the designs made by frost, and are not surprised when strings resound to distant rhythms. But thought produces the most powerful rhythms, and with such vibrations one can create.

Do not consider Us to be magi or sorcerers when you hear about Our mirrors. It is concentration of thought that fixes the images. Thus, first of all, one must refine one's thought.

54. Urusvati has acquired the quality of instantaneousness. This quality is easily spoken of, but rarely applied in life. It is easy to say that thought is instantaneous, but it is difficult to realize such instantaneousness amidst the whirl of events. At times We send one word from which an entire message must be determined. For the majority such a word will flash out without result, but a broadened consciousness will vigilantly grasp each sign. There are many reasons for such brevity. Sometimes the whirl is so intense that it becomes impossible to send each sound. Sometimes there are so many ears trying to eavesdrop on this "radio" that one must be careful not to inform uninvited listeners. For this it is easier to establish an especially inaccessible wavelength during a calm hour, but at a time of raging battle even the best currents can be disturbed and their excessive tension can be fatal for the receiver.

Urusvati has also acquired the ability to recognize the authentic. Our Voices are recognized by their timbre, and a person close to Us will not mistake them. But besides the recognition of the sound there also exists the feeling of authenticity. The broadened consciousness can never be deceived by this feeling. A child senses unerringly the steps of its father and mother. How much more deeply does the heart feel the sendings of the Teacher.

The ignorant say that there could be a mistake, because someone could imitate the voice of the Teacher. But the broadened consciousness cannot make a mistake, for straight-knowledge cannot make mistakes. In a state of great tension a tremor may be felt, but then one can repeat one's question. It is especially difficult, because people cannot imagine what the spatial battles are like. In earthly conditions it is difficult to imagine a battle in the midst of Infinity. Even the Voice of the Silence is not understood correctly. Still, it is recorded and resounds in the consciousness. Each accepted or assimilated thought vibrates and resounds. Also, those who receive a thought frequently repeat it. This process has a special name—the sealing of the thought. You know how often we must repeat what we have received in order that it not evaporate. The least disturbance can break the reception, even with a broadened consciousness.

You are justly astonished that the inhabitants of the Subtle World do not speak about the battles in space. The Great Ones have mercy on the people of Earth, and the small do not know about the battle. Likewise, on Earth there are many wars being fought, but many people either do not know about them, or call them by different names. Similarly, in the Subtle World there is confusion and destruction, but the majority of people on Earth do not understand the reason for this. The lower strata are more numerous than the higher ones. Besides, the confusion does not reach the "Blissful Fields," about which you know. Therefore the great Spiritual Toilers do not remain there, but strive to active service in Heaven as on Earth.

55. Urusvati knows how to bring joy. This quality is contained in the disciplined will. The realization of joy grows through conviction, not through the acquisition of things. There is no condition that cannot be turned into joy. When We speak repeatedly about joy We evoke it as a great reality. One cannot imagine Our Abode without joy. The most tense battles are filled with joy. Without it there is no action. To elucidate the meaning and value of joy is to resolve a great physiological principle.

The ignorant connect the sensation of joy with a healthy digestion or with success in life, but joy is greater than health and success. It can also exist amidst sickness and humiliation. Such a feeling is developed not only through many incarnations but also from a wisely spent sojourn in the Subtle World.

People encumber themselves with objects not only on Earth, but also in the Subtle World, where each unnecessary object will become a heavy load. Equally intolerable is unrestrained, foolish creativeness in the Subtle World. There one can create so much ugliness that it will follow one through all lives. Joy cannot be born when dirty tails are dragged along. Joy is about the future and cannot live in the past.

It should be understood that We wish to explain joy as something creative and inspired. Joy is a reliable magnet. We want people to know where their panacea is. They can conduct a better and higher communion in joy. They will find a firm co-worker in joy. They will wish that the world might live in joy.

We can affirm that despondency will not cross the threshold of Our Abode, for joy lives there. Let people remember that no one can deprive them of their joy. Even a machine works better when it is used with joy. Decidedly, everything can be set right and improved, and nothing can close the way to perfectment.

For Us it is a festival when We see that Our co-workers have understood the shield of joy.

56. Urusvati understands the importance of caution where medicines are concerned. Always, and in all our relations with people, We remain physicians, in the true sense. We continually meet sick people and try first to restore their balance. People seek Us most often when their sicknesses have already begun. Measures should be taken not only to enlighten their consciousness, but also to cure their illnesses.

People do not realize that We have to treat them as dangerously ill. When We advise you to be cautious it does not mean that we consider you careless. On the contrary, We pay attention only when someone finds himself in a state of extreme tension and special caution is needed. If you think of yourself as a physician, your purpose becomes clearer.

Especially now, people are in such tension that they require wise treatment. It is often necessary to agree with them about details in order to protect the most important, and encourage them in order to free them from fear. Thus, the methods of a wise physician must be acquired by a teacher of life. Sometimes an illness can be arrested by a simple word of encouragement. Let us not think so much about where and how the illness began. First of all, a physician does not blame the patient for his condition, but seeks a cessation of decay. In every illness there is evidence of decomposition. Thus, one should apply healing methods in cases of human error.

Recently you heard about an instance of obsession. It was an almost hopeless case because the sick woman was tired of struggling and had become a follower of the obsessor. Also, those who surrounded her increased her sickness. Usually such obsessed ones should be taken to a new place and their surroundings changed. It was not possible to influence her by writing, but through personal magnetism the growth of terror could be stopped. People do not understand how much one's surroundings encourage the development of certain illnesses. Thus one should become accustomed to being in the position of a physician. Our Inner Life is filled with healing activities.

57. Urusvati, together with Us, knows how to be kind. In this one word is contained an entire world outlook. No other concept can be named which is so distorted. From idle hypocrisy to manifest cruelty, all finds its place under the mask of good. One should really know how to be kind in order to benefit others rather than oneself.

We continually send thoughts about kindness, action, and labor. There cannot be kindness without action. There cannot be any good where there is no labor. There will be no kindness where there is no opposition to evil. There will be no kindness if we do not accept the responsibility to discern evil, to recognize corruption, and do not lose the possibility of bringing Light. Beautiful are the words, "Light disperses darkness." However, Light must be brought, and this action in itself is full of self-abnegation. Light will also illuminate and dispel frightful monsters, even when they show themselves in their worst aspect. Every light-bearer has to live through those moments. He should not slacken his pace and should look fearlessly upon the monsters. There will be no complete renunciation of fear if the light-bearer averts his eyes in the hope that Light alone will dispel the monsters. It is not only Light but also the Primal Energy that strikes the blow which destroys darkness.

You have already heard that We send Our arrows at the last moment. You must understand this—know when the last moment for all decisions has arrived—and accept the responsibility. Many people try to avoid it by all possible means, and because of this such warriors are unreliable. We test each co-worker, but few are those who accept the joy of such a task. Most will evade it and try to hide themselves when the time for action has come. Let the co-workers show who is good and who is bad. Let them show who is ready for action and who prefers the lazy twilight. Darkness is not far from it.

Our Abode is most peaceful, but it is ready to fight for good. We are informed when the dark traitors begin new attacks, and can then choose the best hour of battle. Again we come to karmic laws. Each action depends on something that has happened before, and the consequences will flow amidst many secondary conditions. They must be accepted and one's actions taken in conformity with them. I speak about this because many think that We can ignore the Law of Karma.

Many conditions are needed in order to alleviate the consequences. Thus, let us be fully on guard so that the good may not suffer any loss.

58. Urusvati rebels against any kind of cruelty and all torture. This is not through any lack of fortitude, but from the inner knowledge that, in the name of man's dignity, torture cannot be permitted.

There are many kinds of cruelty inflicted upon people and animals. It should be remembered that the karma of torturers is very heavy. The barbaric consciousness should be made to understand what is permissible and what is not. Few torments can be excused by claims of legality.

An experienced physician first of all asks his patients how they feel. Such a feeling is much more important than medicines. But what kind of feelings can there be on Earth if no one is safe from cruelty?

Feelings can solve the most complicated problems of a country, but the inviolability of the individual and his dignity must be protected. Let us not be consoled by the so-called impartiality of the courts, where dignity is trampled by crude arbitrariness. It is easy to talk about sadism, but it is terrible to see that this inconceivable madness is not stopped. Yes, one must expect that the fundamental quality about which We are speaking will not be understood. There are so many small but nonetheless terrible tormentors all over the world! The deliberate torment of one's neighbor is no different from that carried out during the most barbarous eras. You may recall the crowds of the Roman circuses; can today's crowds boast of worthier conduct? Did the change in their attire change their consciousness? One must remember such conditions in order to know what Our Abode must fight.

There are many associations for the protection of animals, but too few for the protection of man. Let those who are cruel not dare to pose as compassionate. It is difficult to overcome cruelty. We labor hard, We send the strongest thoughts, but they seldom penetrate stony hearts.

One may feel the power of the sunrise and store up the solar prana, but immeasurable patience is also required to fight cruelty. We have continually before us examples of the most refined cruelty, as if people had agreed to burden the karma of the planet. Thus, not only war and revolution, but school and family life are filled with mean cruelty. One must realize how much torment and pitiable cries reach Our Abode. Everyone must be helped.

59. Urusvati, through her straight-knowledge, discerns superhuman action. Let us examine the different kinds of human action. There are actions of free will, karmic actions, and actions performed under the influence of obsession. But there can be special kinds of action that do not fit into these categories. We call them superhuman actions. Chosen people fulfill Our missions, consciously applying their best will and abilities, yet their actions do not originate from free will or from obsession. Nor can they be called karmic actions, for in them karma may have been exhausted, or new karma started. Comparing all these, one may come to the conclusion that such action is a special expression sent by Higher Forces.

In antiquity such actions were called sacred, for in them was felt something from beyond Earth, and the discerning of such actions is contained in straight-knowledge. It is difficult to classify them according to human laws, but an expanded consciousness can feel their presence. The higher ranks of the hostile forces especially dislike those who bear Our missions. The dark ones cannot understand the missions or determine their scope, which irritates them all the more.

One can cite many examples from history of people who carried Our missions. These tasks take many forms. Sometimes We assign only one action to be performed, but the mission may last a whole lifetime. We are accustomed to taking responsibility for the chosen ones. Each member of Our Community suggests a person who has been tested and assumes the responsibility for him. We need these lengthy testings that last even for several lives. We must be certain that the essence of the mission will be fulfilled. We do not consider details, because local conditions can bring in new factors. Also, We do not insist upon minor dates, for what is important to Us is the essence of the manifestation. Where is success and where failure? We alone can decide that. The considerations of cause and effect bring many complications. We project Our attention into the future in order to avert untimely conclusions.

It can be asked why We did not speak earlier about the concept of superhuman action. One should not speak too openly about these missions, for many people might feel self-important, and might justify their arbitrary actions with some claim of mission. On the whole, many will not understand this classifying of action into four kinds. But if straight-knowledge does not indicate the distinctions, the intellect will not define them.

Some enjoyed reading *The History of a Piece of Bread*, but for others it was a tedious and boring story. So also, reflections on human action will seem boring to many. Let us remember the guarantees connected with superhuman actions. People should help Us to help them.

60. Urusvati can attest to how empty life is without communion with Us, if one has been previously connected with the Brotherhood. It is often necessary to feel support and to compare one's decisions with Principles already verified by long experience. The Teaching itself comes to life when it is linked with its Source. It is cold and gloomy to walk alone between hostile camps. Of course, the Subtle World dispels loneliness, but it is immeasurably more encouraging and helpful when one is aware of Our Abode. Not in Infinity is the Stronghold revealed, but here. Even those who do not know the exact location of the Abode can turn in its direction, and this direction is given by the striving thought.

If an artist were to depict Our Abode even approximately, the product of his imagination could be used as a teraph. But the best teraph is the human heart. A powerful magnet is developed from heart to heart, and such an attraction can be strong, even physically. The attraction to Our Heart can increase so greatly that it would be impossible to restrain it. This is called "the Fiery Chariot." Such fiery sensations require great harmony, otherwise they can turn into a chaotic whirlwind.

He who knows about Us will not be rejected. His thoughts are known to Us, and great is his relief when he realizes that there is no reason to hide them. He knows that each kind thought strengthens the link with Us; without words, simply by a deep tremor of the heart, every kind sending reaches Us. There can be unnecessary appeals because of inexperience, but harmony and devotion establish true cooperation. We rejoice when the step of true cooperation is reached; then the smallest sign is understood. Wise brevity is appreciated and one might say, "Our joy is your joy."

As long as people are preoccupied with magi and sorcerers, they are not with Us. The heart alone is needed for the Abode. A beautiful heart will always suffer on Earth, but the suffering heart becomes trustworthy. A fish cannot live without water, and the eagle does not rejoice without freedom. We want to suggest simplicity to our friends, for the complexity of life has already become harmful. Therefore We are silent about many discoveries, and although many formulas are ready in Our Abode, it is too early to reveal them to scientists, for their high purpose is too easily turned to harmful applications. Let those people who know Us guard this knowledge. A treacherous apostate will receive a wound that will not heal. But let us not speak about consequences, because some will take it as a threat. Every weaver grieves over a torn thread and rejoices at a strong yarn—thus it is also with the human spirit.

61. Urusvati is not afraid to join Us during the battle. Many become frightened at the mere mention of battle, and others are overcome with confusion when they learn of its long duration. Still others are seized by a deadly terror when they understand that this battle is without end. Most people try to limit Infinity.

One may smile at the mortal fear that strikes even those who imagine themselves to be great occultists. It is easy for them to sit and write articles, but they turn pale at the word "battle!" People who speak pompously about their initiations are far removed from real activity. How can they be taught to love the battle for Good? There are no words to transform a coward into a hero. Only danger can impel one into action, and it is precisely the coward who must go out to meet danger. People often beseech Us to protect them from danger, but dangers are necessary for their inner growth.

The endlessness of the battle will confuse the ignorant ones, and it is better not to speak of eternal battle to the unprepared. Let them keep the hope of a victory that they can understand. Of course, in thinking about such a victory, the phantom of defeat will hang over them. In the battle throughout Infinity We do not know defeat.

Let us not belittle the dark hierophants; they are not minor adversaries. Their ways are cunning, and they are aware of Infinity. But We know something beyond their knowledge, and they sense that there is something they cannot attain. Great is their wrath against such limitation, but that is the law. It is amazing to observe what base means they use to attract people! One must rely not on transient earthly ideas, but on immutable values.

It may be asked whether We become exhausted in time of battle. Such a question is not relevant. It would be better to ask about the degree of Our tension, which is great. If Our Sister Urusvati has heard the fall of the drops of Our sweat, one can imagine the tension of Our energies. If Our hair stands on end in an electric vortex, one can imagine the tension. We do not conceal the fact that the battle has moments of the greatest tension. If one is afraid, he should not approach the battle for Good. If one fears human judgment, let him not think about ethics. If one trembles for his earthly life, let him complete his decay in darkness. One can see that a coward perishes sooner than a courageous man; be assured that he who fears death attracts it to himself. Thus in all manifestations one can see how useful it is to develop the consciousness of Good. Let us not dwell upon these spasms of fear, for when one speaks about Brotherhood there is no place for fear.

62. When in her subtle body, Urusvati usually appears in a purple Grecian garment. The color of one's garment usually corresponds to the color of the aura, and the style of the garment is taken from the era to which the spirit feels closest. Everywhere in the Subtle World the beauty of one's garment is expressed clearly in thought. In the world of thought we usually wear the garment of a former life. Those who have not preserved a clear memory of the past frequently have difficulties in the Subtle World. They remember only random parts of their many garments of the past, and thus create an ugly mixture. They feel a need to create a garment for themselves immediately, but their undisciplined imagination can visualize only scraps of their attire. Seeing different garments on others, the newcomers begin to rush about in thought, and each thought-wave evokes an unexpected fragment.

The same thing happens with all mental construction, and in the end one must destroy all those ugly heaps. We do not idly advise you to concentrate, to develop thought in life, and to understand the feeling of harmony, so that each spiritual accumulation will prove useful in the Subtle World. We like simple and comfortable garments that do not impede Our work. It would be better if everyone could find a comfortable garment that will be useful in the Subtle World, and it is very sad when unseemly earthly garments are worn. Of course, the Guide will explain their ugliness and lack of comfort, but some people are so dull that they do not understand this advice. They wish to communicate with each other only through words and cannot grasp communication by thought.

The lower strata of the Subtle World manifest much ugliness. It is essential that Earth be purified of it. When I speak about the power of Beauty, I have in mind not only Earth, but also the Subtle World. We live half our lives in the Subtle World, and many of Our near ones are already in their subtle bodies. One can imagine the diversity of inner life manifested in Our Abode when the earthly exterior comes in contact with the supermundane worlds. Radiant are the flashes of fire and the rays!

63. Urusvati knows how to appreciate the value of all that exists, for every manifestation is the result of active thought. Even if a manifestation is undergoing involution, somewhere in it is concealed a spark of the highest energy. People will usually reject something completely even if only one part is not understood by them. An unwise or inexperienced person will act in this way, but with accumulated knowledge he will learn to appreciate each creative force, even when it is in an unfit envelope. Even jinn can build temples. They may not understand the purpose of building, but because of their power they make good masons. Every legend contains a particle of truth. For instance, the subterranean people of Agartha are often mentioned, although they do not exist. But the legend itself originated not far from Our Abode, where We do have extensive underground passages, but they are not on the grand scale described in the legend. Other legends tell about "White Waters" and "The Heavenly Jerusalem." Both of these tales relate to Our Abode. It would be unwise to reject legends without pondering over their meaning. Each of them preserves precise indications, often deliberately concealed. Frequently We Ourselves shroud the meaning of a legend, so that the local people will not disclose too much. Sometimes We must sternly forbid the crossing of particular boundaries. In everything one should evaluate situations carefully.

However, let us not be too specific about the details of every problem. Co-workers must understand that everything requires urgent decisions. Let them imagine the quantity of information that pours into Our Abode, all of which demands immediate decision. In this, We must not frighten Our earthly co-workers and must find everywhere an applicable spark of energy. Many useful helpers need repeated Indications, for they will not accept Indications when first given. This develops great patience in the co-workers, who learn that irritability is nothing but weakness of will. Misty thinking loves repetition, but events do not tarry.

We apply the highest measure of caution so as not to subject Our co-workers to unnecessary danger. But one can imagine how difficult it is at times to protect those who rush into danger, indignant at the Guiding Hand. Thus Our atmosphere is saturated. Only the cooperation of the Subtle World enables Us to expand possibilities.

64. Urusvati reveres the dates. Do not be surprised that We return to this question of dates, which are so important in Our Inner Life. Many dates can be communicated to people, but the majority will not be able to benefit from them. For their egoism impedes, and causes them to apply all indications only to themselves. The date of a great event may be indicated, and they will awaken at that time in their beds and ask with irritation, "Where is that special event?" Also, people do not understand that indicated events often take place on another plane. Irritation and perplexity disturb the atmosphere; they serve no purpose, and clearing them away drains the energy. If only people could spare the energy that they turn to their own benefit!

It is harmful when people envy the progress of others. When it is learned that someone has reached Our Abode because of just one service rendered to a Brother, many will think that they are also ready to render a similar service. But they forget that service was simply the last pearl in a whole necklace of self-sacrificing action. It is difficult for people to accept that someone of ordinary appearance might carry many accomplishments in his heart. For many lives the fires of Service may have shone brightly, and who can judge the progress of the heart? In general, people are uncomfortable with the unfamiliar. Thus, much is rejected that could be useful in Our Work. Even We have had to at times assume the most ordinary appearances, and have even been obliged to take earthly titles in order to enter more easily into the most exclusive and corrupt circles.

We are always concerned that each action should take place at the right time. Our adversaries may bring the world into confusion and even into war, and We must foresee the consequences of such events in order to ensure that they be directed to the progress of nations. For these reasons We are called the World Government. Many fear such terms, yet pray willingly to the Highest Concept and readily accept a Guiding Hand. If we can imagine the Highest Concept and have a living faith in it, why can we not accept World Government? Thus, reverence for the Highest Concept of Hierarchy could be manifested.

The dates are indicated. Let people accept them with all possible caution.

65. Urusvati has more than once taken upon herself another's pain. This action becomes part of the Great Service. At first it is difficult, but later such containment and self-sacrifice become second nature. Physicians should observe and study not only the transference of sensitivity, but also the transference of entire illnesses, whose symptoms can be made quite complex by simultaneous aggravation from different sources. Also, the acceptance of the pain of others can be broadened by a person's predisposition. At first, transference of the pain is limited to near ones, but then the self-sacrifice is extended to others over vast distances.

Do not be surprised that Our widespread associations bring Us many pains; man can become inured to any condition. When We advise caution, We anticipate the possibility of the transference of pain. Under the conditions of ordinary life, these pains would not exist, but the conditions We speak of are not ordinary, and are caused by an exceptional life.

Sometimes We ask people not to burden Our Work with such sendings, and not to trouble Our co-workers by heaping physical or spiritual pain upon them. Multitudes cry for help in their sickness, even though they themselves might have created their conditions only the day before. Physicians should be asked to probe more deeply into the study of the causes of illness in order to eliminate them at their source. Many illnesses are contagious not only physically but also spiritually. One can see that spiritual contagion occurs more often, and the transfer of the pain is thus intensified.

One reads about the special pains suffered by remarkable people. This is not only the so-called sacred pain, but also a deliberate acceptance of another's suffering. It can be said about Our Abode that there are no illnesses there, yet there is much suffering. This is unavoidable when one works for and helps humanity.

66. Urusvati has observed correctly that most of those who strive toward Us lose interest when they hear about Our labors. But We do not force Our call on anyone. Only one who is led by karma to the Great Service can become a trustworthy co-worker. One cannot impose a love for labor. Any coercion in this domain will only provoke aversion. He who knocks should be welcomed, but to gather idlers from the bazaar is not wise. Everyone can observe that friends approach by special paths, and neither ancestral nor racial considerations have any meaning.

It is especially important to understand that We do not expect large numbers of co-workers, and We ourselves are not many. But even a small community is valuable, for in addition to earthly assistance, the cooperation of the Subtle World can be summoned. For certain purposes these co-workers from the Subtle World are very useful. They have nothing in common with the husks that parade at spiritualistic seances and suck out the strength of those who are present. Nothing useful can be made from such husks. Of course, sometimes the harmony of those present can provide the possibility for developed spirits to manifest, but such harmony is very rare and requires lengthy association. Our cooperation with the higher spheres of the Subtle World has a different aim. Flammarion has been very useful to Us, and Marconi will also be useful, because such men can use wisely the powers of the Subtle World and understand how to labor for the Great Service on Earth. The inhabitants of the higher spheres can materialize easily, just as the inhabitants of Earth—the best ones—can easily visit the Subtle World.

Urusvati has again heard the expressions of sorrow of Sister Oriole. Of course, it is difficult not to be horrified when earthly decay has spread to such an unprecedented extent. These processes at the end of *Kali Yuga* cannot be stopped on command. They must be outlived, and the dust raised by their whirlwinds must be re-worked. It is difficult indeed for so much litter to be made harmless, but the seeds must be separated from the chaff! We affirm that the care for every grain is great. The manifestation of unfit elements is great at the end of *Kali Yuga*. The fiercer Armageddon is, the better it serves as purifier of the dross. But the Host of Earth thinks otherwise. He values this dross and hopes to increase it. There are those who do not like to clean their own homes, and the resulting accumulations often end in conflagration. Therefore, he who fears labor should forget about Our existence.

67. Urusvati knows well that one cannot use any earthly measures to identify Our friends. It is not possible to demonstrate to an earthly understanding the broad dispersion of Our co-workers. They can be found in many different places, even in opposing camps, and can be found on both sides in a battle. One cannot explain such contradiction to an earthly consciousness, but Our Abode does not act in accordance with earthly laws. A broadened consciousness can understand that there are ties beyond earthly laws. Is it so difficult to imagine that Our friends can be found in different parts of the world and that, using the local languages, they try to restrain human madness? They may not even know about each other, but will nevertheless act for the same General Good.

On many occasions Our friends have asked Us to provide a sign by which they might recognize each other, but such attempts always ended badly, because traitors were often the first to make use of the signs. We therefore rejected these outer distinctions, and only in the smallest groups do We permit the Sign of Our Abode. Thus, it is not possible even in this one respect to adopt earthly conventions. The heart can feel beyond all earthly limitations. Thought about Us can be aflame in the depths of the heart.

Our co-workers will never call themselves initiates, nor will they boast of being superior. Our measures are above all earthly degrees. Even if Our friends are sometimes required to accept earthly distinctions, they at least know their true value.

Once upon a time, when one of Our Brothers appeared at a state gathering wearing decorations, His friend smiled and remarked on how heavy his medals and awards must be. Our Brother answered, "The doorkeeper's keys are not so light either!" Thus must earthly distinctions be understood.

This does not mean that We cannot occupy positions of world leadership. We accept them sometimes, but only as a special sacrifice. One should understand broadly the possibilities that are beyond earthly ones. We are greatly saddened when a Brother or Sister must take leave of Us to go on an earthly pilgrimage. Who will understand this sacrifice? Who will show the needed care and solicitude for this voluntary action? Will not such a pilgrimage be the bearing of a cross?

Beautiful symbols have been given to people, but they seldom realize their full meaning.

68. Urusvati senses even remote earthquakes and changes in atmospheric pressure. Ignorant ones will ask why such painful reactions must be endured, since the earthquakes cannot be prevented. Such questions are like those reactionary doubts expressed about new scientific discoveries. How can anyone say that one who can experience the vibrations of the planet is not of use for the gaining of knowledge? Unfortunately, such refined organisms are not studied, and because of this the possibility of their use for scientific observation is lost. A hundred years from now people will express regret about these lost opportunities, but today, even when faced with them directly, they are full of doubt. The subtle sensibility is linked both to the broadening of consciousness and the science of vibrations. Both subjects are deeply significant and are fundamental to the transformation of life.

One can observe many anomalies when communing with Us. For example, some of Our replies are instantaneous, anticipating a question that has not yet been fully formulated, whereas others are often slow in coming. This can be explained either by atmospheric conditions, or because We are occupied with special work. There may be many different conditions, and they should all be observed. Let us also remember that frequently a delay in responding to a question is caused by care being taken to protect the information from undesired eavesdroppers. The sendings of thought can be intercepted, and that is why We advise you to be very careful both in word and thought. A whole new science can be developed that will study the dissemination of the energy of word and thought. The confirmation of the influence of word and thought on vegetation and on planetary conditions will depend upon this. We experiment with vibrations, and Our Brother Vaughan is also occupied with them. Many scientists should thank Him for his help.

We rejoice when such seeds produce good sprouts.

69. Urusvati knows about those close to Us who have gone to the far-off worlds. The ignorant may spitefully misinterpret these departures, and few will understand that the flights are special missions. It is hard to imagine that between the worlds there exist links of thought. It is not easy for man to detach himself from his earthly solidity and realize that the most important place is not here on Earth but in what he perceives as a void. One must be reborn to understand that earthly beauty seems beautiful only because man does not know supermundane beauty. On Earth many things are understood in a distorted way, and people are always ready to imagine that among the worlds there is as much hostility as there is on Earth.

Many do not understand that the Head of the Brotherhood can depart to the far-off worlds. Nor can they comprehend why certain earthly Leaders, although devoted and enlightened, are willing to leave their Brothers behind. Only man's limited understanding causes him to deny the idea of expansion of the Community to several worlds. It is likewise difficult to imagine that, even in new bodies and in different surroundings, inhabitants can preserve the seeds of their clear, earthly consciousness. Yet the Primal Energy is everywhere one and the same. Such a link is stronger than all existing substances.

People are perplexed about the far-off worlds, but they misunderstand much on Earth as well. For example, it is believed by many that Panchen Rimpoche issues passports to Shambhala. It would seem that this makes no sense, but actually these papers are not *to* Shambhala, they are *about* Shambhala. From ancient times there has existed a reminder about Shambhala that was given to those who were able to direct their thoughts to it, but later the sense was distorted and some ridiculous passports have been seen. Also, many do not understand why some seemingly ignorant lamas can be guardians of Our Brotherhood. One must recognize that these lamas are exceptional; they have preserved the concept of Shambhala as a sacred treasure.

70. Urusvati is right to be indignant at all the falsehoods that are written about Us. Truly, if all the idle stories were gathered into one book, an unusual collection of falsehoods would result. Symbolic expressions, created over centuries, have been transformed into unbelievable fairy tales about treasures that are guarded by the Lords of Shambhala. In the elaborate Tibetan narratives it is hard to understand how the more fanciful exaggerations have accumulated. Through these exaggerations the Tibetan nation wished to enhance its position as a world focus. For example, it is written that the warriors of Shambhala are innumerable and invincible, and their leader defeats all evil and affirms the Kingdom of Good. Such is the belief in the East, which cherishes in its heart the legend about the victory of Light. For the East, each veiled word written for the glory of Light is justified, but the West thinks the opposite and wishes to unveil everything, even to the point of belittlement.

Pay attention to the way people in the West speak about the White Brotherhood. They will say that the members of the Brotherhood sit in restaurants, that they manipulate economic power, that they lie, err, and mislead, and do not know how to choose the best co-workers; that they lure people into sedition and war, that they conspire, plot, overthrow dynasties, meddle in the peaceful lives of families, inflict damage upon the church, and fail to preserve the ancient traditions. In short, one can enumerate all the darkest and most unpardonable crimes, and they will be ascribed to Us. Let us not forget that these accusations are often brought by the very people who utter the most lofty words about the White Brotherhood.

One may hear that Brother R. lives in the Carpathians, but it would be just as true to say that I live in London. Undoubtedly, Brother R. has been in the Carpathian Mountains just as I have been in London, but one should not mislead people by referring to dwelling places as permanent. Likewise, one should not think that Brother H. lives in Germany, although some people would like to limit his whereabouts even more, to the vicinity of Nuremburg. There are many examples of how people arbitrarily dispose of Us, while proclaiming themselves to be high initiates, or even Maha Chohans.

Ignoramuses fill books with information about Our far-flung influence, and then proclaim their own wishes as Indications from Us. One can imagine how complicated Our life becomes because of these inventions. Discrediting Us to the very end, they create and circulate strange portraits, and organize meetings at which the most treacherous individuals do not hesitate to whisper even to strangers about their unbelievable visions.

Of course, there exist special organizations dedicated to whatever is of a destructive nature. We do not speak about them for their origin is clear. We wish now to draw your attention to the conduct of those who continually speak foolishly about the Brotherhood, and by doing so, discredit it.

71. Urusvati notices the change in currents during communion with Us. It should be explained that these changes take place, not because of Our influence, but because the spatial currents fluctuate when they come into contact with Our currents. This should be noted, otherwise one might attribute to Our current qualities not properly pertaining to it. The Teacher always takes precautions so that communion with Him will not be burdensome.

The currents can vary according to the mood of those who are present. Generally, one should observe each change of mood. Often the participants themselves are not aware of their state, and quite sincerely deny their moods. For many reasons, people do not know how to observe them. They are under the influence of *Maya* to such an extent that they think they affirm a truth even when telling lies about themselves.

Our Abode strives to deepen the consciousness in order to eliminate the influence of *Maya*. This is not easily achieved, but it liberates one from being susceptible to false sensations. Efficiency in work increases when one is freed from the burden of doubt engendered by mixed currents. Every refraction of currents produces a kind of electric discharge. Only a refined consciousness distinguishes these discharges from painful sensations. So many times one may observe a sudden rise of temperature, a chill, prickly pains, or a contraction of muscles. The discharges of refracted currents can act in this way, but those who know what these phenomena are will not mistake them for the beginning of some disease.

72. Urusvati knows Our meetings to utilize the

concentration of the will. The will of each of Us is sufficiently disciplined, but there are situations that require group concentration; at such times We advise all close ones to maintain calmness. We know that such advice is difficult to follow, but at times calmness is especially needed. Any confusion in the auras of the near ones harms the general degree of concentration.

It will be asked what calmness there can be when the world is in convulsion, but it is precisely when the world is in extreme tension that calmness is needed. At such times problems are not solved by usual methods. It is necessary to call forth from the depths of one's accumulations all Primal Energy and all the steadfastness upon which calmness rests. However, there is much earthly impatience, which, like a hail of arrows, shatters the concentration. One must stop to remove these arrows and in doing so diverts one's attention from the most important. At decisive times it is most important to take part in Our Concentration.

Sometimes We say, "Strive to Us with all your might." Such a call may seem unusual, but those who know understand the urgency contained in it. It is not easy to concentrate upon one object. People may labor for many years to develop this ability, yet at the hour of greatest tension even a small fly can disturb their striving. All of Us at some time have passed through such a strain. Success depends not on special abilities, but on intensified desire. Each one can try to strive to his Teacher, but he must strive so intently that he forgets all surroundings, whether it is day or night, warm or cold, for a short time or long. All this is within human power. And such striving is decidedly useful to Us, because it creates currents in space that meet in harmony with Our currents. If such beneficial thoughts were to be sent simultaneously from several countries, what powerful discharges they would generate!

We say to people, "Do not ask." We know your needs. People do not know how to concentrate upon the most important, and their requests are only disturbing. We do all that is possible, and people should simply send Us their good will. We are not complaining about those who lose themselves in trying to follow their desires, but We do advise the easy way to escape the earthly labyrinth. It is contained in the striving of the heart to Us. Let this striving be silent. Let the heart give its sign. All of Us have known such striving and We can say the more striving, the better. Striving builds strong blood, and this quality is beneficial if it is based upon calmness. But if calmness has not been acquired, it should be developed by the will.

Everyone must admit that life's events do not happen for the reasons we think they do. One may often find evidence of Higher Guidance. To correlate this Guidance with one's own independence will be to achieve harmony.

Man will ask, "Are You always with us?" We can be, but man must want it. We disclose many features of Our Inner Life to you. We Ourselves have passed through all obstacles, and often when going to sleep, did not know if We would be alive in the morning. Each one of Us learned to steadfastly walk in the path of His Teacher.

In the most difficult days the Teacher says, "Consider yourself to be much happier than many. Be grateful."

73. Urusvati knows how to discern the veils of *Maya*. When We speak about veils, it is because there is something being veiled, and that is Primal Energy. Wise is the one who can perceive in different manifestations where the eternal, indestructible foundation lies. Without this discernment everything will be *Maya*, a baseless mirage. It is impossible to live among such phantoms. The very foundation of eternal life requires a realization of where to find that steadfastness upon which the tired traveler can lean. Inevitably man will come to seek the eternal foundation. Thought about immutability can inspire man to action, and this striving to action is a healthy sign. We may be asked what conditions are required for Us to be able to help people better: of course, the answer is in action. We can say to those who ask for help, "Act!" for then it is easier for Us to help. Even a small unsuccessful action is better than no action, since We can then add Our energy to the energy shown by you. It is no wonder that a substance will blend more easily with one that is similar. When We wish to apply Our energy, We look for its most useful application. We send Our energy not just to awaken, but also to increase the power of those who strive. A person suddenly awakened can perform the most foolish actions. The sleeping one should not be disturbed unexpectedly, but when one is on a conscious vigil, We can help.

Thus, when you are asked what to do, answer, "Act!" In such action Our help will reach you. We and Our Brothers ask you to act. Development of consciousness is needed, and refinement of the Primal Energy is needed, otherwise the veils of *Maya* will prevent all access.

We often advise action. When you write to friends, advise them to act. At present the forces of nature are very tense. He who runs away will stumble, but whoever stands firm will find new strength. We help the daring ones, and in Our Abode everyone takes action. A new tension will not be exhaustion, but renewal.

74. Urusvati is right to grieve over those rituals that although outlived, yet still persist. Eternal wisdom is one thing, but ragged, outdated formulas that impede advance are quite another. In all domains of life one can see harmful survivals. They nestle everywhere, under royal robes, togas, or any other attire. They have grown so distant from their original meaning that it is beyond imagining how such absurd conventions could ever have expressed high symbols. In antiquity many seemingly strange rituals had special meanings which have now been completely forgotten.

Heads of state formerly combined their work with the highest spiritual duties, and often led societies of the highest purpose. In time, these missions were lost and the heads of state remained as servitors to insignificant and even harmful institutions. Such examples can be seen everywhere. It is especially sad that there remain only a few small fragments of ritual that still preserve their inner meaning; in ignorant hands even these scraps bring harm. Thus, We try to purify or remove the remnants of rituals that obscure the consciousness.

People say that We are opposed to all rituals. This is not quite true, for certain rituals can call forth high vibrations and purify feelings. We have spoken many times about rhythm, and none of Us will condemn the rhythms that bring harmony. Beautiful singing can open beautiful gates. Therefore, discriminate carefully between absurd survivals and steps of beauty. The Teacher warns that rhythm can influence the entire nervous system. Some parts of ancient rituals that have been preserved to this day, and now confuse the consciousness, can be very dangerous. Words used today during various services were once parts of incantations to exorcise dark forces, but now they are pronounced without sense and even with incorrect rhythm. Such distortions of sound can have a different effect, therefore one should study the ancient sources in order to wipe away the dust of ages. We are not speaking of crude changes, but of the purification of thought. We grieve when vibrations become distorted and, instead of construction, cause destruction.

75. Urusvati understands the harm in not forgiving. Such feelings can only fester under earthly conditions, since in Our life, with its awareness of former existences, feelings of rancor become impossible. In each life one finds many occasions for malice; to accumulate them throughout one's lives would create a long black tail that drags and impedes. With such an appendage one cannot advance!

People do much harm to themselves by limiting their awareness to one earthly existence. They build obstacles for themselves everywhere. When We direct them into the future, they generally do not understand how to begin to think in this new way. One may think that he will be forever attached to one place; another may tell himself that he must always cling to one vocation; a third may convince himself that he cannot endure a change of location; a fourth may imagine that he will perish from his very first illness. Thus each one invents his own fetters, not realizing that in his former lives he has already experienced the many ways of existence. Such a conventional life on Earth, in complete ignorance of the past, does not allow one the opportunity to think about the future.

Most people leave Earth not realizing that they will have to return again. If they could remember at least something of the past, and learn to think about the future, they would save themselves from many errors.

It is not a fear of hell but a desire for perfection that will lead people to the betterment of life.

We know the past, yet live in the future; We do not fear Infinity, and welcome each advance. The future stands as a great reality, separated from us only by a thin, closed door, and even now is being created by our every breath. When one's consciousness is directed into the future, can one harbor rancor? There is no time for immersion in the past. People should know about the immutable law; it is not for human consciousness to interfere with the Law of Karma. Thus let us learn to fly, not only in the subtle body, but also in consciousness.

Let us understand that each moment is already the past, and that the future is given to us. This is Our advice to everyone who loves Our Abode.

76. Urusvati knows how to guard what has been entrusted. It is not easy to find a balance between withholding and disclosing. Beginners are eager to impart all they have learned, not thinking about the consequences, and many calamities have resulted from their foolish diffusion. But experience forges the measures of wisdom, and with time one can find the true ways of dissemination. The path is difficult, and you should weigh how much those with whom you speak can contain. A panacea must be dispensed in proper measure, neither more nor less. One can recall occasions when, after a long conversation, a question was asked that proved the listener's lack of understanding, the answer to which could have produced harmful results. We advise that the books of the Teaching simply be placed at the crossroads, so that they may find their own destiny. Thus We indicate special means of dissemination.

There may have been pilgrims to whom the books were not given, even though their hearts were burning for the truth, because their outward appearances impeded the right judgment. For example, one may have been too smartly attired, another too poorly clad. Superficial considerations can impede useful meetings.

Among traveling sadhus there may be objectionable people, but one can also find significant and learned ones. A wise observer will not pay attention to superficial details. In everything the essential must be understood. One may meet people who are close to Us, yet not recognize them. We are often saddened when a useful sending is not recognized, but the law of free will does not permit one to insist. Thus, also, the spreading of the Teaching has its special ways. In olden times people would say, "Make haste slowly." A careful balance must accompany the sending of the books of the Teaching. In centuries to come you will see how the Teaching given by Us should be spread.

The great mass of people is beginning to see clearly.

77. Urusvati knows that every physical manifestation reveals some small part of the invisible world. There are photographic films that can record things invisible to the eye, such as a subject's radiations, yet sometimes fail to record parts of the subject's physical body. The powerful radiations of Primal Energy can even conceal someone, completely or partially. Skeptics can ask why such unusual photographs are so rarely obtained. This may depend upon the Primal Energy, or simply be a failure to examine the films with sufficient care. The quantity of so-called spoiled film is great, and no one takes the trouble to look carefully at seemingly unsuccessful photographs.

When one begins to experiment with photography immediate results are expected, but success can be achieved only at those rare times when people are consciously or unconsciously prepared for it. Nothing can happen without cause.

We conduct many experiments with films, and can say that the newest films are quite suitable for experiments which can help to solve problems posed by the invisible world. In addition to photographs made in the camera, images can also be made to appear by holding film in one's hands or by putting it under one's pillow at night.

Knowledge about the invisible world should be spread by all possible means. The success of evolution depends on it. Afterwards will come cognition of subtle energies. When We speak of the visibility of many subtle manifestations, some people regard it as a fiction. Such people cannot be brought to Our Abode, for they would be too frightened! All subtle signs would seem to them to be unbelievable and inaccessible.

Our apparatuses may resemble simple telegraphic receivers, but they are designed for more subtle vibrations. The necessary tension requires an increase in prana. The breathing of Our ozonizers can be likened to the breathing of living beings. Our lighting system, which resembles neon tubing, can burn very brightly. The effect of such mechanical devices can be increased by cognition of the Subtle World.

78. Urusvati has seen explosions of black projectiles. What does this mean? Should it be understood as something symbolic, or as a vision of real projectiles? We must acknowledge, with great sorrow, the real existence of such dangerous projectiles even in the Subtle World. They spread a poisonous gas that reinforces the brown gas that contaminates the planet.

The dark forces utilize the most destructive means to pierce the earthly atmosphere and project the deadly peril. They defy the laws of the Universe, and hope to attain their victory through confusion. They are not only dangerous adversaries, but also unwise ones, for they have no thought for the planetary balance. One who has seen the terrible explosions of these black projectiles can understand what extreme countermeasures are taken to dissipate their harmful effects.

Urusvati knows what destructive effects these battles have upon the health. In addition to poisonous fumes there is an electrical discharge, which causes earthquake-like tremors equal to the most violent shocks. Even strong people may experience unexpected pains, but since these pass quickly, they do not think about them. Nevertheless, the organism is undermined, and illness results. Thus do the dark forces rave in madness against humanity.

You can imagine how much energy is poured out to defeat these attacks of darkness! We have stated that We are on vigil, not for observation, but for battle. People could help, but they are unwilling to believe that everyone can apply his thoughts and power for the Common Good.

He who has seen the black projectiles, he who has heard the wailing in space, will not forget his duty to humanity.

79. Urusvati has experienced the most distressing earthly manifestation—the sensation of absolute darkness. It is terrible, for the intensity of the anguish it causes is equal to that of asphyxiation. Whence comes such injurious darkness? It might seem to be no more than a spiritual prevision, which, like straight-knowledge, plunges the entire organism into experiencing the feeling of an impending event. But in reality it is

far more dangerous, for it is an emanation of planetary decay. When people come into contact with this darkness, their unspeakable anguish is understandable. These contacts are usually subconscious, for few have seen the pernicious darkness itself. For those, the feelings are especially strong. When contact is made with absolute darkness while in the earthly body, there may be extremely painful sensations, and even inflammation of the centers. We know this contact; it attacks the psychic energy. One must have a store of prana to withstand the attack of the poisonous substance. Contact with darkness is like touching a decomposing corpse. When We expect a particularly heavy pressure of darkness, We determinedly increase Our vital forces. Those who are under Our care receive a special measure of energy in order to withstand the attack of darkness.

For many, this account about darkness will seem to be a fiction, but even skeptics know about the lethal gases that escape from the soil. Continuing this line of thought, we come to the last measure of absolute darkness. We have shown it to Urusvati, so that she might be a living witness to the mortal anguish that one feels when making contact with this enemy of the planet. One who is attacked by a boa constrictor has a similar feeling.

One should not think that darkness touches only certain people; the traces of these poisonous influences are everywhere. Reactions to them can vary from just a bad mood to a dangerous illness. If black projectiles are falling from above, and darkness emanates from below, it would seem that humanity's condition is hopeless. But the Wise Ones say, "Do not think about conditions, it is better to think about moving forward."

80. Urusvati has heard the hymns of nature, which

is what We call the harmonies that resound at the conquering of darkness. They resemble the music of the spheres, but belong more to Earth than to the higher realms. Most people reject every hint of the highest harmony, and when it resounds, would rather say that it is just a ringing in their ears.

Thus many who consider themselves to be occultists shut themselves off from their natural feelings. Too many books confuse them by prescribing practices that were once intended for other purposes. We prefer to meet new people, who are unencumbered by useless formulas. The music of the spheres and the hymns of nature are more easily heard by those whose hearts are full of love. Those who insist upon formulas for the heart, for love, for compassion, will not open their ears to higher harmonies.

Do not think that We reject the books and works of those who seek to understand the Universe. Not at all. We regret only that their knowledge is unsuccessfully applied in life. Our close ones do not resemble those preaching pseudo-initiates. Those who wish to participate in Our Abode must commune more often with their own hearts, and through them send Us at least silent calls. Sometimes these calls are referred to as "without thought," because they are expressed in feeling rather than thought. The boundary of thought and feeling is tenuous, but you understand such boundaries, which are like those between the facets of a precious stone. Only light can reveal these facets, and the light of the heart will be like the manifestation of a precious stone. One may think that all this is very complicated, but in fact, it can be put into four words, "I love Thee, Lord." This is the conduit to Us. Such a conduit is much stronger than the request, "Help me, O Lord." We know when it is possible to help, and help flies easily upon the wings of love. It passes through the sharpest obstacles. Let us love each other.

81. Urusvati is right in affirming the love of motion. Without love, one cannot understand the necessity for motion. One can listen to instructions about the law of universal motion, and can acknowledge that the least suspension of motion will disrupt the entire Universe, but it is impossible to apply this knowledge in one's life without love. Universal motion is not the hustle of the bazaars, or the bustle of the public square, but the nerve of a creative life that propels the consciousness toward perfectment.

An idler will not understand the kind of motion We speak of. He prefers inactivity and wishes for the cosmic motion to roll him along like a dead grain of sand. True, we are all less than grains of sand in Infinity, but each movement of the consciousness will be a great cooperation. It is not easy to instill in people a love of motion, but they must remember that We work continuously, and thus manifest the motion of the Universe.

Urusvati is right in insisting upon unity. We call unity a healing infusion, a harmony of motion that cannot be summoned or created by coercion. Some people regard advice about unity as fetters. They prefer to evoke the destructive forces of the elements and be trampled, rather than make an effort toward cooperation. We shall not tire of showing compassion to the unwise ones preparing for their own destruction. But is it not clear what has been said? Does humanity learn only from bitter consequences?

Let Our Advice about motion and unity go forth. Our Abode rests upon these principles.

82. Urusvati knows how unexpectedly great manifestations can occur. Thus, she has seen the strata of the Subtle World, not in her subtle body, but in the physical one, with open eyes and fully awake. She has seen the crowding in the Subtle World, and was astonished at the crowds that roamed idly with no work to do. True, she was shown that stratum of the Subtle World which especially concerns Us. In it were seen the contemporary clothes that reinforce an earthly way of thinking, and people crowded together as in the square of any modern town. We are greatly saddened that such crowds are the least accessible for evolution.

It can be observed that their thinking is so egocentric that they cannot see beyond their own crowded and motionless circle. They contaminate each other and, as on Earth, fail to look up. Urusvati can attest to how densely crowded these strata are.

One cannot often permit the observation of the Subtle World with open eyes and while fully awake. Such an experiment can cause great tension of the organism and is harmful for the eyes. But in honor of St. Sergius' Day We wanted to show Urusvati a striking picture. Usually, it is only in dreams and in the subtle body that people can contact the Subtle World and allow these invisible images to be remembered.

We can see the Subtle World with open eyes, but it is not easy to acquire such clairvoyance. Of the several kinds of clairvoyance We experience, that with open eyes is the most difficult. Urusvati is able to see with open eyes those in the Subtle World who wish to become visible to her, but in the previous example, We are speaking about becoming an observer, and simply finding yourself on a street in the Subtle World without any participation in that World. The evidence of that life should be remembered sometimes so that one is encouraged to vigorously strive to rise above these strata.

83. Urusvati understands the uniformity of law in all worlds. People usually think that the laws of the physical world do not apply to the spiritual world, but every event in life reminds one that the essence of a law is immutable. For instance, when climbing a mountain one leaves all unnecessary loads behind. Is it not the same in the spiritual world? A man falling from a height increases speed as he falls and not even the softest mattress will save the falling one. Is it not the same in the spiritual world? One can compare the foundations of all worlds and come to see the uniformity of laws. One should approach the Subtle World with this measuring rod. Some qualities may be less perceptible than in the physical world, whereas others will be exaggerated. In the lower strata lust is increased, and in the higher spheres the best qualities are enhanced. There, one's sense of duty grows, and is especially evident at the time of reincarnation. A high spirit does not resist moving naturally into a new life. It rejoices at the possibility of self-improvement, and actively seeks more difficult tasks in order to test its renewed consciousness. The high spirit strives to a difficult path, while the weak one clings to laziness and cowardice.

People come to Us only by difficult paths. Not one Brother, not one Sister can be named who did not come by a difficult path. Each One could have chosen an easier path, but did not in order to hasten the ascent. One can imagine the atmosphere that is intensified by such labors! The vibrations are so powerful that they cannot be endured by those unaccustomed to them. Joined with the power of the vibrations the unified tension radiates brightly to form a beautiful rainbow.

The atmosphere of Our Abode radiates in this way.

84. Urusvati knows how much man is constantly guided by the Primal Energy. From the greatest achievements to the most ordinary, everyday events, people are under the influence of the Primal Energy, which has been given so many names that it has lost its identity in the eyes of humanity. It is time to restore its basic significance, and not use any of the former names but retain only the simplest and most expressive one, Primal Energy. The most important thing is for people to learn to sense its presence, then cooperation with it will be realized.

One should not be surprised when We speak about cooperation with an energy that is within us. How can one cooperate with one's self? Let us not forget that the Primal Energy exists everywhere, and our spark of that Energy must cooperate with the highest currents. Thus we can better understand the guidance about which so much has been said. Truly, Guides exist as well as tempters. Every incarnate man is surrounded by both friends and enemies. Without fail, the many cares and hatreds of former lives gather around one. When a man asks for help, he feels that there must be something real near him during his lifetime, and truly he is not mistaken. In addition, if he could realize the presence of the Primal Energy his call would be still more effective.

We wish to create thoughtful cooperation everywhere, and would rejoice if people addressed themselves to their surest Guide. It is precisely the Primal Energy that shows man the measure of possibilities. He hears the voice of his conscience, but it is the Primal Energy that provides impetus to this voice. Each resolve is the result of this Energy, and is better developed by acknowledging it. Such acknowledgment is like an invocation of strength. Among the rituals of the ancient Mysteries one may find the invocation of powers. This should be understood not only as a protection from dark forces, but precisely as the invocation of powers that are concealed in the depths of the organism. Thus, everyone can perfect his powers by acknowledging them.

85. Urusvati senses the magnetism of objects. This ability is made possible through the synthesis of many subtle feelings. We are not speaking about a detailed explanation of the history of each object, for many accumulations on an object can give different indications from different eras. Those who hold an object and start telling stories about its life serve no purpose; however, it is important to feel the essence of an object and sense its harmony.

It is equally important in life to avoid objects that have had unpleasant contacts that influence them during their existence. Even recently produced objects keep the emanations of those who made them. Therefore one should not become immersed in the details of objects. The Primal Energy will warn about the essence of things, and one should not keep things nearby that bring sad and unpleasant feelings.

The magnetism of objects can be seen in rings that change color, depending on events. The magnetism of water is known to you, but the magnetism of certain metals is manifested with more difficulty. Thus, We took Urusvati's ring to Our Abode to magnetize it. Let us not call such objects magical; they simply harmonize with the Primal Energy of the one who wears them. It is not the ring that indicates the events, but the Primal Energy of its possessor. Only pure silver can vibrate to the Primal Energy. Urusvati's ring could become red, black, or yellow, depending upon the events. We conducted this experiment because the radiations of the Primal Energy are of special interest to Us.

Contact with the Subtle World helps greatly. The three fundamental worlds are often likened to the three kinds of ocean currents. An experienced seaman pays no attention to the drift of surface foam, nor does he fear the middle turbulence, but he forecasts storms according to the deepest currents. Thus, let us not fear the foam of the physical, but let us pay attention to the subtle manifestations. We should understand the essence according to the fiery signs. The Primal Energy is the fiery substance.

Truly, We are Brothers and Sisters born of Fire. Therefore, when you visualize Us, surround Our Images with fire. And We will recognize you by the fiery seed.

86. Urusvati knows the significance of great tension. We say, "Turn to Us," but one should ask how, and We will reply, "With all your mind, with all your heart." This is easier to say than to do, for to offer the entire heart is to be in love, and where there is true love, there is no place for doubt. Those who love will not criticize something they do not understand. Where there is criticism, there is not complete love.

Half-felt measures will not suffice in days of great calamity, when there must be a unity that bars even the slightest discord. The hostile forces dwell in such little cracks and poison seeps into shields damaged by discord, against which Our defense is perfect love. Let all Our friends wear this trustworthy armor. Do not mislead yourself by thinking that small splinters are harmless, for they cause terrible infection. In Our intense life the cracks of doubt are the most dangerous.

We stress that care be taken of one's health. Can We permit Our co-workers to be careless? Indeed We cannot! We foresee the attacks of the dark ones, who try at all costs to shorten the lives of workers of Light, taking advantage of each weakness of the organism to cause injury at the vulnerable spot. Do not think that Our help can be shaken, but any false step can prove fatal, and We can protect only those who accept Our help. Any unworthy thought can sever the thread, and people often unknowingly project harmful thoughts. In times of great distress one must be able to turn to the Teacher with one's whole heart, knowing that His help will not be delayed even for one moment.

Faith is true knowledge, and trust is the way to success. Distrust is the result of ignorance about Our work. It is essential to relate every individual situation to world conditions and to recognize how much Our help is complicated by human error. People defeat their best possibilities. We point out the necessity for unification, but there are not even three people who can fulfill Our requests!

At least when in danger, people should realize the need for unity—if not with their hearts, then through reason. Thus must one think in times of great disaster.

87. Urusvati knows how absorbed We are in astrochemistry. Interplanetary chemistry is a science of the future. No matter what name it may be given, this subject will be attentively studied even in the schools. It would be more correct to call it psychochemistry, for not only every heavenly body, but all that exists produces strong chemical reactions. It is time to pay attention to these interactions, not only from the point of view of so-called magnetism but also from the point of view of chemistry.

A chemical reaction is created in every handshake. Not only can physical infection be transmitted, but a chemical substance is also created. People deny the existence of these reactions, not realizing that all of interplanetary space is permeated with them. Much has been said about spectrum analysis and its application, but such theories have for the most part remained abstractions. Nevertheless, all this has a significant influence on earthly life. If people recognized that all objects emanate, the next step would be the acceptance of the chemical aspects of these emanations. From small facts one can march on to great discoveries, even concerning interplanetary influence.

We are occupied a great deal with the study of psychochemistry. The Subtle World helps in this research because it is replete with the subtlest chemical activities, which facilitate distant communications and create the circumstances for sensitive discrimination. Everyone can begin such experiments by observing why he feels attracted to or repelled by certain objects. In time, this type of experiment will be taken up by chemical laboratories, but even now careful observation will help to analyze such phenomena, and the effect of psychochemical reactions on the most elementary substances will be discovered.

Thus, let us be cautious with all surrounding objects without losing efficiency of action!

88. Urusvati grows indignant when she hears about war, Sister Oriole is terrified, and We are all saddened by the barbarism of humanity. The most negative manifestation of free will is seen in outbursts of war. People refuse to think about the terrible currents they evoke by mass murder and the consequences it will bring. The ancient Scriptures correctly warned that he who lives by the sword will perish by the sword.

There is a difference between the karma of aggression and that of defense. It can be shown how aggressors suffer the most grievous consequences and how terrible their condition is in the Subtle World. People delude themselves by thinking that great conquerors do not reap bad karma during their earthly lives. But karma has its own timely approach, and does not show itself immediately. Life is continuous, and the wise ones understand their lives as a single necklace.

Aggressors burden their karma not only by killing but also by polluting the atmosphere, which occurs during war. The poisoning of Earth and of the other spheres is long-lasting. You who intrude into the lands of your neighbors, has no one told you the consequences of your fratricide?

Our Abode has witnessed many wars, and We can testify how this evil is increasing in the most unexpected ways. People know that explosions can cause rain, but what about poison gas and its possible effects? How sad We are to see free will, which was bestowed as the Highest Gift, manifested in this horrible, uncontrolled way.

89. Urusvati understands the significance of silence. But what kind of silence must this be? People think that silence is simply not uttering any sound, but true power comes when the whole being is overwhelmed by silence and an energy is generated that permits communion with the Higher World. We know these hours of surging energy, and can affirm that this kind of silence is the highest tension.

One must practice to attain this state, but it can only be acquired gradually. One may trace in one's various lives how awareness of this energy develops, thus broadening one's possibilities, whatever the circumstances may be. The sooner one begins to expand on his experience, the better.

When silence reigns in Our Tower it means that We are experiencing this powerful tension, and communion with the Higher World will result in a renewal of forces. We need such an accumulation of new forces, just as all of life needs it. It would be a mistake to suppose that We do not need replenishment of energy. In revealing Our human side to you, I am strengthening Our bond with humanity. We certainly do not want to appear as "Beings beyond the clouds"! On the contrary, We want to be close co-workers with humanity. Therefore, let a closeness be created that will be the threshold of cooperation. It is especially needed.

90. Urusvati has experienced the way in which a special concentration of the eyesight can help one perceive former incarnations. One would think that such concentration of the gaze would be natural for everyone; however, there are two conditions that make it exceptional while in the earthly body. An extraordinary intensification of psychic energy and tension of the optic nerves are required. The images of former lives are brought forth from the depths of radiant accumulations, and just as in a kaleidoscope, these separate fragments join together to form a complete picture. Such an experience is therefore difficult for those in their earthly bodies, and We rarely allow it because it can harm the eyesight. Even though it would be possible to see many remarkable things in this way while in the earthly body, the conditions of life do not allow frequent use of these natural possibilities. Even those of Us who are in physical bodies must experiment cautiously along these lines. People probably will not understand why, even in Our Abode, earthly laws must be applied. To most of them, everything is either possible or impossible. They do not want to understand that the laws of the Universe must be respected.

Most of the time people rebuke Us before the completion of their deeds, or think of Us only after their actions have already taken place. We wish to establish as many conditions as possible that will facilitate normal contact with Us. There was a time when We preferred not to tell people how to communicate with Us, but now We find it necessary to remind people that We are ready to help them when conditions are appropriate. In the previous books many conditions were mentioned that promote the harmonizing of human consciousness. Those who study the Teaching attentively can easily understand the way of communion with Us.

We are not fortune tellers, We are not avengers, We are not oppressors; We are the Weavers of Wings, the Forgers of Shields, the Guides of Thought. It must be understood, however, that this complex energy requires careful application, for calamities can be provoked if it is applied wrongly. We have given you an example of how incarnations can be visualized, but at the expense of the eyesight. In working with Us the power of the Heart must be applied, not by forcing, but by the most natural striving, which must underlie the foundations of one's whole life.

91. Urusvati knows the ways of striving. Such techniques should be transmuted in the consciousness, for one cannot command them intellectually. Only with the eyes of the heart can one see whether there are still more ways to increase striving. One should rejoice at each act of full striving. Such fullness gives birth to the music of the spheres. An intensified harmony arises when all the strings of the heart resound. Do not take such comparisons as mere symbols; long ago We spoke about the eyes of the heart. Indeed, man sees through them, and hears with the ears of the heart. How could we exist without such senses?

In Our Community We use special apparatuses to

broaden the capacity of the heart. We would be happy to share this knowledge freely, but human hands would only cause heartache. These apparatuses should not be used without having control of one's thoughts, otherwise the heart would be overburdened. In addition, the surrounding conditions should be suitable. You know how easy it is to contact Us when the fires of the heart are kindled, and the spirit rejoices in exaltation. Beware of irritation and fear, those petty obstructions that not only separate you from Us, but also burden Us. Seek nearby, seek in the small things, seek in everyday life. We are talking about the ways that lead to the far-off worlds. Petty obstructions are out of place in such preparations.

Examples of communion with the Brotherhood can be given. A great measure of inspiration can be seen throughout the centuries. When the Brotherhood commissions someone for great sacrifice, could that person remain without inspiration? The degree of striving is determined by inspiration. We help such lofty achievements. Let waste and dust not obstruct the beautiful path, and doubt not obscure the details of the path, for even rapids can be crossed on a rainbow of Light. But the rainbow comes only after the storm. Thus let us understand the highest degrees of striving.

No human confusion or slander will obstruct the beautiful path of sacrifice.

92. Urusvati knows that working with Us is a Great Service and a reverence of Hierarchy. So many divisive ideas have permeated the world that we must seek the common thread in all concepts. We are called by various names in the world's many languages, and Our work is understood differently by different people. But further division should not be allowed. There is not one Teaching that has not been rent by distortion. Even the Teaching given late in the last century has already split into many rival groups. Hence, the unification of ideas is essential.

Many names are given to the Primal Energy. It is amazing that people can argue about different names for the same thing! Thus We advise you to forget all random names and accept "Primal Energy." Such an inclusive name should not be offensive to scientists, because they know that within each of their various experiments and searchings is concealed one and the same energy—Primal Energy. The same is true of Our Names. Let the name "Brotherhood" remain, and pay no attention to any other.

Every age has its times of discord, and also its times of unification. Therefore, one should prepare for the time of unification. This should be understood neither as advice, nor as a means of collecting ideas, but as help in harmonizing a divided humanity. In this action is contained the concept of Great Service and the idea of Hierarchy, of which people have only a vague idea.

You are right to use great discrimination in distributing the books on Hierarchy. There are many who will not accept Hierarchy, and one must not impose such ideas on those whose consciousness is clouded. Only the free will can, in time, prompt one toward great Unity.

Thus, one can observe the direction of Our Inner Life. Meditate upon the Unity of all, particularly during days of dreadful discord.

93. Urusvati knew long ago the identity of the Founder of the Brotherhood. It is possible to trace the long chain of incarnations and the periods in the Subtle World, yet in all this diversity the fundamental, unchanging goal of existence should be discerned.

Similarly, one can see how, though earthly temples and strongholds have perished, the ideas that brought them into being have not died. Not only do they nourish entire generations, but, as centuries go by they continue to flourish beautifully with a new understanding. We pay no attention to superficial fluctuations, knowing that the essence is unchangeable.

The different incarnations of the Founder can be observed in their amazing outward variety: at times the Master, or the suffering Spiritual Teacher, or the Hero; at times the Hermit, or the Leader of nations, or the wise Ruler; then the Monk, the Philosopher, and finally, in the Subtle World, the Healer of the people on Earth. It would be too much to enumerate all the former lives, but in all there was the same Service and the same persecution. In the Subtle World, Service was more peaceful, because it was possible to remain in a circle in which the energy was not aimlessly consumed. But on Earth more energy must be used for defense than for productive activity, and this is burdensome. It takes centuries to grow accustomed to directing energy where it will be useful. But you must remember that every transmission of energy with a benevolent purpose brings its good result.

We have had opportunities to visit the ruins of temples erected by Us ages ago. There are many such temples in Egypt, in Greece, and all over the world. We know that these walls served their purpose and are no longer needed, but their essence remains and does not lose its freshness. Thus We testify, We who have experienced much and seen much. People often do not understand the correlation of the past with the future. Our Community has preserved many examples of Service, and We can testify to the continued vitality of all the Sacrifices.

Amidst Our labors We do not forget all those who have offered beautiful sacrifice.

94. Urusvati knows well that the most difficult task is to harmonize the currents of human free will. There are no cataclysms destructive enough to turn the attention of humanity to the true nature of its deeds. Let us recall how those who survived the great cataclysms of the past did not care to think about the causes of the disasters, preferring to consider themselves innocent victims of some cruel fate. They did not want to purify their consciousness and instead began once more to indulge their free will gone mad.

The currents of will come into rapid collision, and undisciplined thinking fills space with destructive explosions. Probably the ignorant will again declare that We threaten and frighten them, but they should turn to the pages of history in which they can trace the calamities of humanity. These calamities are not sent by heaven, but are caused by human society. People persecute their own Saviors, acting like a mad musician who tears out the strings of his instrument before the concert!

When We point out the natural consequences of ignorance and madness We are well prepared for accusations of cruelty. But there are no words in human language that can warn people sufficiently against self-destruction, the destruction of the planet, or the pollution of space. It is Our patience, acquired over centuries, that helps Us to continually offer salvation to humanity, in spite of its ingratitude and cruelties. Each day and every hour We are cursed, and Our helping Hand is rejected.

One can imagine what violent currents of willful madness inundate every movement for good! Why think about remote hierophants of evil when ordinary people, who seem to be struggling against evil, are actually increasing it to the maximum. Such is the situation on Earth. The ungrateful sons of Earth are hastening to bring catastrophe closer, and each warning is taken as an offense. Thus the world has inscribed the truth about Golgotha.

Therefore you must know this aspect of Our Inner Life. Realize it and work with a proper understanding of existence.

95. Urusvati is familiar with earthly suffocation. This is what We call the atmospheric condition produced by heavy spatial currents, which, intensified by subterranean fires and by human insanity, cause unbearable depression. We know such times! People may attribute these conditions to sunspots or to the passing of comets, but external events could hardly cause such unbearable tension. Even the subterranean fires themselves are not capable of penetrating the planet so completely without the cooperation of man.

People feel this depression. They become possessed by a nervous madness, but cannot distinguish its cause. Many attribute it to epidemics, or to new forms of disease, but they overlook the main cause—their own behavior. Thus the earthly suffocation builds up, and sensitive hearts are deeply affected by it. Even physical suffocation is felt, and the heart is depressed. Extra care should be taken of the heart. There is consolation in the fact that such tension cannot last for long. It must dissolve into the currents of prana, or else it will cause cataclysms. But sometimes even a cataclysm is better than this deadly suffocation!

We know this suffocation.

96. Urusvati knows the significance of synthesis. If this foundation is not accepted, the most useful works will be destined for destruction. The essence of Our

Abode is not properly understood because people arbitrarily categorize. Some consider Us to be Hermits of Kailas, while others think that We are Beings of the Subtle World. Such distinctions destroy the synthesis of Our Existence.

People refuse to accept the logical explanations that are given to broaden their knowledge, and by refusing, they diminish the very meaning of Our existence. If Our Center exists as the link between the worlds, in it must be expressed the conditions of both worlds, physical and subtle. But such a simple idea can only be understood by one who comprehends the great importance of synthesis.

Humanity can be divided into those who accept synthesis and those who deny it. Those who deny the benefit of synthesis do not recognize the history of the human race. The epochs of upliftment were also the epochs of an understanding of synthesis, when each harmonization of the centers resulted in a broadening of consciousness.

Please do not think that narrow specialization makes the glory of an era. Only benevolent, all-embracing synthesis can give impetus to the new progress of consciousness.

Thus, let us not forget that categorizing prevents a proper understanding of Our Brotherhood.

97. Urusvati knows the balance between harmony and evolution. These correlative concepts are often taken as being contradictory, but, in reality, can evolution ever be inharmonious? And how can harmony be created without evolution? Yet people prefer to understand harmony as an immobile and inactive state, and use it as an excuse for their irresponsibility. While the world is in convulsion people prefer to sit in sweet oblivion, and call their benumbed condition by the lofty word "harmony."

However, the strong chords of harmony are tensed, and as they expand they contribute to evolution. Similarly, the benefit of evolution is in its continuously accelerating motion. It is beautiful to realize that the world is perpetually evolving, in ever-increasing striving and motion. People do not look into the future, but secretly dream about an impossible static condition. But there can be no static evolution. The spiral of evolution is an eternal ascent that even the convulsions of chaos cannot arrest.

In their earthly condition people cannot always notice the beneficial growth. All growth comes with pain, with lightning, and in storm, and only a perfect consciousness can perceive the radiance of Truth. Every evolving thinker must transmit his understanding of Truth while on Earth. If he does not apply Truth in life, man is not worthy of being called a thinker. Thought is life, and life is moved by thought.

Thus you realize the two foundations of Our Life. We live in harmony for the sake of evolution. We must evolve, otherwise We shall be transformed into mummies.

One must be able to love the movement of evolution, for in it eternity is realized.

98. Urusvati practices austerity and courage. Both of these attributes should be developed through attention to the examples of heroes. One should be reminded of those who overcame superhuman obstacles, and understand the complexity of the circumstances that surrounded them. History did not record all the dangers that threatened them from near and far. People suppose that heroic deeds are performed spontaneously, without preparation, but in reality many thoughts must take form before a firm decision to carry out a selfless act can be made.

The most valiant heroes have recollections from early childhood, when they had visions and dreams and heard voices that called to them and led them. Certain ideas were formed during their childhood that manifested much later. Heroes can describe how certain invisible forces directed their actions, and how they at times would spontaneously utter words whose meaning they did not understand until later. Thus, Our influence flows to many co-workers and strengthens their courage. We appreciate the gratitude We receive for the constant care that We bestow upon heroes.

Our Abode is the focal point of stout-hearted decisions. But We have to practice great patience so that these decisions do not interfere with free will. Thus, with regard to Our patience, We can be considered examples.

Not all potential heroes will reach their goal, because their free will often rebels against their own determined decision. But if people realized how ardently We try to help them succeed, they would see how beneficial it is to cooperate with Us. Then *podvig* will be kindled, and felt as the highest joy.

99. Urusvati agrees with Us that the present century is the century of thought. Only in the present century have people begun to accept that thought is energy. None of the thinkers of past centuries could reveal that thought is the motive force of the world, because in order to understand the process of thought a knowledge of physical sciences and of many other discoveries was first needed.

It is true that Plato knew the power of thought, but he revealed only a clue to its power, because it was dangerous to give this knowledge prematurely to the masses. Only now are some researchers beginning to realize how accessible are the many hidden qualities of thought. Centuries were required for such simple observations, but now it has become possible to prove that thought is a tangible motive power.

How much more quickly would a broad knowledge of thought penetrate humanity if people realized Our existence! The most powerful currents of thought vibrate from Our Abode, and it is easier to decipher thought transmitted over a distance when it comes from such a powerful Source. But when people experiment with thought transmission they pay little or no attention to their own spiritual condition. Once again we are reminded of the old saying that one must wash one's hands before starting an experiment! Researchers should pay attention to harmonizing their own condition before experimenting, for a discordant mood will not permit positive results. The first stage of transmission can be reached easily, but it is desirable to press forward with the development of thought transmission over great distances.

Certainly one should be grateful to those scientists who have overcome their prejudice and are helping people to understand their birthright. We constantly send arrows of thought to penetrate the consciousness of humanity. May people sense how many messengers are knocking at their doors!

100. Urusvati remembers that the events in Spain were predicted ten years earlier, and that the dates of other great events were also given. Some may wonder why certain events were predicted far in advance, whereas others, apparently far more significant, were not pointed out at all. From an earthly point of view, this question is quite reasonable, but on what basis should some events be considered more important than others? Let us remember that beyond worldly understanding there is a supermundane one. Some events may greatly influence human affairs yet leave no trace upon the pages of history. On the other hand, events may occur that seem to be only local, but in reality are most significant and become turning points in the history of the world. Such seeming contradictions between earthly and supermundane evaluations can create confusion in people's minds.

We have often been accused of being interested in insignificant events while being deliberately indifferent to important ones. To this We say, "You of little faith, where are the scales on which you can weigh with such precision the events of the world? Can you assume the right to judge nations and the actions that fulfil their karma?" Even individuals must be judged sparingly.

Often a leader is unworthy of the esteem that he enjoys during his lifetime, and only later do the results indicate how unfruitful his activities were. Today can be seen, but tomorrow must be imagined. The events of the world can be likened to mosaics, which are seen clearly only from a distance.

Karma is made amidst storms and tribulations, and the inevitable takes its course. The country that yesterday was a giant may be a dwarf by tomorrow. Such destiny may amaze people, but We can see the chain of causes.

One must learn to discriminate between the great and the small.

101. Urusvati realizes that, although on the reality of the physical plane some people at times seem alive, from the viewpoint of a Higher Reality they are quite dead. It might seem puzzling that those defined as dead by a Higher Reality continue to move about on Earth. But why should such determinations be limited by only physical manifestations? When Our apparatuses indicate death, this indication is more correct than earthly evidence. We could mention several such "living corpses," each of whom is afflicted by some physical ailment. But their physical condition is a secondary factor, the primary one being the condition of the subtle body, which is ready to leave and may no longer be fully connected to the physical body. Such automatons can no longer be independently creative, and are easily led by others without realizing it. They are strongly earthbound and dread the idea of death, yet sense that they no longer belong fully to physical existence. Usually they are so-called materialists, and fear even a hint of the continuity of life in the subtle body! They may even fear to think about their own deeds. One should be able to recognize these living corpses and regard them as empty shells. I know that they would be enraged if their names were mentioned, and We shall not do this, for you know whom I have in mind. You also know whom We consider to be vacuums.

Let us not calculate by earthly measures, and let us take the future into consideration. The complexity of relationships is such that neither jinn nor fools should be dismissed immediately, even when they seem insane. We are in the midst of the world's events, and cannot cut karmic knots, for this might cause catastrophe. People often suggest that We put an end to certain circumstances, not realizing that the ends of such threads can turn into snares for them by enmeshing their own karma.

I must emphasize this, for some people have strong

ideas about Us and think of Us as beautiful angels, dwelling in the clouds and playing harps!

May the true description of Our concerns and labors be given to the people.

102. Urusvati senses the correlation of the worlds, whose limits are not usually perceived. The worlds exist in many forms, and interpenetrate each other. Only straight-knowledge can recognize the borderlines of such subdivisions, and it is even more difficult to realize their evolution. If all of life is in motion, then the condition of the worlds also depends on motion.

We have already discussed the densification of the astral body. Conversely, the material essence of flesh is considerably refined by the energy of thought. This means that between the subtle and the physical worlds there are new forms that are not quite visible to human eyes. New forms have their origin between the Subtle and the Fiery Worlds. These transitions evoke the striving for perfection. There can be no doubt that such limitless intensification is possible in Infinity.

If we were to imagine the greatest Spiritual Toiler on Earth, we would associate Him with tremendous power in the Subtle World. But contact with the purified Fire of Space would direct Him even to the Fiery World. There is no force that can prevent the ascent of the spirit that harbors no doubt. Doubt is like a hole in a balloon. Everything is in motion and is carried into Infinity. I say this to remind you that the natural direction of man is upward. Doubt is nothing but holes in one's pockets, and diamonds cannot be carried safely in such pockets.

In Our Life there is no such thing as doubt. The attraction to the higher worlds is tremendous, and We must exert great effort not to be torn away from Earth, where Earthly burdens have been chosen voluntarily and consciously. Such sacrifice is forged by love and by the experiences of former lives that kindled love for those who suffer. Experience can either kindle love or sharpen hatred, and who will be the one to burn on the stake of hatred? Will it not be the one who hates? Love must become wise and active. This concept is very subtle and one can easily stumble over it, or fall prey to hypocrisy. Only labor for the good of the world will afford the proper balance. Labor evokes joy and cognizance of Infinity, and imparts a realization of the mobility of the worlds.

One may ask, what is the best *pranayama*? What instills the best rhythm? What can kill the worm of depression? Only work! Only in work is the attraction to perfectment formed. During labor the Fiery Baptism will come.

103. Urusvati knows the urgency of the hour. It is difficult to combine urgency with harmony, or excess with moderation. Many seeming contradictions exist, but life provides the proper place for everything. If we establish activity as the foundation, straight-knowledge will indicate the rhythm of labor. The world is carried forward irresistibly, and the tempo of work must keep pace with the race into Infinity.

We have already discussed the striving upward, but there can also be an eternal fall down into the abyss, and only work can provide the trait of excellence that will safeguard against it. One must learn to love this quality in all aspects of life, for its least violation arrests all progressive motion. Thus, it is right to feel sad for those nations that have forgotten the need for maintaining quality in all aspects of life. But one should not despair, for the potential of the heart is great, and the urgency of the hour intensifies all the forces of the human being.

Do not think that Our Abode ignores the urgency of the time. This urgency is manifested in many ways, and can be recognized by the general tension it creates in various groups. And now, too, it is possible to see how the seeds of events hasten to flower. People prefer not to notice this tempo, but their attitude resembles the unsteady walk of the blind.

Let us realize the urgency of the time.

104. Urusvati maintains solemnity even in moments of danger. Few can appreciate the power of this shield. Amidst stormy currents the rock of solemnity holds firm. With it, man can draw upon any force within himself and forge from it an invincible armor. People should realize that solemnity is the best bridge to Us. Our help reaches them most easily through the channel of solemnity, whereas the more difficult way is through terror and depression. Every human force can be studied scientifically.

One should know how We send the blue rays of help in the hour of danger. For example, at one time seismologists predicted an earthquake, which then was barely strong enough to be recorded. Some thought that the seismologists were mistaken, not realizing that We had prevented the catastrophe. So often people look for events far away when they take place right behind their backs. The White Swan of Solemnity flies by the straight path.

Let us remember that all offered help should be accepted. When We advocate unity as the means of achievement, Our Advice is simply scientific. We require an intensification of energy that can be achieved only if the co-workers are united. Every breach tears the valuable tissue, and who can tell whether it will be possible to restore it? People refuse to consider such simple facts and are ever ready to risk their own welfare. Who is the one willing to endanger himself in this way? Who is the one to judge which violation of Our Advice will bring disaster? We often direct the attention of people to Us so that contact can be easily established. But they have freedom of will and rarely choose to follow the Voice of the Brotherhood.

105. Urusvati knows how great earthly achievements could be if true collaboration were practiced. No one knows how far human thought can reach without distortion. No one can fully comprehend the task entrusted to him from the Subtle World. To each is given a seed of Goodness as a foundation for his earthly challenges. But people do not cultivate these benevolent gifts, for they cannot perceive the higher worlds from which are sent such waves of Goodness.

If people could remember the grains of Goodness entrusted to them, many evil manifestations would be destroyed. We send thoughts of Goodness; however these messages are misunderstood and even indignantly rejected. This indignation stems from an unwillingness to remember those Realms from which earthly life appears as nothing but a particle of dust.

People dislike the idea that their overblown earthly concepts are colorless compared with the mental creativeness of the higher realms. This earthly egoism makes cooperation impossible. Yet, without cooperation, how can one hope to learn about the higher spheres? It is essential to recognize the higher realms. It is essential to start thinking about them. Such thinking will revive the memory of the entrusted grains of goodness. In the early hours of the day one will recall how it was ordained that subtle and beautiful ideas be brought to Earth. Indeed, everyone who is ready to incarnate is entrusted with a mission for the Common Good according to his individual capacity. One may reject this worthy mission in the whirlpool of free will, but someday will return to pick up the scattered grains.

Amidst Our intense labors it is especially difficult to continually remind people of their mission. In spite of the fact that people connect Us with the Invisible Government, they refuse to follow Our simplest Advice. Just think how often the best advice has been ridiculed! They call Us sages and saints, but will not listen to Us.

106. Urusvati knows that clairaudience is the most difficult of the subtle senses, because so many intrusions obscure subtle hearing. It is interesting that even strong voices or thoughts can be distorted by a single sound. Thought resounds, but people do not understand this, and do not perceive that a word that is emphasized mentally will resound more clearly.

During unfavorable currents mental messages can be colored by unexpected influences. We are sending Our Discourse at this time under such burdensome conditions. In ancient times it was well known that difficult cosmic periods could be long-lasting, but today, despite the phenomenal progress of science, such cosmic conditions are not taken into consideration. There are still arguments about the effect of sunspots and embarrassed hints about the possible influence of the moon, which is thought to be associated with sorcery. Few scientists have the courage to speak about the moon as it relates to earthly conditions, and they allude timidly to the forgotten Teachings of the East, where the significance of the moon was well-known.

The *Puranas* contain much scientific data. Several years ago, Urusvati heard from Us about the significance of the year 1942. And now this information is broadly disseminated and is common knowledge. The end of *Kali Yuga* is significant, for many cosmic events are connected with this period. For certain reasons the true dates were concealed, and only few could perceive that the enormous numbers that were cited were mere symbols. Likewise, certain references to Krishna, Avatar of Vishnu, are also symbolic. You know very well what particular event was meant by these indications. Now everyone can notice the unusual accumulation of events. Armageddon was predicted ages ago, and the abnormalities at the end of *Kali Yuga* were described in the *Puranas*, but even keen thinkers underestimated those clear indications.

However, the unusualness of the events does not impress humanity, whose mental confusion was also predicted ages ago. The onset of this important period intensifies the general rhythm of Our Abode.

People may feel that for some reason they cannot start doing anything. Such a mood is caused by a change of rhythm. One's inner consciousness may have already assimilated the future, but the mechanical routine is the result of the hypnotic effect of *Kali Yuga*. This is a state of divided consciousness, which also affects the general rhythm of Our Work. Various calamities threaten Earth. Karma works intensely. It must be realized that the karma of the Devas is also accelerated. Thus the forces are intensified during the change of Yugas. Let us be aware of this and let us fill our hearts with courage.

107. Urusvati knows that most diseases come from suggestion. They may be attributed to autosuggestion, or to suggestion from a distance, about which little is known. Just as one can heal from a distance, one can also inflict disease. In the future, science will prove the existence of powers of suggestion, but at present very few understand that disease can be caused by suggestive thinking directed from a distance. It is significant that thought can be direct or indirect, and that the arrows of thought can pierce the cells of an organism that is predisposed to illness. The so-called evil eye has a concrete, occult meaning. A particular thought may not be intended to cause a specific painful reaction, but the energy of an evil will strikes at the weak part of an organism, and overwhelms its self-defense.

It is important to recognize that thought can not only create the outer symptoms of disease, but can also compel dormant embryonic diseases to arise and begin their work of destruction. What better proves the existence of the power of thought? There are innumerable such thought messages roaming the world.

Medical authorities believe that infection is transmitted only physically, and they ignore the main cause of infection. The science of thought should be studied in its many aspects. For example, just as radio waves interfere with one another, mental messages can cause a similar confusion. Many such facts still go unrecognized.

This will provide an idea of the complications in Our Work. We transmit benevolent thoughts and ideas, and must also work to counteract the numerous malicious carriers of infection. We are in a position to observe how people themselves spread dangerous earthly infections by thought, infecting one another with damage, in the true meaning of this word. Such malicious influences used to be attributed to sorcery, but even today there are more of these "sorcerers" than one might think.

Certain unusual diseases are now spreading rapidly. People either ignore this fact, or if they do notice it, prefer not to look for the causes. One can argue that from the point of view of the average person this is neither new nor unusual. However, one must remember that this is the age of new energies, and the daily life of even the ordinary man is charged with numerous highly concentrated currents which produce new impulses in human minds.

Man must assimilate many new ideas.

108. Urusvati saw the Ray that was filled with numerous eyes. Such evolutionary forms should also be faced and one must learn to accept their existence. A special ray is required to establish the visibility of these spatial forms, which are the prototypes of future creatures. These traces of great thought-creativeness are registered upon the layers of *Akâsha* and are an illustration of the creative work of the Great Builders, who fill space with their ideas. By the currents of such powerful thought are born multitudes of forms.

Let us examine the laboratory of eyes, which differ in size and expression. Some are already awakened and full of luster, and others are half-closed; some remind one of Eastern eyes, whereas others are the eyes of the North. One can see how thought creates inexorably out of the treasures of *Akâsha* and supplies the needs of the worlds.

And now, for example, a school of fish can be glimpsed in the ray. Thought must be unusually clear to create such harmonious forms, for obscured thinking creates monstrous forms. It is most important to look at least once into the treasury of *Akâsha*, but such glimpses are hard on human sight, and We must practice caution with Our co-workers. However, in this book We can record that Our Sister was able to see such treasures of thought-creativeness even while in her physical body. These observations should not be repeated often because people have polluted the lower spheres, and some experiments are dangerous to the health. Our Blue Ray can reveal many subtle forms, but seldom can We allow such manifestations. Urusvati saw this Ray in single combat with the destructive fire. Only in an extreme case can such a powerful Ray be applied throughout the whole world.

You may remember how We observed Our own Images reflected upon the surface of a polished board. The same principles operate in the subtle spheres as they do in television today, but you saw this phenomenon seventeen years ago. Such experiences should be recorded and eventually compared with new scientific discoveries. Much has been projected into the world, but it takes time for it to be realized.

109. Urusvati realizes that psychic energy should be carefully conserved. This may sound strange. Can people regulate the Primal, all-permeating Energy, and would it not be arrogant of mankind to assume such authority? Can one pretend to be the guardian and controller of such immeasurable, infinite power? Yes, for man has the responsibility for the Primal Energy since he is capable of co-measurement and of knowing exactly when he violates the beatitude divinely entrusted to him.

Abuse of the Primary Energy has been compared to the abuse of alcohol, which is beneficial in small doses during certain illnesses, but harmful in large doses. So also, psychic energy can be used for benefit or destruction, and only a broadened consciousness will understand how much can be drawn from this source of energy without abusing it. People have the idea that they can use the beautiful energy without limit, but they forget about the creative laws that provide all possibilities and at the same time limit them.

The Blessed One Himself preached the Middle Way. Only the Middle Way can engender true reverence for the precious Primal Energy. Our Abode lives by the law of the Middle Way. He who desires to ponder upon Our Abode should ask himself if he understands the beauty of the Middle Way. The foundation must be laid upon the best, with the best, and for the best, and it is the Middle Way that leads the best ones through the best fields. Work itself, when done in the spirit of the Middle Way, will never be disharmonious, and will lead toward the foundations of the Subtle World.

Urusvati has seen the crowds of the Subtle World, but those of whom We speak do not live amidst these strata. One must learn to know the various spheres, and must realize by what Earth is surrounded. Thus, one will better understand why We must be so vigilant.

110. Urusvati knows that he who strives to discriminate between the laws of the three worlds during his earthly life approaches the fullness of self-realization. Where then should one look for the sparks of the Fiery World? Can they be found amidst the earthly dust? Of course, it is precisely in every earthly manifestation that one can find the sparks of the Fiery World. Therefore, each one should be more observant in his daily life. One must learn to refrain from hasty conclusions, which may result in harmful reactions. One must understand the harm of baseless accusations and thoughtless complaints; otherwise one will act like the man who, instead of expressing gratitude when he was saved from drowning, immediately began to complain that his clothes were spoiled! Frequently lives have been saved by the loss of a mere finger, but We hear more complaints about lost fingers than gratitude for lives that were saved. However, We will not forget those things that are far removed from the Fiery World, but will continue Our help, and will speak firmly about reverence for all the treasures of the three worlds.

Urusvati sensed correctly the state of consciousness of some of the spheres of the Subtle World, in which hopeless grief reigns simply because of the inability to think or to imagine. No one teaches how to discipline the mind, and no one cares to develop the imagination, but without these wings it is impossible to soar to the higher spheres. One should know that there is a realm where purified thoughts reign. One should realize how beautiful is the path to this realm, where thoughts become feelings. Earthly hearts can respond to those benevolent, purifying thoughts and sense their creative grace.

May we make our earthly life full, and, not missing a single moment, achieve a fullness of being that can be defined as exaltation or spiritualization. Such a state of mind transforms one's whole life.

Thus let the smallest sign be reflected in your heart and remember that on the far-off mountains you have Friends who care for you and labor for you.

111. Urusvati realizes the multiformity of the Great Service. This great concept of Service is usually completely misunderstood, or if accepted at all, it is mistaken for monastic monotony. But the Great Service responds to earthly needs, and the true servant of humanity must know all conditions of life. He must spare the feelings of the ignorant, he must soothe the desperate, and must appreciate the various fields of labor in order to be able to give wise encouragement. In this way Service will bring benefit everywhere, and the servant of Good will know how to find the word that will lead people to a brighter future.

Let us not think that a better future is only *Maya*. Especially now, at the end of Kali Yuga, we should realize that the brighter future is a reality, and that only human malice can retard the coming of the new, luminous age.

They will ask you how it is possible to reconcile the threatening signs of the destruction of the planet with the possibility of a harmonious and auspicious future. The fact is that humanity has a free choice, either to enter the new life, the age of great discoveries, the Era of Happiness, or, by the power of free will to choose catastrophe. Thus, people cannot complain that they are deprived of a beautiful destiny, for it is only their evil will that could lead the nations to planetary cataclysms. Free choice is man's birthright. It provides endless possibilities, but people do not care to apply their freedom in the right way.

We observe quite fantastic and contrasting ways of thinking. Scientists come together to work for the future and ignore the barbarians' clubs poised to strike just above their heads! Thus Our Abode is constantly sending warnings, but unaware of the danger, people ignore them. They want to be saved, but do not want to be disturbed.

This age is difficult. People refuse to heed the significance of their destructions and wars, which cause great upheavals in the Subtle World.

112. Urusvati knows how strong is the shield of the one who fully realizes lawfulness. One must have not only trust, not only faith, but also a sense of righteousness. Otherwise, how could the great saints and martyrs have withstood their hardships? Truly, only through an awareness of righteousness were they able to accept abuse with a joyous heart. It is the same in Our Abode, where the foundation of Our Work is righteousness.

You should not think that We are so distant from

Earth that no earthly problem can reach Us. Each earthly commotion strikes against Our Stronghold of lawfulness. In the Great Service there must be an invincible constancy in the realization of righteousness. People lose their strength when they lose their sense of righteousness, and how can one advance if one's feet do not feel the firm ground? The spirit must lean upon the solidity of consciousness.

People who have gone through many dangers can testify that only their sense of righteousness carried them over the abyss. Let each one think about the moments of danger and ask what actually saved him.

Certainly, We are always ready to stretch out Our hand, but absolute trust is necessary for such a handshake, and complete trust can flourish only when there is awareness of one's own uprightness. We insist upon this type of consciousness because it makes collaboration easier, and the purified energy reaches its destination without causing painful reactions.

Let people remember about the strong shield of lawfulness.

113. In her flights to far-off worlds, Urusvati sensed their differences. It may seem strange that in spite of their foundation of Oneness there are so many differences, even in manifestations that seem to resemble earthly conditions. In addition, the inner atmosphere of those worlds is wondrous! The colors at times may remind one of earthly colors, but their substance is entirely different. The colors of the oceans of Earth cannot compare to the depth and transparency of the waters of the Subtle World. The atmosphere of the Subtle World resembles a rainbow, but its subtle colors are totally unlike the colors of earthly rainbows. The fish can fly, but their coloring has no equivalent in fish of Earth, and the most luxurious feathers of earthly birds cannot compare to the plumage of the Subtle World. The people resemble earthly people, but amaze one by the subtlety of their features and tissues. Their voices remind one of the finest singing on Earth, yet the meaning is entirely different. Such differences are striking to the human consciousness, and one must become accustomed to them.

Blessed are those who, while in the gross body, are already prepared to accept the manifoldness of the worlds. Do not think that such acceptance comes easily, for one must be spiritually experienced to be able to accept Reality. The word "accept" signifies the very essence of evolution. There are even cultured and educated people who cannot comprehend the many and varied worlds, and therefore do not have access to the Subtle World. Subtle feelings can never be forced.

Whoever rejects the idea of the Subtle World is preparing a miserable abode for himself. One must cultivate a broad expansion of ideas, for without it one cannot hope to have flights in the subtle body. A timid subtle body, even if it succeeds in leaving the physical body, will be terrified and will remain motionless. It is not easy to enter the Subtle World without fear, and to calmly observe and study. The crowds in the Subtle World are as unusual as the beings on the far-off worlds. The luminous matter is different from the earthly matter, but even amidst endless differences, one must adhere to the idea of Oneness. Our Abode is One, yet it is multifaceted.

114. Urusvati is well acquainted with the so-called sacred pains, and also with other painful sensations whose origins are not known. One should look for the cause of these strange pains in one's contacts with the Subtle World. Just as the gross body can receive "shocks," which are followed by painful reactions, so can the subtle body be influenced by various forces which it then transmits to its physical counterpart. Many nervous reactions are linked to the reflexes of the Subtle World.

One cannot remain physically insensitive to experiences in the Subtle World. One is subject to many painful reactions, similar to stings, which in turn will affect the nerves and cause pain in the nerve centers.

Urusvati has met pseudo-teachers and their followers in the Subtle World. Such contacts are quite usual, and are by no means pleasant, but one should know that they exist. Such instances teach us to be cautious and give one an idea of the unusual variety of manifestations in all existence. Only one who has gained knowledge from personal experience will refrain from drawing hasty conclusions, and will carefully record all new impressions in his Chalice of Accumulations.

We have learned much from Our experiences in the physical and Subtle Worlds. We observed and then preserved in Our Chalices the individual experiences, marveling at their variety. We advocate the same practice for Our co-workers. However, it is especially harmful to proclaim laws when one has experienced only a minute part of the manifestations that are the evidence of those laws. It is not out of a sense of modesty that I say this, but out of a realization of the grandeur of Cosmos.

115. Urusvati remembers how she could change the moods of some people by a simple touch of her hand. We, too, raise Our left hand when We transmit thoughts. One can actually make use of the gross magnetism located at the finger tips, and one should learn to sense it, especially when it has been reinforced by the intensification of thought-sending.

In Our Abode it is customary to send messages

while standing with one arm raised, but some sendings require a relaxed seated position with the arms folded on the chest or the hands placed on the knees, in order to stem the outflow of magnetic currents. These different positions of the physical body illustrate how psychic energy is connected with other bodily functions. Today these reminders are especially timely, because people are beginning to study thought-transmission without sufficient knowledge of the essential peripheral conditions. In the East the physical body is studied, but serious attention is also given to the many additional surrounding conditions.

In the ancient records one finds many symbolic expressions whose original meaning is now lost. The ancient tradition of oral instruction had a profound purpose because the Teaching could be transmitted directly to the deserving disciple without the need for symbolic veiling. However, conventional written records contain many harmful errors. Dense ignorance can obscure small parts of the given Truth, and deliberately malicious statements distort even the most obvious facts. One can imagine how much effort is needed to direct human thought to the intelligent eradication of such shameful distortions.

It is regrettable that most people do not realize how much of their strength is wasted in attempts to depress the mood of those intimately connected with them. Some day people will be censured for trying to spoil the mood of others. It is reprehensible enough to break a musical instrument, but how much more valuable is the human mind! It is impossible to restore a broken mood.

116. Urusvati knows that there is a correlation between battle and creation. From the mundane point of view these concepts would appear to be opposites.

But We say that creation is the dispersing of darkness, therefore there exists not opposition but a correlation between these two seemingly opposed concepts.

We are often accused of frightening people by putting so much stress on the concept of battle and for saying that Our Battle is endless. People assume that creation is peaceful, and battle destructive, but how can one think of creation without mastery over the elements, without a courageous struggle to overcome obstacles? Thus Our Battle, too, is mastery over chaos. If there were no such defense, the waves of chaos would overwhelm all achievements. It is important to realize fully that battle and creation are active principles of Be-ness.

When We discuss motion, We have in mind the very same dispersal of darkness. We advocate battle not as fratricidal slaughter, but as a beautiful defense of the whole manifested world. One cannot remain at peace when chaos is raging. It would be appropriate to illustrate this idea by the ancient maxim that to appreciate safety one must experience several earthquakes. Only on life's precipice can one perceive Infinity.

Most people will not understand this, since for them battle is the opposite of creation. One cannot speak effectively to the crowds about endless battle, and only a few true seekers will realize how much their bold experiments resemble a battle. The ancient images of the Luminous Spirits always depicted them with armor. Every scientist has his own armor, which is knowledge.

We use both physical and spiritual armor, and suggest that Our followers acquire the armor that will protect them from the blows of chaos. Please do not take Our words about armor as symbolic, but realize that there is need for a weapon created by your consciousness. The stronghold is strengthened when the bridge to the Tower of Chun is firm.

117. Urusvati is aware of the concept of victory. When We start creative work that is protected by the battle, We affirm victory. May the tautened string of victory resound! May the signs of forward motion become visible, for there is no defeat in Infinity. May Our Call be accepted as living advice.

Urusvati knows well the communications link with the Brotherhood; only by means of this link can one know the varied states of existence. Our Brotherhood is like a laboratory of all branches of life. The new Teaching is now being spread throughout the whole world, introducing a new knowledge of the subtle energies.

Our victory too, is subject to subtle conditions. Sometimes years are required to make the right path, already outlined by Us, visible to earthly eyes. Later, people will remark on how specifically events were foreseen, and some will then appreciate Our sense of co-measurement in revealing the truth. Thus, learn from Our patience. May the adamant aspiration of the Brotherhood be an example for you in all your actions.

Our Inner Life contains a subtle reflection of earthly ways in all their multiplicity, therefore We advise that a keen and agile mind be developed. The ancients taught the possibility of all impossibilities, and in so doing taught how to broaden the consciousness. They often repeated the parable about an inept general, who, standing on a hilltop, was so concerned about the defeat of one part of his army that he failed to turn in time to see the other part of his army win a major victory.

118. Urusvati is familiar with the many details that have been given to people about the Brotherhood and the Subtle World. We have records in which all such messages have been entered, and when We gather together all Our words We have a precise record of the many details which together provide a clear picture. These messages were deliberately scattered, and can be found in the historical records of various nations.

We have never permitted Ourselves to force ideas or to use complicated discourses. The human consciousness should, like a bee, collect knowledge from all sources in order to build its own concept of truth, freely and voluntarily. Only such laborious effort accelerates self-culture.

There are many people who would welcome a ready-made pattern of truth. Such people wish to be led like the blind, but Our ancient method declares: Man, know thyself! We are ready to share generously fragments of the world's mosaic, but everyone must create his own design.

People complain that they cannot find sufficient information about the Subtle World, yet there are many indications to be discovered if people would pay attention to the many shelves of books and realize that historical legends are not meant for the delusion of human minds!

Each of Us, in the course of many and varied lives, has appeared in the subtle body and witnessed many events. Is it conceivable that when I appeared from the Subtle World in the capacity of a physician, My healing visitations could have been attributed to mere delusion? We can point out volumes of such phenomena witnessed by people on Earth. It is important that such earthly witnesses be given the opportunity to testify to their experiences, no matter how unusual they might seem. One cannot assume that all people, of all beliefs, are liars!

Much information about the Brotherhood has been given, but the aspirant must collect it himself. Even now Our words will impress only a few; nevertheless, the words are uttered and recorded.

119. Urusvati correctly senses the disturbance of the currents. We concentrate intensely on the task of maintaining balance during such periods of agitation, for it is essential to protect the apparatus of psychic energy. One may experience a kind of withdrawal of the whole organism or at times feel a burdensome inner bloating. I advise you to eat lightly at such times, but this advice is relative, depending on the individual and the circumstances.

Psychic energy in motion can be likened to a turbulent sea. When its balance is disturbed, the ebb and flow of energy becomes excessive. When waves of beneficent energy are being sent out it is important to be aware of that part of the body, and that center, from which they have been sent. The waves of energy may flow away and become available to others, but the important question is how this help will be received. Without conscious receptivity there may be a reverse blow, which can have serious consequences. Often these waves can be of such dense quality that they affect the Chalice, and a heavy sensation will be felt around this region. A specific tension is observed when the spatial currents have been intensified by free will and form a knot of densified energy. Every impulse is a double-edged sword.

We cannot help feeling these storms, which tear the tissue woven over centuries. Let us not underestimate the dangers created by free will: a high gift, its misuse can drag humanity into the greatest dangers. It is impossible to convince people not to harm one another, but it is possible to continue the battle for equilibrium.

You can imagine what tension surrounds Our Tower when the waves of energy are raging in space, but We continue Our work, and Urusvati has sometimes heard Our forceful exclamations and urgent indications.

120. Urusvati knows the significance of the moment that separates sleep from the waking state. This moment is called "the diamond of consciousness." During this transitory condition of consciousness man belongs simultaneously to both worlds—the physical and the subtle. If people perceived such conditions consciously, they would grasp more easily the idea of psychic energy.

No mysterious initiations are needed for the realization of the sacred moment. Everyone is given the opportunity to perceive both worlds, but their free will must not interfere and prompt deadly denial. We do not like the word "death" and all that it implies, yet all ignorant deniers may be called dead.

It is correctly observed that a special vibration is needed for the realization of the diamond of consciousness. This vibration originates in pure aspiration, for which conscious knowledge is required. There is neither magic nor sorcery in the ability to perceive this beautiful moment. When man brings impressions from the Subtle World into his physical life he may also perceive the Fiery Gates.

We intensify and deepen these diamond moments through a clear understanding of their significance. Indeed, they are so brief that no effort is required. Prolonged communication with the Subtle World can be achieved, but simultaneous awareness of the two worlds is momentary. We are not referring to Our guiding powers and Our messages to the world. Our discourses, and My words, are not coming to you now from the Subtle World, but are the result of the transmission of thought from a distance. When Urusvati sees the events taking place in Our Tower it is a special function of telepathic vision, whereas discourse with Us corresponds to direct radio messages. That channel cannot be revealed to everybody, nor can everybody have access to Us.

What We are speaking of here is something else, the diamond moment between sleep and the waking state, at the moment of the return of the subtle body into the physical one. Each human being has the power to experience this moment that connects the two worlds, but for this one must develop a subtle awareness. All recollections of the Subtle World are extremely useful for human evolution, and even reminders about the lower strata of the Subtle World serve as a useful warning. Human thought moves in the direction of cognition of the various realms, and even the fiercest Armageddon is helpless to prevent the predestined knowledge.

There are those who define all the worlds as material, but in the final analysis one comes to understand that all is spirit-matter. Hence, the worlds are material, after all. Indeed, the Tower of Chun is built of matter. But let us not complicate our thinking with nomenclature; the signs of all the three worlds are being manifested, and earthly man can even see the sparks of the Fiery World.

121. Urusvati knows how persistently We try to impress predestined discoveries upon the human mind. Let us take aviation as an example. One might think that after the flying ships of Atlantis, thought about victory over the air would have been abandoned for a long time to come, but thought about flight was destined to survive. People began to dream about airships, iron birds, and flying carpets. Solomon used a flying apparatus, and, finally, Our beloved Leonardo laid the foundation for scientific aeronautics. Thus one can trace in many fields of knowledge how ideas expressed in poetic legends gradually grew into scientific achievements.

One should remember the myths about Icarus and Simon Magus, which suggest flights into the Subtle World. Some day man will again develop the power of levitation, but first he must understand psychic energy. Similar predictions can be traced in other fields. We do not fail to remind people about those possibilities that are knocking at their doors and can accelerate their evolution.

One should remember that modern calculations are far from perfect, because certain factors are not taken into consideration. Until now, Primal Energy has not been taken into account, and the effects of many potent chemical combinations are not known.

Sometimes it seems that certain discoveries were made as if by chance, but was there not a whisper of help from the Tower of Chun? Scientists seldom heed Our Advice however, and We are often compelled to give an indication, not to the specialist, but to a receptive worker in a related endeavor. Wives, sisters, and other close co-workers of inventors can testify how sometimes they led the scientists to predestined discoveries because of their straight-knowledge.

We will remind you untiringly about the most urgent needs of humanity.

122. Urusvati remembers how steadfastly We care about protecting the Beautiful. Foreseeing the events of Armageddon, We work to spread abroad Our suggestions about the best methods for preserving the world's treasures. We know that the forces of darkness will use all their efforts to prevent the fulfillment of Our urgent precautions. They understand very well that a work of art emits the most powerful emanations, and can serve as the best weapon against their attacks.

The forces of darkness attempt to destroy art, or at least divert the attention of people from it. It must be remembered that a work of art deprived of attention loses its power of transmission, and its benevolent energy is arrested. There is no living contact between a cold spectator or listener and art that is beyond his understanding.

The concept of creative thought is profound and such thought permeates a work of art, which then becomes a strong magnet and a collector of energy. Thus, each artistic creation lives and assists in the exchange and accumulation of energy.

Even in the midst of Armageddon one can experience the influence of works of art. Concern about precious art can preserve a whole era. Our repositories are filled with objects that people considered lost. Perhaps some of them will eventually be returned to the nations that failed to protect them.

We have saved many works of art. We can foresee how the dark ones will apply all their skill to minimize favorable conditions, and from the highest spheres of existence We know at which time We must help humanity. These preliminary plans are in the Subtle World well in advance. We do not conceal the need for urgent measures, because, in the ongoing Armageddon, the dark ones hope to corrupt all human energies. But We know how to oppose them. Thus, observe where We direct Our care.

123. Urusvati notices how the cosmic currents

affect not only world events, but also the lives of individuals. One can observe unusual illnesses and even epidemics that cannot be accounted for by usual causes. One can notice how sometimes people become susceptible to colds and sudden nervous pains. The treatment of such unusual ailments should also be unusual.

All this confirms that during these periods the psychic energy is in an unusual state. The protective net is agitated; it is inflamed, and outer influences can easily pass through it. We warn people to be especially careful during such days. We do not mean to say that these days are more dangerous than others, but that one's sensitivity becomes more acute. And let us not forget that the dark forces prefer to use these times for their own purposes. It is essential to protect not only physical health, but also nervous balance. In general, one must have an intelligent attitude toward the existence of the dark forces. It is ignorant to deny their existence, but it is just as harmful to be afraid of them. Urusvati has seen their images, some disgusting and others beautiful. They have the ability to surround themselves with luminosity and they also know how to offer various advantages.

It may be asked, "Can the hierophants of evil approach Our Tower?" Indeed they can, although these approaches are very painful for them. Their fury gives them a strong impulse. At times We are obliged to use powerful discharges of energy to repulse the uninvited visitors. With such discharges We vanquish the enemies who try to approach Our Brothers. You can remember special currents that you sensed during the night. These currents are salutary and protective. Striving to Us will intensify them. Other influences may cause tears in the protective net, but Our currents do not delay in protecting you.

124. Urusvati has seen Our protective tissue. We speed invisible currents of this luminous tissue, which blocks the attacks of the dark forces and protects *Dokyood*, where Our co-workers relax before undertaking their new work.

It is important to realize that Our rays and currents are helpful when they are accepted consciously. We can testify that the benefit of Our influence is increased a hundredfold if it is accepted through the heart.

People suffer because they do not grasp the reality of Our Messages. Although their complaints are constant, Our Messages are rejected and ridiculed. Every aspiring thought directed to Us will bring a good harvest, yet Our most obvious manifestations are forgotten and explained away in the most commonplace manner. Let Us choose the best ways.

Urusvati can notice even the briefest changes in the protective tissue, but most people are not able to pay heed to even prolonged signs. How, then, can We trust them with the details of Our inner life? Instead of benefiting from the knowledge, they will only concoct new reasons for doubting. Thus, We and Our true co-workers will always discriminate in what can be said that will be beneficial. One should not force the Teaching on anyone, for unless the heart has been opened, it cannot recognize either benefit or beauty. A deep understanding of the Teaching requires an open heart. Let people turn their hearts to Us more often, and let them learn to love to think about Us.

125. Urusvati knows how highly We value the feeling of solemnity. Indeed, it is solemnity that stabilizes Our upward soaring. This feeling is intensified during days commemorating Great Heroes.

Humanity pays tribute to many of Our Brothers, although under different names. People think that their heroes have no connection with Us, little realizing that among the most revered and worshipped giants of mankind were the very Founders of Our Brotherhood.

Let us remember that they appeared on Earth under a special Ray, and therefore their birth is associated with particular legends. We shall not contradict these legends, because they encourage solemnity and help humanity to perceive the Great Images. Nor do We correct the dates that have been established by convention. On the contrary, We send forth benevolent thoughts at each of humanity's holy days. Solemnity is intensified if one is aware of the great achievements that are honored by these memorial days.

People are only dimly aware of the significance of the Great Teacher's glorious achievements, and have turned the most beautiful self-sacrifice into things common and selfish. But even while belittling, they may preserve a small particle of solemnity. Let us with all patience help to cultivate this beautiful feeling of solemnity, which transforms life, creates heroes, and leads to the far-off worlds. Let us observe memorial days with positive, good deeds.

Service is expressed in good deeds, which are possible under all circumstances. Great achievements contribute to Our joy. We show the way, but it must be trod by human feet—such was the law given by the Great Savior.

All such Great Achievements are recorded in Our treasuries. The ignorant attempt to deny these truths, but fortunately We preserve the proof of these deeds. Thus, let us dedicate a special day to Great Achievements.

126. Urusvati rightly encourages co-workers to copy paragraphs from the books of the Teaching dealing with Primal Energy. One should gather the pieces of the mosaic into a complete book. At the same time, we must remember that some people complain that the books of the Teaching discuss one and the same thing over and over. These ignorant ones do not read with proper attention and fail to notice that in each approach to an idea We introduce a new detail. That is why extracts must be introduced in sequence; only then can one notice the turns of the spiral of Our Messages. People should learn to enjoy this work, for through such thoroughness they will be able to observe Our methods while gathering together Our Indications and Advice.

What merit is there for the student who repeats Our words without applying his own effort? Consciousness is enriched only in the process of right thinking, and mechanical repetitions cannot lead to the new synthesis. One should observe how We lead thought without interfering with independent activity. We show the way, and point out the possibilities without violating karma, but each turn of the path must be recognized by the person himself.

Our Inner Life is conditioned by definite methods which are based upon immutable laws. Our Abode can exist only in fulfillment of the laws of evolution. You have witnessed how, quite unexpectedly, scientists sometimes confirm what the Teaching has already proclaimed. It would be appropriate to point out that in addition to the given Teaching certain unexplainable impulses are received by scientists. Our thought-messages fly all over the world, and We sow the seeds generously in space. Space is full of ideas. This condition is called the "digestive power of Infinity."

It is of particular importance to develop a love for thoroughness. Only in this way can you become familiar with Our methods.

127. Urusvati remembers how, when she met Us for the first time, passers-by seemed to disappear as if they had been dispersed. It would be correct to assume that this was the result of Our mental command, but these are times of such unprecedented tension that no such message can be given. In comparing these times we can see the influence of Armageddon.

Some may ask if it is possible that within only two decades such a powerful cosmic tension can develop. Such a question proves that the significance of Armageddon is little understood. Anyone who knows about the approaching end of *Kali Yuga* recognizes that it cannot occur without world upheavals. The forces that were particularly powerful during the Black Age must now struggle for survival, and they prefer a general catastrophe to defeat. We must co-measure Our forces according to the planetary situation, for during such tension the least exaggeration of effort can destroy the equilibrium.

Most people are unable to understand the importance of co-measurement and goalfitness. They think that Our Power can overcome any resistance, regardless of the cosmic imbalance. It is a simple concept yet it must be repeated constantly, otherwise even the most learned people fall into despair and wonder why something that was possible ten years ago is not possible today. Such a question is evidence that they do not understand cosmic motion. Not without reason do We call for courage and patience.

We send forth information about the dates pertaining to the end of *Kali Yuga*, and multitudes pay attention to it. The *Puranas* provide many obvious indications regarding these events, but the most important conditions could not be indicated in the old manuscripts. The tension of spatial currents and the discovery of Primal Energy could not be mentioned in the *Puranas* even though they were intended for the seeking, advanced thinkers. But both of these conditions have now been manifested in a pronounced form, making the significance of the approaching end of *Kali Yuga* the more obvious.

128. Urusvati was restrained several times from undertaking extremely dangerous flights. The Teacher must protect one from over-courageous investigations. The higher spheres scorch like the heat of the sun, and the lower spheres are oppressive for the higher consciousness. It is impossible to fly through all the spheres, for the subtle body would be consumed. The division of the spheres of the Subtle World is determined within one's own consciousness. The transfer to the higher spheres must be gradual. Just as physicians supervise their patients, Guides are appointed to help the disciples to preserve their balance so that this transfer may be performed intelligently. In the Subtle World each violation of equilibrium causes a shock.

Thus We too preserve balance in Our Abode. This is especially essential at the borderline between the physical and Subtle worlds, which is clearly defined in Our Lives.

It is difficult for people to understand that the knowledge acquired on Earth is essential for their experience in the Subtle World—not only the knowledge itself, but also the degree of perceptiveness and tolerance. When people demand these qualities of themselves they will automatically develop an open-mindedness that will bring them to the Fiery Gates.

Such discipleship is easy for those who realize and

accept the existence of the Brotherhood. At a time of great danger the Guide will protect and warn, but only at the very last moment.

Urusvati remembers the difficult ascent of a smooth mountain wall, deep in snow, when the Hand of the Teacher was stretched out to offer support. Urusvati did not doubt and therefore conquered all difficulties. This should be an example to co-workers of how difficult ascents are achieved. One should ponder how other Brothers have succeeded in their efforts.

There cannot be an effortless ascent.

129. Urusvati attempts to compare a flight to the far-off worlds to a flight into the higher spheres of the Subtle World or up to the Fiery Realm. Fundamentally, both flights are performed in the subtle body, although in different dimensions, and there is danger in both of them. A definite change of pressure is felt when approaching the far-off worlds. For example, let us remember what happened to Sister I., whose flights nearly tore the connecting cord. The dangers are even more grave when we prematurely attempt to contact the Fiery Worlds. The subtle body can be consumed if it has not been prepared by a lengthy, gradual approach.

Do not forget that a subtle body, even of high refinement, remains a material body, and is subject to laws which, though of a higher order, are nevertheless material.

Fiery phenomena, rare on the earthly plane, affect the human heart, and transform all the spheres that they touch. Such instantaneous transformations can cause an extraordinary shock against which the physical surroundings provide no protection. In other words, the fiery sword will burn through the physical sheath.

Only seldom are We able to be in touch with the Fiery World. Normally, these contacts occur through the corresponding spheres of the Subtle World, and in this way the law of goalfitness is obeyed. With the broadening of consciousness this sense of goalfitness is applied more intelligently. The physical world envelops Our Abode and We take upon Ourselves the task of maintaining the balance.

Our Brother V. remembers that He once foresaw an explosion that was about to take place in the heart of a city. We are responsible for all karma that comes Our way, and such misfortunes should not be allowed. Also in flights goalfitness should be applied. There is no benefit in being burned before the Fiery Gates have opened. We are responsible for all karma that comes Our way.

May the striving toward Our Spheres be a beautiful ascent!

130. Urusvati is aware that We are not immune either to the dangers that surround Us. In ignorance people assume that We face no danger in Infinity! Certainly, thanks to Our knowledge, We are sufficiently protected in earthly conditions, but everything is relative, and when thought strives to Infinity standards of measurement differ.

A heroic attitude should be maintained in all circumstances. This is a test that must be passed if true evolution is to be supported. We divide heroes into the unconscious and the consciously determined ones. Those who understand what they labor and suffer for are truly heroic. Knowing the truth of their situation they still do not turn from danger. Amidst the currents of space, amidst evil will, amidst terror, courageous heroes labor and create. Heroes know that their earthly life can end at any moment, but they do not reduce their efforts. They realize that their selfless *podvig* will continue even under the harshest circumstances. Nothing can stop their will from manifesting itself in any sphere.

There is a great difference between the unconscious and the consciously determined heroes. In the first there may be a spontaneous exaltation. But although temporary reactions may occur and cause the determined ones to pull back, they will never give up, and will continue on their path, applying the cosmic knowledge accumulated through centuries. They know how to transmute knowledge into feeling and how to fill their hearts with it. Where the heart is full there is a soaring into the future. An austere knowledge of danger inspires the hero.

I speak of this to emphasize that heroism is the fundamental stronghold of Our Inner Life. Examples of heroism can be seen in the past lives of Our Brothers. Will not Our Life serve you as an inspiring example of beautiful, though weighty, armor?

131. Urusvati understands the beauty of collaboration with the Subtle World. Anyone who imagines that such contact is with a dead world only displays complete ignorance. We constantly work with this living world. We are particularly strengthened by the broad knowledge transmitted by Our co-workers in the Subtle World. Those who are limited by physical existence are able to learn only one aspect of truth, but the broad scope of Our science is acquired through knowledge that We derive from the Subtle World. One should not be limited by the physically visible horizon. The time will come when people will be able to enrich their lives by natural means, but this will require the ability to perceive life everywhere.

People may ask whether it is confusing to work with

disembodied entities and densified astral beings—not in the least. Such collaboration takes place on the plane of unified consciousness, and because such co-workers are of similar mentality, the unification forms a true community.

It is correct to say that a community of people represents a crown of achievement, but for a perfect community there must be refinement and unification of consciousness. It is not a small task to unify consciousness in true collaboration. In the higher spheres of the Subtle World the soul begins to understand that collaboration brings power and success, but when people return to Earth, they forget the value of reciprocity. They also forget about Our existence, though they were aware of Us in the Subtle World, met Our Brothers, and understood the significance of *Dokyood*. Nevertheless, the appointed hour is approaching, and people will either understand what is predestined or choose catastrophe.

132. Urusvati remembers her visit to *Dokyood*, where it was a great joy to see children striving for heroic deeds. It is also interesting to see those who have not yet outlived their physical experiences. They are unable to approach the physical atmosphere from the Subtle World, because such an approach causes tension in the subtle body, and results in the secretion of an unusual sweat that decreases the vital force. Thus, the Guide must regulate the inner condition to conform to the degree of desire for Service.

Recently Urusvati visited places where those people dwell who left Earth in an aged condition. It is easier to work with children, and with those of advanced age who have outlived their tasks in the earthly body. Most difficult are the middle-aged people who are still filled with unexpressed accumulations and discontent, and are unable to accept the Hierarchy. They are victims of their own vague desires and are dissatisfied with everything.

Among those who have experienced a long earthly life there can be found an organization that helps others to recognize Hierarchy. The beings from the Highest Spheres are not always perceived by those in the Subtle World, and though their presence is more pronounced than on Earth, there are many disbelievers even in the Subtle World. Those who were ignorant on Earth are stubborn and carry their doubts and negations with them into the Subtle World. One should remember this so that one may be ready to follow the Teachings when in the Subtle World.

Urusvati saw those who were eager to see their Teacher. Remember that We do visit the various spheres of the Subtle World, although it is difficult for Us to remain in the lower strata. Brother K. fell ill while fulfilling His mission on the earthly plane, and the lower layers of the Subtle World are just as dense. Urusvati is aware of this denseness and suffocation. It is better to know of all the difficulties of a dedicated life than to dream only of "heavenly harps and songs." We purposely emphasize the difficult side; first, in order not to hide the truth, and second, if man realizes the joy of spiritual achievement, he will also realize that even the greatest difficulties are nothing when compared with the grandeur of illumination.

A young boy whom Urusvati met was striving for great achievements, and will indeed find joy in all fields of endeavor.

133. Urusvati knows how extremely difficult it is on occasion for Us to visit meetings of earthly people; visiting the Subtle World is easier. We all realize that to achieve results on the earthly plane more energy is needed than in dealing with the Subtle World. Where the energy of thought can be applied directly it is easier to establish contact, but thought in earthly conditions is so confused that the sending requires an increased tension.

Urusvati also knows that it is very tiring for the invisible witness to remain in the midst of earthly gatherings, yet such attendances are frequent. People can sense the invisible presence, as if someone had questioned or answered them. At times this is felt so intensely that one is prompted to ask his neighbor whether he has spoken. One can recall episodes in history when statesmen clearly heard voices and warnings. Unfortunately, most of them paid no attention to this help.

We warned Napoleon more than once, and he admitted that he "heard voices," yet he continued on his path of error. Over eons it has been Our duty to warn those in high places who are in a position to hinder evolution.

Urusvati recently visited some military gatherings. The participants sensed that they should speak plainly about their problems, but had no idea who it was they were confiding in. Thus, decisions are often made which otherwise would remain unspoken. We call such influence "inaudible Advice."

134. Urusvati knows about teraphim. Some may wonder if the idea of teraphim does not contradict the idea of power of thought. If thought is the strongest manifestation, why then would an object be needed to serve as a focus for concentrating it? It is true that teraphim are not needed for a powerful mental message, but they can be used to economize mental power. Each kind of energy must be used intelligently. The object that serves to accumulate energy also serves to multiply it. Such objects preserve the precipitations of energy, which can be gradually intensified. From ancient times teraphim have been regarded as sacred, but today this concept has become a scientific one.

We have a number of teraphim which facilitate the sending of help to Our dear ones. It is important to understand that such accumulated energy can be a healing power by helping in the transmission of certain vibrations. All beneficial measures should be taken into consideration.

The Stone from the far-off worlds is a significant teraph of the Brotherhood. Much has been written about this Stone. A part of it performs the duty of a messenger throughout the world, carried by the hands of the chosen. People call the Stone "Grail," but it has also been called by many other names. Legends of all times reveal some of the truth regarding this Stone, but its most significant aspect is not mentioned—the Stone is permeated with a substance that helps to preserve the vibrational communications with the far-off worlds. Likewise, a small particle of the Stone serves as a link with the Brotherhood. Thus again there is a scientific basis for a legend which has become a part of human history. We purposely emphasize the scientific aspect of this legend because the ignorant ones are ever ready to attribute everything to the darkness of superstition. Urusvati knows this Stone of Our Abode. We preserve it in a special place so that the vibrations may retain their original power.

We must point out that the vibrational energy of meteors has not been studied. Some contain particles of remarkable metals which, though small, can still be traced. The mind of the researcher should not be limited by old methods.

Some people may be interested to know more about

the whereabouts of the Stone. The place where it was first revealed became the foundation of Shambhala, and it intensified the chemical significance of the Abode. Many stories could be told about this messenger from the far-off worlds. You already know about certain guardians who have particles of this Stone, and you can confirm how the Stone reveals itself. You will be astonished to know how many different countries and heroes are connected with it, and how many great deeds were inspired by the legends pertaining to it.

The fierce adversaries of the Brotherhood have also heard about the Stone, and its saga is extremely repulsive to them. They do not understand the essence of this phenomenon and thus are full of hatred and fear of it.

May reliable friends guard the story of the Stone.

135. Urusvati knows that thoughts about beautiful legends lead to the Teacher. And even in the most difficult hours, thoughts about the Brotherhood will create the best bridge to it.

Thoughts should be directed to the Beautiful, as a salutary medicine. People do not understand what a powerful remedy has been given to them, and they prefer to complain, feel discontent, and weep, not understanding that such ways only limit the best possibilities.

Upâsikâ provides the best example. Even in the most difficult moments she was striving to Us. Such will power inevitably results in a powerful vibration. Nothing could compel her to criticize the Teacher, even indirectly. No misfortune could make her forget the Brotherhood. Not even the shipwreck could interfere with her concentration. She held firmly to the thought about the Brotherhood, and this focus intensified the sacred vibration.

Urusvati also knows that talk or thought about Us brings the sacred vibration closer. We, too, know the power of exalted thought, and come together for the purpose of thinking unitedly about the Beautiful. However, We do not suggest one particular image; each individual selects the most beautiful according to his affinity. Thus, a symphony is created which comes close to the music of the spheres. Its chords ring out like victorious trumpets, so harmonious that their very sounds fill the heart with joy.

Amidst the most grievous struggles, remember the Beautiful. It can be a panacea for the heart of the toiler. Know that this Advice is given not only to you; in Our Abode it is also applied. Everyone has his dangers and sorrows, but it is a joy to know that there is the one protecting remedy for all.

136. Urusvati knows what it means to be amidst earthly battles while in the subtle body. Physical weapons can be used against any entity, and it may seem puzzling that they do not injure the subtle body. The reason for this is that during earthly battle a weapon is used consciously and with free will, but there can be no conscious will directed at an unseen target. This is a good example of the increased potency of conscious action.

One can find ancient images that depict "heavenly" participants in earthly battles. Urusvati can testify how swiftly and safely she was able to fly amongst the combatants. You can imagine how often We participate in such earthly battles. We are invulnerable to human weapons, yet can suffer injuries from the hierophants of the dark forces, whose ruinous attacks fill space. Such invisible battles are not fairy tales. It is one thing to send a Ray from the Tower, but it is an entirely different thing to fly to participate in the righteous battle in space. Flights are possible even in the physical body, and, despite the sceptics, flights in the subtle body have often been proven.

In both earthly and subtle battles, decisive results come from the quality of aspiration directed to Us. One should repeat without end that aspiration to Us is a strong shield. Help can be immeasurably increased where there is no room for discontent, complaints, depression, and mistrust. People, give your Invisible Helpers the opportunity to stretch out their hands! So many luminous wings have withered away because of human distrust!

If a conscious attitude can add potency to a weapon, then pure, enlightened striving can certainly attract help. This is not a moral admonition, but scientific fact. Selfless flight is already an act of faith and straight-knowledge. Urusvati voluntarily aspires to join the battle. Her motto is, "Be strong for victory." One can participate many times in the battle, and We value each effort for the sake of Truth and Light.

Hypocrites will plead, "Who are we? We are so small! How can we help the Great Light?" But it was said long ago, "Each breath should praise the Lord."

In a word of kindness is born an act for Good.

137. Urusvati remembers the attractive, brilliant appearance that can be assumed by the hierophant of Evil. One should also bear in mind that the dark ones constantly attempt to touch Our Rays; this is analogous to intercepting a telegraphic communication. Thus, one should remember the many tactics of darkness.

Never forget the brilliance of the emanations with which the dark ones can surround themselves. For beginners this fact is rather puzzling, but when one has studied the science of radiant energy it becomes clear. However, because the power of pure radiance is not available to all, the emanations of the dark ones can never achieve the level of vibration that can shake one's entire being.

We have already mentioned various places where the dark ones gather. We could repeat them, but this would not help. If We were to mention B., or N., or E., it would not be an address, and even the name of a street or the description of a house would not help in locating one of their dark nests, which would have a very innocent appearance. There are certainly no images of Satan, but religious objects will be plentiful. Only the sensitive heart will sense where the evil ones are. Let us not forget that they are skillful and fierce, and that no one can compete with them in these qualities. Thus, the dark ones can bear suffering and even destroy themselves in order to participate in destruction.

Much of Our Strength is used to counteract the tricks of the dark ones. We consider that day a victorious one when the hierophant of Evil is obliged to retreat.

138. Urusvati knows that We never regret the past. Precious is the striving to the future, and a special energy is attracted when thought about the future is alive. The most brilliant past cannot compare to the possibilities of the future. Science confirms that thoughts of the future are salutary, and regretful thoughts about the past are poisonous.

We offer knowledge about the past, but the heart should be filled with striving to the future. Let the ability to perceive better possibilities for mankind be developed out of such thoughts.

Do not think that it is easy to reject the past. Great knowledge must be acquired before one can recognize the spiral of evolution, which perpetually surges forward. Usually people dwell on yesterday, not realizing that each tomorrow brings new knowledge, and the day that is hardly over has already engendered new accumulations. Night brings communion with the Subtle World and the renewal of energies. In the morning people seldom remember their experiences of the night just passed, but they feel the increase of energy. Scientists explain this phenomenon in a narrow materialistic way, but more experienced observers perceive different causes.

I am now referring to those who are able to greet every morning as the beginning of a new experience. The Pythagorean hymn to the rising sun was actually based on the joyous recognition of the new day, and of new knowledge. In such an exalted state there can hardly be regret for the past.

A thought about the freedom of the forces of the spirit brings creative joy. We do not regret the past.

139. Urusvati knows that many decisive moments pass in silence. First may come a storm, with lightning and thunder, but the foundation is silence. When We suggest unification in silence, then somewhere something significant is taking place. Such concentrated silence gathers a special energy, which potentially is more powerful than even the loudest words. Very few understand silence as action. Our entire Abode sometimes merges into profound silence when something of great importance is taking place.

Often people feel the need to go into silence before undertaking a dynamic action. Thus, an experienced speaker will be momentarily silent and take a deep breath before uttering a decisive word. Some know the importance of such an intake of prana, but others do it quite unconsciously. The potency of one's psychic energy increases with the expansion of consciousness. There is joy in Our Abode when We learn that some great task was performed consciously. Thus, a current of striving can benefit human endeavors.

Perhaps just now an event of great significance may be taking place, but no one realizes how essential it is. Only in years to come will historians evaluate the true meaning of present events.

140. Urusvati knows that many would consider Our commissions beyond their abilities. Such people measure everything in life by ordinary standards. They would not attempt to develop adamant striving in themselves, and are limited by the phantoms of their current illusions. Meanwhile, so-called present time is simply the interval between visible lightning and audible thunder, when lightning has already struck and thunder is inevitable. What then can the interval between two joint manifestations mean? Thus, the present is confusing to people, because it is nothing but a mirage.

When people learn how to grasp the significance of a past event, they will be able to accept the inevitability of its consequences; such a future is a reality.

We do not commission Our messengers to perform impossible tasks. We know the limitations of human ability, and We also know what can be expected of a human being in the building of a realistic future. We can just expect the highest degree of striving from Our messengers. When there is such intensity Our Magnet is active and serves as a strong shield. However, for the long journey timidity is not suitable. Everyone knows, in the depths of his heart, whether he is led by the highest degree of striving or is just being dragged along in fear.

Let man recall how many dangers he escaped

when he was striving forward with all his heart, and how many gates that seemed to be locked were transformed into curtains of light! Thus, he who strives forward adamantly can accept the reality of the future. Let people recall how successful they were because of Our Help, and how they actually felt that a Leading Hand had touched them. Some may have brushed it aside as if it were an annoying fly, but there were those who accepted it with gratitude.

Strong are those who are filled with gratitude, for their wings can grow! They will not be afraid of Our commissions. They know that We are greatly burdened, yet rejoice on the way to the Garden of Beauty!

141. Urusvati knows how much decisiveness is needed for the fulfillment of Our commissions. Those who are unprepared will regret giving up what must be left behind, and others will bemoan the need to leave the vicinity of Our Towers. They forget that spiritual contact is indestructible and that distance has no meaning.

But he who is armed with the power of decision will not regret anything from the past when he knows the path leading into the future. It is not just readiness that is needed, but decisiveness. You understand the difference between these words. We teach how to develop decisiveness so that no earthly circumstances can influence the ability to decide. There were times when attachment to insignificant earthly objects influenced not only the destiny of individuals but that of entire nations. It is shameful when an object made by human hands can interfere with the path of true achievements.

We teach people to resist transitory values that can veil the great Infinity, and point out the supermundane spheres to broaden their scope of thinking. If people become accustomed to thinking about the higher worlds, they will not claim the superiority of mundane life, and will find within themselves the strength to live a life of achievement and the ability to fulfill Our commissions. They will not be perplexed by the problems of earthly life, knowing that these problems can be solved by a higher degree of inspiration.

One must have such confidence in Our Help that the magnet of faith will attract the adamant energy. Our Inner Life is one of readiness to render help.

142. Urusvati knows how attentively one must follow Our Indications, but unfortunately people relate even cosmic events to themselves. Concentrated attention to the words of the Teacher can only come with great love and devotion. In the coming years you will realize how timely were all Our Indications. Often, for the sake of reference, We mention only the country, or the city, or a name, but if these notes are compared, an obvious chain of events will be seen.

Armageddon began in 1931, and now the year 1942 is pointed out as an important one when the next series of world events will be decided. We have spoken of the year 1942 before, and it is significant that this same year is resounding also among humanity. An epic of planetary significance unfolds around each Indication.

Let us recall how brief were Our words about the destiny of China and related events in other countries. Only a sensitive ear could catch the names that were so quickly mentioned. Sometimes We change the names slightly so that the message will not be intercepted, but when, in the course of events, one comes upon such a name, straight-knowledge will at once draw one's attention to it. The technique of foresight will become a great science in the future, but it can be given only when human consciousness gains its sanity.

You are right in disapproving of the neglect shown to the humanities. Only intelligent cooperation among all sciences will create an understanding of the unity of knowledge. But any excess of zeal will prove to be corrupting. One must understand that fanaticism is a form of ignorance, and is based upon negation and condemnation.

Thus you can see what We have to struggle with, yet people never tire of criticizing Us. Not only the fanatics but even good thinkers attempt to correct Our Instructions. May We remind you about a writer who proposed to limit the tasks given by Us, without even taking the trouble to read Our Advice! There were many who tried to hinder the activities of the Brotherhood. Later, some misguided critics repented, but the harm caused by their judgments had to be outlived, and such karmic wounds constitute the most bitter earthly experiences.

The current burdensome days are nothing but the outliving of countless accumulations. We harken attentively to the groaning Earth.

143. Urusvati knows that psychic energy is subject to many physical influences. We have already mentioned that the currents of space affect the entire human organism, but in fact any physical manifestation of energy can heighten the tension of the centers. For instance, strong electrical energy can be most helpful in the transmission of thought at a distance. This is most evident in America, where electrification is presently more widespread, but people there are not usually aware of how this energy assists their experiments. In advanced stages of development psychic energy is not affected by outer influences, but beginners are greatly affected by them. Every intensification of energy further increases one's powers. One scientist declared that he could think with the greatest concentration in front of a blazing fireplace, and another discovered that he was influenced by the sound of boiling water. A third found that thunderstorms increased his mental faculties. Many examples illustrate that even the most ordinary concentration of such natural energies aids the power of thought. One must learn to observe what it is that particularly increases or decreases the thought energy.

We fully possess this ability to observe, and apply it to all aspects of life. The power of thought will act at the greatest distances when increased by natural conditions.

We have already mentioned that those who rebel against the Brotherhood are struck as if by a boomerang. The ignorant will attribute this to Our vengefulness, but the fact is that it is due only to a discharge of energy. If one touches both poles of a charged battery he will receive a shock, but it would be ridiculous to accuse the battery of being vengeful or malicious.

One simply must pay heed to life's manifestations, and admit that there exists an invisible world, even on Earth.

144. Urusvati can testify to the great variety of vibratory cures that have been effected at a distance. This kind of healing will eventually be known to medical science, but at present the very notion would only irritate physicians. We are particularly aware of vibratory influences and apply them far more often than people might think. One should bear in mind that such influences can be intensified by conscious receptivity.

With few exceptions, Our healing remains unnoticed. People are inclined to explain the vibrations by absurd guesswork, and will note every minor symptom of their indisposition, ignoring the strong sensation of vibrations. Sometimes, they will tremble under the currents of the rays, yet will immediately fabricate some explanation for them. Most people will not accept that it is possible to transmit vibrations to a distance, and even the knowledge of radio waves does not convince them that parallels exist in other fields.

Urusvati can testify to how often vibratory energies are applied to the various centers, and how quickly pains are relieved. It is wrong to take these diverse vibrations for granted, and to attribute them only to the patient himself; external influences should also be considered.

We affirm that among future human discoveries there will be such vibratory cures. Many diseases, nervous afflictions, and psychic ailments will be cured. Cancer, in its early stages, can be arrested by such vibrations, stones can be dissolved, and glands normalized. Similarly, certain skin ailments will be cured easily.

Some may wonder if conscious receptivity will promote the success of the cure. Definitely so, and to the greatest degree, for conscious receptivity activates the psychic energy of the organism. Such an ally is always essential.

145. Urusvati knows that unknown names, unknown places and unfamiliar words often come to the surface from the depths of consciousness. Scientists call this the subconscious, but they are unaware that communications from space accumulate in man's Chalice, and when given an impulse, are transferred to the brain.

What is this impulse? Often it is Our Ray, which kindles the surface of the Chalice and evokes the corresponding Sacred Knowledge. Therefore, one should pay heed to such flashes of consciousness. They resemble clairaudience, but in reality are brought forth from the depths of consciousness by Our Ray. In everyday life one should learn to recognize these messages which always come at the right moment.

People complain that they are deprived of lofty Guidance, but such a strong statement is unreasonable. We give much, and it is they who perceive little! Therefore, We remind people to pay more heed to words that spring forth suddenly in the conscious mind. Such words should not be dismissed, but should be carefully applied in life. Many other useful ideas come in a flash, like flying butterflies, but people only brush them aside.

We never tire of disseminating useful information, and We advise you to treat it with care, for it will be of use in the Subtle World. Thus, one should develop the particular ability to catch the thoughts of space.

146. Urusvati has notes pertaining to certain days of the Great Pilgrim, and has preserved His Image in her mind. The Great Pilgrim chose the fervor of great spiritual achievements, which were crowned with amazing success. Those who worship Him fail to understand that He dealt directly with the common people, and that He laid the foundation for a new understanding of the position of woman.

In the ancient Apocrypha one can find mentioned certain stories that were preserved by His faithful followers. It would be a mistake to reject the so-called Apocrypha, for who can prove that they are false? They may be fragmentary and may have been written at different times, but they are based upon treasured memories. The quality of devotion is little appreciated.

Despite the slander of enemies and the errors of

His followers the Beautiful Image remained luminous. Thus we may approach the Great Ones, and no one is forbidden to emulate Them in the proper way.

It should be pointed out that the main Teaching was given by Him when He was in His subtle body. This consummation corresponded fully with the brilliant Truth proclaimed by Him. Wisely He gave a simple word to the people regarding the foundations of life. It was possible for only a few followers to be entrusted with the Teaching that came from the Subtle World since, in accordance with tradition, the Teaching was transmitted orally. However, the Apocrypha do not contain His last instructions, which dealt with the power of thought and would not have been understood by the majority of people. The Teacher knew that ignorance could distort Truth and that only harm would result.

The manifestations in the subtle body were the pinnacle of His Great Achievements. The Teaching was continued without interruption, and some hints indicate that even the disciples were startled by His powerful manifestations. One of the Apocrypha describes how some of them collapsed, while others died from the shock. Yet the most amazing, significant fact is that the Teaching survived, and no distortions could obscure it.

It does not matter that people misrepresented the Beautiful Image in their clumsy efforts to depict Him. The Images familiar to us do not resemble the Great Pilgrim. Some may ask why His true Image has not been restored. But portraits seldom bear a true resemblance, because people usually prefer the Image that most pleases them. The most accurate depictions are not generally known.

Nor did people accept the true way of life of the

Great Pilgrim. They would not believe that He worked hard and had more than one skill. One could find in His land a great variety of ceramic objects created by His own Hands. These objects became healing talismans. But who knows now about these benevolent signs? The path of the Great Pilgrim was filled with benevolent signs.

147. Urusvati remembers the striking features of the Great Pilgrim: the eyes, the forehead and the light brown hair, features that overwhelmed one with wonder, and were so unusual that they provoked exaggerated rumors among the local people. It should be remembered that everything that amazes can cause distorted and absurd interpretations.

History knows little about the Mother of the Great Pilgrim, who was as exceptional as Her Son. The Mother came from a great family and was the embodiment of refinement and nobility of spirit. She was the One who laid the foundation for His first high ideals, and sang a lullaby to Him in which She foretold His miraculous future. She took great care to safeguard Her Child, and was a source of strength for His great achievements. She knew several languages, and thus made the path easier for Him. Nor did She object to His long pilgrimages, and gathered all that was necessary to make the travels easier. She rightly valued the common people and knew that they would guard the treasures of His Teaching. She recognized the grandeur of the Culmination and thus could give heart to those of diverse character who were weakened by doubt and rejection. She was prepared to experience the same achievement as Her Son, and He entrusted to Her His decision, which was confirmed by the Teachers. It was the Mother who understood the mystery of His wanderings. For the fundamental truth about the Mother's life to be clear, one must understand the local conditions of those times. However, She was led by Her insight into the future and was able to rise above the customs of Her country.

In truth, very little is known about Her, but when one speaks about the Great Pilgrim one has to say a word about the Mother who led Him to the Highest.

148. Urusvati will not forget to write about the music of the spheres, which she heard today. In it were expressed the fundamental details of coming events, their grandeur and their sadness. Great is the creation of these events, and profound is the sadness that success should be achieved at so great a price.

Remember that We are ready to hurl portions of Our Aura to strike at and defeat darkness. We are ever ready to sacrifice, but it is sad to waste such power in opposing the dark forces. May this symphony resound as a symbol.

149. Urusvati remembers the Great Pilgrim. In the Arabian desert He was in solitude, but in a sheik's tent He found friends and helpers. He often remained alone, and one should not think that His journeys were always with wealthy caravans. Remember that everyone, when clad in an earthly sheath, is subject to the conditions of the physical world. It is usually supposed that when Our Brothers go into the world they will be placed in special conditions that are unnatural to them, but nature is a state conditioned by law. Every one of Us knows this and selects His path consciously.

It was to be expected that the Pilgrim would meet the dark ones on His path. The story about the meeting of the Great Pilgrim with the Prince of Darkness should not be thought of as imaginary, or symbolic. Urusvati can affirm that she saw various dark entities more than once, including even the Hierophant of Evil himself.

One may wonder what difference there is between such attacks and the usual pressure of darkness. The difference is great, but Our Brothers do not fear them and therefore cannot be hurt. The Great Pilgrim often saw such dreadful images, but He was never afraid of them.

Some may wonder why such a Great Spirit had to face the imperfections of dark entities. But the power of the Magnet attracts even the dark ones, who long to confuse and injure wherever they can. For example, even the slightest doubt will make it impossible to walk on water or fire, or to levitate. I mention this because the Great Pilgrim could perform these acts easily. His great power was in His absolute fearlessness, and He proceeded unwaveringly, for in His heart He had chosen the life of great deeds.

150. Urusvati knows how the Great Pilgrim directed and guided human consciousness toward the Highest. He understood that people were not yet ready to go by the Middle Path. Thus, even when someone attempted to utter the unutterable the Great One would allow him to address the Highest, rather than let him lower the process of his thinking.

The Great One taught people to pray within their hearts, upon the mountain, amid inspiring summits. It is impossible to grasp the full depth of meaning of the Sermon of the Great One, because He gave instructions for the whole of life in the simplest words. The key to this greatness was in His simplicity, which not only allowed Him to more easily communicate with people, but was a beautiful way of expressing the Highest in the simplest words. One should learn to make the complicated simple, for only in simplicity is kindness reflected. Such was the work of the Great Pilgrim.

Great is His luminosity in the Subtle World, and He loves to descend into the lower spheres so that His prana may purify the dark realms. It is not easy even for Him to descend, and one should appreciate all the more this example of His selfless healing of those who suffer there.

It is customary for Us to visit the lower spheres of the Subtle World where a compassionate heart can save multitudes.

151. Urusvati knows that every Great Teacher is associated with healing and the arts. Only a few of the Great Pilgrim's Indications and Advice about healing are recorded in the Apocrypha, but one should not conclude that these few recorded miracles comprise all of His healing activities. There was much healing, mainly of two kinds, when people came to Him, or when He Himself would touch a person because He saw the onset of an illness. Often the ailing one did not understand why the Stranger had touched him. Such an act represented true generosity on the part of the Great Spirit, who, like a tireless gardener, sowed such seeds of goodness.

His words about Beauty also do not appear often in the Apocrypha. The Teacher drew people's attention to beautiful flowers and to the radiance of the sun. He also encouraged group singing, for it is the most powerful method of achieving harmonious vibrations. The Teacher did not emphasize this specific aspect of music and singing, but simply advocated joy and inspiration.

There were those among the disciples and followers whose lives were filled with misery and daily hardship. The Teacher would first help them by uplifting their spirits, and only when balance was established would He discuss their problems. He never condemned their past, but led them into the future. The Teacher could clearly see the future, but only revealed it according to the consciousness of His disciples. Nor did He hesitate to use severe words to revive the dead consciousness.

Thus the Healer and Creator proceeded on His Way.

152. Urusvati has heard both the majestic music of the spheres and the uproar of chaos. Out of confusion and wailing the Great Teacher composed harmonious symphonies. Only the ignorant assume that celestial harps will sound at the first request. From the abyss of chaos to celestial harmony the way is indeed long. This is why the Great Teachers are also the Great Toilers, and only those who have heard both extremes can judge the extent of this evolution.

People wish to see the Teachers just as they see themselves, and if the Teacher differs in some way they will disbelieve. The ignorant demand, never realizing that their demand is based on ignorance, and that the image they have invented is belittling. In general, most pictures of the Great Teachers are tasteless. People want to see their Teachers as exceptional, even in their outer appearance. If people have such an attitude toward true greatness it indicates that they would not have recognized the Great Pilgrim.

He did not avoid mingling with people. He visited their festivals and discussed their daily needs, but few noticed the many wise warnings that were given with a beautiful smile and words of encouragement. His intimate tenderness was not always appreciated by the disciples, who sometimes even criticized Him for it, believing that He should not have given so much attention to people of no importance. However, wonderful souls were revealed and made manifest by His smiles. He was criticized for talking to women, yet it was women who preserved the Teaching. He was also criticized for association with so-called heathens by those who forgot that the Teacher came to all people, not just to one sect. It was part of His lofty achievement to accept insult with equanimity.

We mention these condemnations because through them the Image of the Great Pilgrim is shown to be more human. If He had not come into contact with life and had not suffered, His deeds would not have been as great. No one realized how tormented He was by the many disturbed auras He came into contact with in this way, but the thought of great achievement never left Him.

Thus the Great Teacher followed His ardent Path. We love to dwell on such examples.

153. Urusvati knows from the Apocrypha that certain people wanted to acclaim the Great Pilgrim as the People's Hero. Such a wish is often expressed in connection with a Great Teacher, but this can lead to sad misunderstandings. A Great Teacher is certainly a hero and a leader, but people usually cannot comprehend the true significance of these concepts, and thus is woven the crown of thorns.

Urusvati heard the voice of the Great Pilgrim; how could such a voice belong to a mere leader of crowds? It was precisely the crowds that were the cause of His particular sufferings, shouting in praise of His Kingdom, and then hurrying to His crucifixion. Thus, in their way, they helped to fulfill the prophecies. It is impossible to imagine what karma awaited those crowds of madmen! People are now witnessing events that have burdened the lives of many generations. This is not a punishment, but the consequence of the madness of free will. When I advise restraint from unwise words and thoughts, by this very request I make you think about the future.

The Teacher could have lived His Great Life without the crowds. Even those whom He healed polluted space with their threats and curses. Such a manifestation of free will may be called by many names, yet it remains a form of free will. It is correct to consider free will as the highest gift, but how wisely this precious treasure must be used!

In Our Treasuries there are many objects connected with the life of the Great Pilgrim, and it is amazing how well His emanations have been preserved during these many centuries. They are significant proof of the potency of accumulated psychic energy, which is deposited not only when the hand or breath intentionally sends forth the power, but even when unintended touches leave imperishable traces of the energy.

Thus you must remember the remarkable primal power of the Great Pilgrim.

154. Urusvati is aware that the Great Teachers converse with animals. The Great Pilgrim was remarkable in this respect also. One should understand such contact with the animal kingdom. Although human beings do not pay much attention to animal sounds, they can understand them, since psychic energy can contact its equivalent energy in animals and thus create a bridge of understanding.

An absence of fear and anger is needed on both sides. In addition, there must be truth and good will, for to pretend in these cases is impossible. Cowards may claim to have courage, and the cruel can pretend to be kind, but then the natural bond between the worlds will not exist because the living creatures will have lost their mutual trust and there will be no communication. Nowadays it is considered a great rarity when animals of different types can live together. When people approach animals with a doubting attitude there can be no mutual understanding.

If one could see how the Great Teacher related to animals and birds, one would be convinced of the living bond between the kingdoms. He could call a bird to alight on His arm and then send it in a particular direction, or calm an animal simply by a mental suggestion of calmness. The old legends tell us that sick animals would come to Him to be healed, and many true examples could be cited.

Verily, the Teacher had the right to call the animals His smaller brothers. There was nothing contrived or forced in these communications. Nor was it a relationship of master and slave, but simply cooperation between man and animal.

155. Urusvati knows that animals long remember the emanations of their master. If this is true for the ordinary person, then how much more powerful must be the accumulated emanations of the Great Teacher! For this reason the Teachers must sometimes destroy personal possessions that have been imbued with their magnetic aura, in order to avoid the possibility of their intense emanations falling into the hands of the ignorant. Similar was the fate of the objects that had surrounded the Great Pilgrim. I say "surrounded" because He did not see them as His possessions. Such rejection of possessions was natural for Him because His path was a path of striving.

History has recorded that objects belonging to the Teachers were scattered in various ways. For example, paintings by S.G. were left in France, England, Germany, and the Netherlands and attributed to others.

Most of His paintings were destroyed by the artist, but a few were left with the Van Loo family.

One should carefully consider and understand the distribution of the magnets that were left by the Great Pilgrim. They are not many, but their places are significant. He instructed His disciples to carry such magnets to the far-off countries. It should be remembered how far His messengers went. People did not know them, but they sensed the significance of these envoys and hated them as they hate everything unknown.

156. Urusvati knows that the Great Pilgrim could direct people to the Highest just by His glance. His disciples were surprised when He wanted to labor with them in order to earn their daily bread. This principle was used by Our other Brothers, too. One of them, when He was an emperor, loved to say at the beginning of meals, "It seems that I have earned my bread." Several of the most zealous disciples have fallen away because of the demands of continuous labor. You know one such example in a Northern country.

The Teacher used to say, "Friends, you find ample time for everything, but for the Highest you have only a few moments. If you had dedicated only the time you waste in the dining-hall to the Highest, you would have become teachers by now!" Thus, in practical terms, He taught the advantage of elevated thinking.

He also used to say, "When you offer your whole heart, you will feel the strong cord that binds you to the Great Heart."

He also said, "Do not disturb others when you see them immersed in prayer. You can tear their hearts by thoughtless interference."

He said also, "Be clean. Rinse your mouth after eating. Do not take intoxicants, for in the madness of intoxication man becomes lower than a beast."

And He also taught, "Do not partake of flesh if you can avoid it."

Thus one may find in the Apocrypha many hints about all aspects of life, and besides the already known Apocrypha, new chronicles may still be found. One cannot try to trace the chronological dates of these writings, for they were rewritten and translated many times.

Let us remember that these writings were taken at random from the many that were at hand. Thus, you should pay equal attention to all that has come down to us from the early centuries. Although the Apocrypha were written during the years immediately following the related events, fragments of the ancient writings are still being discovered.

157. Urusvati has experienced the feeling of separation from Earth. This feeling, and the powerful magnetic attraction to Earth, can only be understood by those who have experienced them. They can also appreciate the extraordinarily powerful attractions the Teacher is exposed to. He has earned the right to separate Himself from Earth, but chooses not to, and in so doing experiences a tormenting weariness whose depth words cannot express. Only the power of consciousness can liberate Him from this overwhelming anguish.

We should also point out the divisibility of the spirit of the Teacher. Those who have this ability know that during the moments of the dividing of the spirit a complete absence is experienced. Usually these moments are brief, but when divisibility of the spirit is more developed, they may be profound. One can imagine the moments of absence as experienced by the Great Pilgrim! This is not a loss of consciousness, but a partial absence when psychic energy acts at great distances. It was at such times that the Image of the Great Pilgrim was revealed simultaneously in various places. People saw Him quite clearly during their waking hours and in their dreams.

Because the heart is very tensed during the dividing of the spirit, it is dangerous to disturb the body during these absences, which are almost equivalent to flights of the astral body. But people pay little attention to these conditions and can sometimes cause much damage.

158. Urusvati knows the Sacred Pain. Physicians today would call it neuralgia, rheumatism, nervous spasms, or inflammation of the nerves. There may be many diagnoses, but even an earthly physician will notice that something unusual is taking place. This "something" is a pulsation of psychic energy in Infinity. One can observe that these pains appear without evident cause and disappear without any effect. They are never the same, and it is impossible to foresee which center will be affected.

You can imagine how often the Great Teachers are subjected to these tensions! It cannot be otherwise, because the Primal Energy is pulsating in new spheres and rushing into those spheres whose vibrations correspond with its own. But the free will of the Teacher binds this Energy to Earth for the benefit of mankind.

The cure for such pains can only be by vibrations. We send forth such currents, which sometimes reach a high intensity. These pains tormented the Great Pilgrim, and at such times He went into the desert, where it is easier to receive the healing vibrations. People assume that the Teacher is free of all human limitations, and cannot imagine why the Great Pilgrim was required to suffer such pains.

The Great Pilgrim did not conceal his need for the

cooperation of people. The action of psychic energy can be evoked only if one fully realizes its presence, and it will serve properly only when there is purity of heart. He constantly repeated that all is given according to one's faith. In this way He taught the significance of Primal Energy.

Thus one may see manifested in the life of the Great Pilgrim the most human and also the scientific.

159. Urusvati can describe the features of the Great Pilgrim to artists who have a talent for depicting the human face. At least in a general way this Image should be given to the people. Here We shall once more recall His features. His light brown hair was rather long, with soft waves in noticeably separate locks and ends that were slightly darker. His forehead was broad and bright, unwrinkled, with eyebrows somewhat darker than the hair, but not too prominent. His eyes were blue and raised at the corners, with lashes that gave them great depth. His cheekbones were somewhat high and His nose not large, but gently rounded; His mouth was not large, but with rather full lips, His moustache not thick, and not covering the mouth. His beard was parted in the center, and not heavy. These features were appealing, but it was not so much the beauty as the expression of His face that made it unforgettable.

Whoever turns to the Teacher should fill his heart with love since reverence and respect without love cannot be true. Some think that love will diminish reverence, but this indicates a misunderstanding of that high emotion. The true disciple is the one who loves his Teacher. All feeling is based either on love or fear, but fear is not appropriate where there is striving to Light.

Urusvati remembered that once a lotus served her

as a boat! As frail as such a boat was she felt no fear, because her love for the Teacher gave her fearlessness. Only ardent love can create such fearlessness, and one should intensely cultivate it. Without the protection of love one cannot withstand the attacks of chaotic forces, and even one's health will suffer.

When thinking of the Image of the Teacher one is overwhelmed with love. Yet, it should be remembered that this love cannot be exclusive. A disciple may have his own Teacher, but he will feel love for other Teachers, too. It is true that the chosen Teacher will be the closest, but when one knows the Great Achievements of other Teachers, he will feel sincere love for them also.

160. Urusvati knows that the Great Teacher would sometimes trace various signs in the sand and then erase them. The disciples were puzzled and asked the Teacher why He did not write these signs on something permanent. In response, He drew a line in the air and said, "This is the permanent law. Nothing can erase this inscription." Thus the Teacher explained the power of thought.

Some used to say that the signs in space were as bright as lightning. The Teacher did not deny the possibility of such radiance and said, "The time will come when people will learn how to transmit their signs to distant places." The disciples could not understand what He meant by these words.

The Teacher also said, "Beware of negative thoughts. They will turn against you and will burden you like an abominable leprosy. But good thoughts rise upward and will lift you with them. You must know the power of the healing light and deadly darkness that man carries within himself."

He also said, "We part here, but we may meet

again, clothed in raiment of Light. We need not be concerned about shopping for garments in the Kingdom of Light, for they will be created at will. We must not be too attached to Earth when our best Friends await us with joy."

He also said, "Let us not lament those things that perish quickly, for imperishable garments await us."

He also said, "You are used to fearing death because you were not taught about the passing into a better World."

And He also said, "You must realize that good friends will continue to work together there, just as here."

Thus the Great Pilgrim continued teaching about the eternal values and the power of thought, but His Teachings were comprehended by only a few. Though the Teacher spoke briefly and simply, very few were those who remembered His words.

In Our Abode, We value the ability to speak briefly. Such hieroglyphs are clearly outlined in space.

161. Urusvati knows that the Great Pilgrim was frequently attacked by the forces of darkness. These incidents were mentioned in the Scriptures, and one might question how occurrences that no one had witnessed could have been recorded. It was the Teacher Himself who wanted to prepare His disciples for that battle and therefore, rather than conceal the struggle that was taking place, He recounted His own experiences to illustrate it.

He said, "Every human being constantly finds himself in three battles. Although he may imagine that he is completely at peace, he actually takes part in three battles simultaneously.

"The first battle is between the free will and karma.

Nothing can excuse man from taking part in the struggle between these two principles.

"The second battle takes place between the disembodied entities of good and evil, which surround man and influence him in one way or another. It is difficult to imagine the fury of the dark forces when they attempt to take possession of man.

"The third battle resounds in the Infinite, in space, between the subtle energies and the waves of chaos. The human imagination is too limited to envision these battles in Infinity. Human intellect comprehends earthly collisions, but is incapable of looking into space and imagining the powerful storms and forces working there. Only when human emotions are completely controlled can man start thinking about the invisible worlds. One should develop such thoughts, for they alone will make man a conscious co-worker with the Infinite forces."

Remember that you are always facing the Infinite. Even the loftiest words cannot express the Most Sublime, and only during brief moments can your heart record the exaltation of realization. Learn how to remember these moments, for they are the key to the future.

It is impossible to comprehend the fullness of the numberless worlds, but the Teacher leads toward this knowledge. Learn to give Him your trust and reverence, for without this bridge there is no passage.

162. Urusvati knows that the Great Pilgrim mingled with both the rich and the poor. Not all the rich were advised to give away their wealth, for when the Teacher saw a right attitude toward earthly treasures, He did not indicate a need to renounce them. In interpreting the attitude of the Teacher toward earthly riches, it is important to know that He advised giving up possessions only when they were dragging down the spiritually weak ones. He did not reject earthly riches, for how can one deny what already exists? He taught that it is essential to find a sensible attitude toward all that exists in life. Indeed, the Teacher did not want to see uniform poverty. He used to emphasize that even people of small means should cultivate pure joy, without envy of wealthy neighbors.

The Teacher shared the company of both rich and poor and in each case was equally kind and ready to help. Indeed, it is the rich who are sometimes most in need of help.

The Teacher was ready to help when He saw injustice, and knew how to inspire heroism in the persecuted. Yet He knew that all His blessings would be condemned. He cared little for gratitude toward Himself, but in His Teachings He did not forget to point out the great power of gratitude. Thus, let us pay homage to that Wonderful Life, which nourished so many hearts.

163. Urusvati knows that the best sayings of the Great Pilgrim and much of the most remarkable healing that He performed remained unrecorded. He not only spoke to the people and to His disciples, but also spoke privately to many others. Who, then, could have recorded these remarkable Teachings?

The Teacher did not speak about reincarnation to the people because in His country this truth would not have been understood. Even among the disciples very few could fully comprehend the Law of Reincarnation. Some sects knew about reincarnation, but the idea provoked strong arguments and the majority doubted, just as it doubts today.

The Teacher preferred to discuss those subjects that caused arguments with each person individually, for only in this way could he transmit the Truth according to the listener's level of consciousness. There were many such talks with individuals, which at times dealt with elementary subjects. At other times highly educated philosophers came to Him. Some came timidly and only by night, while others were bold enough to come during the day. He practiced great patience with all of them.

One can imagine how filled His time was during that short life of heroic achievement. His disciples often wondered when He found time to sleep.

Much remarkable healing was performed unnoticed. People saw only the obvious things, such as the healing of insanity, of paralysis, blindness, and deafness. This healing impressed the crowds because it was plainly evident. Indeed, when the dumb began to speak and the lepers became clean, the crowds were stunned. But, from a scientific point of view, there was even more remarkable healing: the Teacher could stop the internal destructive processes just by the power of His will. Even His immediate followers could not fully appreciate such powerful manifestations, when at His Command, dead muscles began to move and afflicted tissues were healed.

The power of thought that was manifested in these cases was such that an ordinary man can only imagine it. Such influence cannot be called suggestion, but rather the victory of mind over matter. And now, when people begin to study the power of thought, they must pay homage to these remarkable victories of the mind. If a sense of co-measurement is a guiding principle, the energy will always accelerate through the shortest channels.

164. Urusvati knows what cosmic conditions accompanied the transition of the Great Pilgrim into the Subtle World, but besides the known violent disturbances there were many others. Is it any wonder that earthly events coincide with cosmic ones?

It is time for people to realize that all events are connected and that unity reigns throughout Cosmos. Many different manifestations follow each step of evolution, but during those solemn times of transition people become particularly stubborn, reminding one of travelers who refuse to alight from the carriage when their journey is over. Similarly, during the consummation of the achievement of the Great Pilgrim, people did not want to leave their carriage, and were unable to perceive the significance of the events that were taking place in front of their eyes. An incredible injustice was being committed, and no one dared tell the people how dreadful was the crime.

The Great Teacher had the wisdom of Pericles, and certainly knew that He should not expect justice from the mobs. He who gave so much knew that the law of proportion had been violated, and simply warned the people not to overload their karma.

Thus, the Teacher knew that the events had been inevitable, and began to teach from the Subtle World. These Teachings also remained unrecorded, and thus arose one more example of injustice. In the manuscripts that have come down to us one comes across brief hints about His visitations from the Subtle World, but even the disciples failed to take the opportunity to reveal to others that His greatest Revelations were given when He was in His subtle body. Yet this information would have been of great value to the whole world. The Teacher did not insist, for He knew that space would guard His Teachings in a far better way.

Similarly, We now warn about the cosmic tension,

but few pay heed. We have pointed out the unusual events, but in a true example of the lack of co-measurement, people consider them accidental.

165. Urusvati knows the many different qualities that are required for self-perfectment. At times it is difficult to recognize their various combinations through intellectual reasoning alone. Let us take the example of Joshua, who was the leader of an unruly nation. Since his mission involved constant dangers, not only for him but also for the entire nation, he had to concentrate his will upon leadership, and could not allow himself to be distracted by basic theoretical tasks.

Imagine a shepherd trying to lead his flock through a thicket—how many branches he must break and rocks he must push aside to clear the way! The shepherd's task is to bring his flock home before dark, and he is well armed for protection against the wild beasts that will threaten him on the way. Such is the role of the leader who must possess courage, decisiveness, aspiration, and self-denial.

Now let us examine another path, that of the intellectual leader, the leader in creativeness, after whom a whole century of the highest achievements is named. We refer to the Age of Pericles, an era that is associated with the most refined manifestations. Science and creative power characterize this era. Pericles knew recognition and also the blows of Fate. He was surrounded by the finest intellects of his time, philosophers who left to humanity the legacy of an entire age of thought. The Great Pilgrim was a friend to Pericles, and highly approved of this unforgettable and brilliant era of knowledge and beauty. It is interesting to note how the finest spirits are brought together, so that later they may meet on the field of labor. One should watch attentively the accumulation of diverse qualities that will lead to creative work on a world scale.

166. Urusvati knows how the historical records concerning remarkable leaders are lacking in important details. But something besides human injustice causes such scarcity of information. In fact, the Great Workers themselves avoided public recognition and did not wish to have biographies written, sometimes even destroying such chronicles. The fundamentals of Their Teachings were recorded, but the details of Their Lives were not written down. Now, We too are giving the idea of the Teaching simply, without dwelling on small details that might be interpreted in a mundane way.

Let us now turn to the great philosopher, Anaxagoras. The foundations of his Teachings seemed new for many centuries. Even today, his theory of the indestructibility of matter as the fundamental substance can be considered new, and his idea of the Highest Intelligence could easily have been conceived by modern scientists. He absorbed the refinement of Greek thought, loved art, and frequently helped Pericles with his sound advice. He was therefore an inner director of many decisions. He possessed great dignity, defended his friends, and preferred exile to dishonor.

The biographers of this philosopher did not depict the worldly side of his personality. His career was brilliant, but he did not care for transitory events to be recorded. He knew in the depths of his heart that his path was one of renunciation. Many Great Teachers combined the Teaching with Their future Paths, and one can thus perceive an entire chain of precious lives. One should not be surprised that certain links of the chain were obscured, for they were thresholds, preludes to an urgent inner accumulation.

167. Urusvati knows that persecution pursues a Great Teacher like dust after a horseman. One should observe not only the followers of the Teacher, but also the persecutors, among whom can be discerned certain individuals who, in the course of many lives, tried persistently to undermine the Goodness that was brought by His Teachings.

One might ask why these evil beings, while in the Subtle World, do not learn that their dark attempts are fruitless. The fact is that their protectors are vigilant! Remember the ancient legend about the demons who concealed the Light from the sight of the disciples with their wings, and know that in the lowest strata of the astral spheres such obscuring of Light is indeed possible. This happens on Earth as well. The persecutors of the Teachings of Light inflict harm consciously as well as unconsciously, and grow increasingly furious as, against their will, they are magnetically drawn to the Teaching.

Examples of this madness can be observed in various eras, and when these persecutors are asked what causes their fury and makes them attack the Teaching that they hate so persistently, the answer is almost always the same—they are unable to stop their attacks. Such lack of self-control indicates obsession.

It is customary to apply the name Judas to betrayers as a symbol of the grossest unfaithfulness. Let us ponder upon this. Was not Judas in his previous lives also connected with crimes? Remember that in the greatest periods of Greek history there were cases of venomous betrayal. We could mention names, but it is not wise to pronounce names that indicate only evil. It is enough simply to remember that every great Teaching has had its betrayers, with demonic wings on their backs.

Urusvati recently glimpsed a dark hierophant who attempted to approach her, but Our fiery arrows threw him off, and his hand was stayed by lightning.

168. Urusvati knows that every good deed transforms some particle of chaos. Each kind action is a burning away of chaos. This description has a basis in reality, for every impulse toward kindness and Light kindles the best fires, which transmute chaos into a new, purified form.

Some think that collaborating with the Brotherhood will evoke the fury of darkness, but it would be nearer the truth to say that each good deed attracts the fury of the dark ones. Timid souls will probably wish to refrain from performing good deeds for safety's sake, and there are many such people who for this reason refuse to be compassionate. They have extinguished their fires and merged with the darkness. But the ghosts of darkness are repellent, and whoever fears goodness will sink into chaos.

The Great Pilgrim taught the love of goodness, but His Teaching was greatly distorted. Even His simplest words could not save the Teaching, for people found ways to interpret Truth for their own profit. The expulsion of the merchants from the Temple is a symbolic warning, and the Temple should also be understood as the human spirit from which mercenary thought must be ejected. No one can forbid the exchange of daily necessities, but merchants must attend to their business with enlightened hearts. Even the basic elements of life can be spiritualized.

I hear laughter and ridicule—chaos is in convulsion and hopes that its servants will cling to it tenaciously. Thus, a good thought provokes the convulsion of evil. Be not frightened by even the most awful grimace of evil, for our main task is to increase the reservoir of Goodness.

169. Urusvati knows that those who burn away chaos and those who create it co-exist on Earth. Chaos accumulates here and it must be destroyed here, not in the supermundane spheres. It is people, not just demons, who are trying to increase chaos and bring it to the point of absolute darkness. Urusvati has experienced this absolute darkness, to which nothing can compare.

It is a mistake to apply to the spherical Earth the symbolic protection of the circle! The fact is that the currents of chaos surge in to destroy the equilibrium as fast as the rays of Light restore it.

Darkness is filled with poisonous currents that attempt to arrest striving thought. This statement should be understood realistically. Truly, the current of thought can be obstructed, and then its energy must be intensified in order for it to succeed. However, such an application of one's great force exhausts the heart.

The Great Pilgrim used to emphasize the necessity of balance, and one might wonder if by this He meant cosmic equilibrium. He affirmed the existence of many worlds and directed thought toward the Highest. Such affirmation was needed because people thought of Earth as the only abode of humanity, and even today many limit their thought to Earth alone.

The Teacher called for the realization of Cosmos. He continually confirmed the existence of the beings of the Subtle World, particularly in His last discourses.

170. Urusvati knows that cosmogony and religion should be carefully studied. One should appreciate the words of the Great Pilgrim when He said that He had come to fulfill the previous Law.

In His thoughts the Teacher could separate the

strands of prejudice and ignorance, and He chose words to correspond to the consciousness of His listeners. Thus, when they pressed him with questions such as whether Earth is flat, for some He would answer that it is flat, and for others the answer would be adjusted according to the level of their consciousness. In everything the Great Pilgrim always answered according to the listener's capacity, and one can learn from the simplicity of His answers. The Brotherhood stresses the importance of speaking according to the listener's consciousness.

Many of His Teachings were profound, but His listeners could accept them only according to the level of their thinking. The task of the Teacher is the same in all centuries. He must continually deal with the same questions without hurting the feelings of those who ask by telling them that their questions have already been answered in ages past. If one could imagine the mental level of those who questioned Him, one would be amazed at the inexhaustible patience of the Teacher!

One must live through many lives in order to acquire such patience and understanding in how to help humanity. Thus the love for humanity grows, not just for individuals, but for all mankind. It is extremely painful to watch the abuse of free will, this greatest gift, yet, in spite of it, one becomes even more determined to help those who err. Thus you can imagine the Inner Life of the Teacher.

Understand the joy of self-abnegation, which dwells in the heart of the One who was sent to save humanity. We do not hesitate to call this Service the salvation of humanity.

171. Urusvati knows that it is by the power of free will that people create their existence in the Subtle

World. When the will is pure and strong, when the Primal Energy is not weakened by base instincts, then passing into the Subtle World becomes easy and the higher spheres can be reached. Verily, man creates his own destiny. The Great Pilgrim said this also, and He warned that on the way to the higher spheres many hands try to impede the ascent, but the will and the Primal Energy carry the aspirant upward.

Pure will can be cultivated in all environments, and psychic energy can be preserved in all circumstances. Each person, small or great, is equally endowed with free will. Everyone has this highest gift and may either accept it or, in ignorance, prefer to squander the entrusted treasure. Everyone has sufficient psychic energy for fearless flight into the Subtle World, but must first of all overcome the fear of the unknown and learn something about the Subtle World.

Even the humblest aspirant can find information about the Subtle World. One need only sharpen one's free will in this direction. Unfortunately, most people resist the idea that their true home is not on Earth, but somewhere in space.

The Teacher's task is to develop the thinking of the students in the direction of the far-off realms.

172. Urusvati understands the receptivity of children. Particularly during early childhood, and up to the age of seven, recollections of the Subtle World can be awakened. Children sense that they have experienced some kind of unusual life, and it can be helpful to ask them to recall any memory they may have that is of an extraordinary nature. Such prompting is called "the opening of the memory," and even if the memories should diminish with the passing years, some sparks of an earlier beautiful existence will always be felt.

The Great Pilgrim loved to open the memory of children. He brought them close to Him, questioned them, and touched them with His hand to intensify the clarity of their recollection. He treated children as equals, for when the remote past is recalled the mind becomes more mature. Children will never forget the one who treats them as equals, and will preserve such recollections all their lives. Perhaps children remembered the Great Pilgrim better than did those whom He healed.

The Great Pilgrim loved children and saw in them the evolution of mankind. It is they who will carry life forward, and each of us must share his experiences with them. But it is still wiser to awaken in them recollections of the Subtle World. The most profound spiritual life will be formed where the consciousness is opened to the perception of the Subtle World, and the Invisible becomes accessible.

The phenomenon of the materialization of the subtle body of the Teacher strengthened the belief of the disciples in the reality of the Invisible World. Not all of them were able to perceive the essence of that world, but the window had at least been opened to a certain degree.

173. Urusvati knows that most people are unable to attain the attitude of alert expectation. The Great Pilgrim taught how to wait without thinking, so that the whole being would be permeated with expectation. With such an attitude, expectation will not be limited by thought. Man knows well enough what he is striving for, and with what his consciousness is joined. Through this awareness the Great Pilgrim maintained His adamantine will.

He knew how difficult it is to give people a new consciousness directly through the heart, without intellectual reasoning. Intellectual reasoning can make things seem logical, but the heart knows that people do not easily relinquish their antiquated concepts.

We have said that one should give according to people's consciousnesses. But what can one do if, instead of consciousness, there is only a wavering, ignorant mind? The Teacher is then obliged to constantly repeat simple ideas, and therein lies the tragedy for Teachers in all ages. Only a consciousness tempered through many lives can safely tread the thorny human paths.

Hard is the task of the Teacher, and especially so because the Hierarchy is misunderstood by most people. This was quite clear to the Great Pilgrim and that is why He hastened to the fulfillment of His Achievement. One Achievement is fulfilled in the course of a century, another in only a few years. On what kind of scale can such Services be weighed?

The deeds of Truth cannot be measured in earthly terms, but great is the joy that such offerings take place. They teach humanity to strive, and thus renew human consciousness at all times.

174. Urusvati knows how certain sayings are misinterpreted. It is well known that the words about turning the other cheek have led to many errors. Indeed, if this saying is interpreted simply in the physical sense it results in absurdity, because this was spiritual instruction and was intended to mean that when there is inner balance, the attempts of evil can do no harm. The Great Pilgrim valued human dignity and knew from the Teachings of India that nothing and no one can harm the balanced human spirit.

We greatly appreciate the ability to maintain equilibrium, whether in success or in failure, and the ability to continue to strive toward the chosen goal whatever the difficulties. But first one must have a goal and realize that without it there can be no advance. From such an attitude comes the possibility of great achievement. Achievement is demanded of everyone, and the idea of great achievements should inspire, not frighten.

The Great Pilgrim also taught about the quality of achievement and said, "Whoever improves the quality of his labor is already performing a good deed. Even if he acts only for his own sake, he contributes to the benefit of others. One's labor has a special effect on others and everyone benefits from it. Not only on Earth are great deeds appreciated; the Subtle World, too, watches beautiful labor attentively."

He also said, "You judge the coming day by the sunrise, paying attention to whether the atmosphere is cloudy or clear, and whether the sun is bright red or obscured. In life, too, it is possible from early childhood to foretell the development of human character. One can observe those possibilities in a small child that eventually will be manifested. He who loves work in childhood will remain a toiler all his life."

A laboring or idle nature is formed in one's previous lives. Many do not learn to rejoice in labor during their stay in the subtle spheres. I affirm that the quality of labor builds the future ascent. It is wrong to think that only kings ascend and peasants descend, for the quality of labor can be improved in all circumstances.

The Great Pilgrim also taught the advantage of knowledge over ignorance. "Knowledge is achieved as the result of great labor. People will never succeed unless they strive to learn. Few are those who are qualified to help others to learn. Glory to such enlightened teachers! Each of them teaches what has already been written, but also includes a drop of his own knowledge. Such a drop is a gift from Infinity."

175. Urusvati knows the ways in which cultural

activities are ridiculed and abused. Of course, you also know this, but I stress it once more because the Great Pilgrim was constantly asked why the best deeds are rejected by people.

He trained His disciples to bear insults with courage, and said, "Darkness battles with light in an effort to preserve its identity. We may fear darkness, but darkness also fears us. Can Light ever be reconciled with darkness? Can one serve darkness and at the same time be a Light-bearer?" Thus the Teacher illustrated that one cannot serve two principles.

He impressed upon the minds of His disciples that each one must contribute to the Service of Light by personal discipline. Such an idea of service cannot be understood without the realization of goal-fitness, and such a concept can be realized only when the spirit is aware of its goal. Courage and wisdom come from the same source of goodness.

Man carries within himself the evaluation of his deeds. It is impossible to predict how and when the fatal hour will strike, but deep within our hearts we know when the time has come, and only wisdom and courage can help us to realize the responsibility we take upon ourselves when we dedicate our life to the welfare of humanity.

During His life, how wisely the Great Pilgrim took upon Himself a life of achievements!

176. Urusvati knows how unpredictably the mosaic of life falls together, but such unexpectedness is only from the earthly point of view. A person may think that he speaks or writes with a certain intent, but he is directed to an entirely different goal by the Higher Forces. He may think that he is finding success in a desired direction, when in reality he is achieving greater success in some unexpected way. He may, for example, write to a certain person, then find that the response comes from an unexpected source.

Often, one action can produce various results. If We listed all the possible consequences, people might become confused, their consciousness might narrow, and their psychic energy weaken. Only an expanded consciousness can maintain a broad outlook.

The Great Pilgrim advocated the broadening of consciousness, and repeatedly taught, "Open your eyes and ears." Certainly, He did not invite people to open their eyes and ears only to His particular Teachings, but meant that only the expansion of consciousness leads to profound realization. But, alas, one cannot thread a needle with a rope, and a great message cannot penetrate a small ear.

One can imagine how much of His Teaching never reached the consciousness of His listeners. Much was only partially remembered, and the sequence, the original meaning, and the beauty of His words were lost. In the same way, many Great Teachers suffered the distortion of their thoughts.

In the records of space the thoughts of the Great Teachers are preserved in a better way. They descend like a refreshing dew to those who can receive them. Knowing this, the Teachers do not pay much attention to earthly distortions. That which is preordained will come, and the receptive heart will receive it.

Human thoughts also grow in space. Every heroic, unselfish thought can be a seed for generating the future world. The Great Teachers are Cosmic Creators, but every thinker can also become a creator of good.

People do not want to think about the distant worlds, but such thoughts can become excellent purifiers of consciousness. On the paths of space there will be no envy, hatred or coarseness.

The Great Teacher often directed the gaze of His disciples to the planets, saying, "Many are the homes, and there is life everywhere." He wanted His disciples to love Infinity.

All Our Sisters and Brothers commune with the distant worlds. When Sister Urusvati turns her gaze to the Radiant Planet, she recalls her flight and rejoices at the distant worlds.

177. Urusvati knows that miracles cannot always take place. In addition to cosmic reasons and interference from the negative forces of the Subtle World, human disbelief can be an obstacle. It is difficult to discern the line between disbelief and doubt; both snakes come from the same nest.

The Great Pilgrim often taught that all is given to us according to our faith. It has been recorded that Christ Himself could not perform certain miracles because of the people's lack of faith. Today scientists would probably replace the expression "lack of faith" with "non-acceptance of authority," but it does not matter which expression is used, the meaning is the same.

This lack of faith begins with ordinary daily occurrences. When We warn against doubt, We are speaking about a physical law. People can reject the strongest help, because their free will can negate even the most favorable circumstances. For instance, an angry man can push aside the Hand that is stretched out to prevent him from falling. The Teacher warned against the harmful effects of doubt.

We remind you that when the disciples doubted the power of the Teacher, they immediately received a shock, which they wrongly interpreted as fate. What kind of fate is it when man himself severs the salutary bond!

The Great Teacher openly emphasized the foundations of faith as a vital cause of evolution. The Teacher was filled with great knowledge and transmitted it in simple words.

178. Urusvati knows how persecutors can sometimes be transformed into co-workers. We can point out instances when persecutors became pillars of the very Teaching they had been persecuting. The Teacher searchingly evaluates His persecutors. They sometimes have tremendous power, and just one spark is sufficient to kindle the flame of goodness within them.

Ferocity usually comes from ignorance. The Great Pilgrim used to say, "When dogs are taken off the chain, they attack the first person they see."

The Teacher pointed out many times that the conversion of adversaries can be beneficial. However, His attitude toward betrayers was different. He said, "If a man has been entrusted with guarding a treasure, and instead of guarding, steals it, he certainly cannot be trusted, and has prepared a hard destiny for himself. Sometimes it overtakes him quickly, but at other times the predestined is delayed, causing an especially difficult karma."

Thus the Teacher weighed the degree of betrayal. He knew when betrayal was about to happen and consoled those disciples who already suspected the traitor.

Ferocity cannot be arrested, and the current must take its course. But hard, indeed, is the karma of the betrayer, for betrayal is the most terrible of all earthly crimes.

179. Urusvati knows that some people believe that everything should perish with the Earth, and condemn those who leave the earthly spheres to join the far-off worlds. They call them deserters, or even cowards, and cannot understand that there are self-sacrificing heroes who maintain the cosmic balance, and who, by introducing the supermundane path, become the Saviors of humanity.

He who undertakes labor in the far-off realms can be called "the Striving Light," and his difficult task, undertaken amid strenuous conditions, should be looked upon as a heroic deed.

It was not by chance, but only after deep and long contemplation, that the Great Thinker decided to bring His knowledge from the new planet. This was not desertion, but the realization that ideas rule the world, and that thought is limitless. Thus He made known the new communication.

The actual withdrawal from this world to the far-off worlds, in itself was not new, but His conscious attitude toward the responsibility He assumed, was. The far-off world, even in its purely physical condition, cannot be easy for the Teacher, and is especially difficult because of His continued collaboration with the Brotherhood. Earthly rays, in their present condition, cannot be considered beneficial, because the planet is sick and its balance is lost. In ordinary earthly communications, atmospheric conditions may vary greatly, but how much more varied and powerful are the emanations of the far-off worlds!

The Teacher had been thinking for a long time about the far-off worlds, and He allowed Himself to be sold into slavery so that His earthly path might be fulfilled as quickly as possible. He knew and profoundly felt all earthly hardships in full measure, and succeeded in gathering vast experience during His life on Earth. Many remarkable contemporaries shared His company and ideas.

180. Urusvati knows that people try to belittle and limit the highest manifestations. The Thinker said, "A salutary shield is spread from Heaven to Earth, but instead of raising themselves to it, people use every device to bring it down to their level. They do not realize that even the most beneficial remedies can lose their power in the earthly mire."

Once a man came to the Thinker and told Him of a strange dream in which he saw a friend who lived far away rearranging everything in the man's home. The Thinker said, "Perhaps he intruded into your house mentally. Indeed, the power of thought can move objects."

And again the Thinker was asked why clouds form so quickly over mountains. He answered, "Besides the forces of nature, the thoughts of man can produce various phenomena." Thus, He used every opportunity to teach about the power of thought. Most people could not understand this power, which is the birthright of everyone, but still their knowledge was enriched.

When the Thinker was asked why He did not mention the power of thought in His writings, He answered, "The time will come when mankind will be ready to cognize this truth, but each premature transmission will only create obstacles. People must climb every rung of the ladder."

181. Urusvati knows that most people refuse to recognize the advantages of collaboration. The Thinker directed people in many different ways to this salutary concept. He said, "Not by beastly ways will man perfect himself. He is a social being and each thought, each word, is social property. Man cannot live without associating with other people, and he must learn to understand this most noble existence.

"Obscene words and evil talk pollute the atmosphere and are in defiance of the Divine Principle. One can sell his body into slavery, but not his soul. Love for humanity is the result of the development of the heart, which is achieved through thinking.

"Wisdom cannot survive in thoughtlessness.

"The consequences of discord, like the consequences of a terrible disease, come gradually. Fools think that, as long as they awake in the morning, they have avoided any consequences. The violators of collaboration must be judged as detrimental to the public welfare and expulsion will become their lot."

He also taught, "If a traveler knocked at your door at night, you would ask what he wanted, and probably let him in and give him shelter. Why then do you so persistently drive away the thoughts that knock at your door? A guest from a distant land is welcome, but a wise thought from a far-off world is driven away. You look for news in the market-place, but ignore the Messengers of Light.

"Fellow citizens, you are not wise. You pay gold for rotten food, but are too stingy to pay even a copper coin for the nourishment of your soul. Every injustice destroys space.

"Fellow citizens, if you feel no shame for each other, then turn away from the starry sky, which is watching you with disapproval."

Thus, the far-off worlds, thought, and collaboration were favorite topics of His Teaching.

182. Urusvati knows how difficult it is for people to perceive through straight-knowledge. This happens because their inner feeling has been separated from their thought. But how can feeling exist without its foundation of thought? People do not differentiate between the process of thinking and thought itself, which is swift as lightning. Thus taught the Thinker.

He spoke of the role of thought in all creation, but this simple affirmation was rejected by people who had made up their minds not to accept the power of thought. In this way the Teacher suffered greatly for thought.

He taught, "Thought is like lightning, and not knowing where a thought originates, you are unable to transform it into words. A thought may strike your consciousness, but without the process of thinking, it will remain unrevealed and lie ungerminated, like a seed in infertile soil. Such dried up thoughts sadden the Teacher, who sends these salutary signs through space. Centuries may be needed for the proper growth of a seed of thought.

"In schools the art of thinking should be studied above all. One should be trained in the art of constant thinking and learn to be ashamed of thoughtlessness. Man is unable not to think, but there is a great difference between harmonious, disciplined thinking and the oscillations of chaotic thoughtlessness, which not only influences man, but space itself. How can man dare to pollute all of space?

"Indeed, the time will come when mankind will finally realize the power of thought. And when man starts to study thought as a special science we may already be on the far-off worlds!"

Thus taught the Thinker, knowing how long it will be before man emerges from the waves of chaos.

183. Urusvati knows that in all ages the Great Teachers stressed the power of thought, the far-off worlds, the continuity of lives, and the Subtle World. In India, Egypt, China, Persia, in Palestine, and later in Europe, almost the same words were pronounced. And now We must reiterate the identical truths. The affirmation of the same facts nearly five thousand years ago ended in martyrdom, just as it does now.

People assume that they have progressed in so many ways and proudly point to their technical achievements, but they have advanced very little in the cognition of truth. One can search throughout the world and will discover the shameful fact that only a few strive toward the realization of Truth, and these few will only whisper timidly about the Subtle World. If one were to explore the history of human enlightenment, one would discover that there exists an immobility of consciousness.

Be assured that only a few contemplate the far-off worlds, or think about the continuity of life, and the very ideas that would help to improve life are neglected. It is not the acceleration of technical discoveries that leads to concentration of the mind, but the desire of people themselves to learn something new. Yet, how can they learn if the most fundamental truths have not found a place in their consciousness? One must do more than listen politely to these truths; one must apply them as reality.

The Thinker spoke precisely about this over two thousand years ago. Does this not ring out as a great rebuke to humanity? Men have perfected themselves in the techniques of killing one another, but have lost the ability to contemplate Truth. And these words were repeated by the Thinker more than two thousand years ago!

If in those times the Thinker was appalled by the ferocity and cruelty of people, what can one say about today? The bloody sacrifices to Moloch appear merciful compared with the murders that are now taking place! How many times must We stress these words! How can people contemplate truths when their minds are filled with a craving for murder? This, too, was said by the Thinker, and because of these words He was persecuted and sold into slavery.

Now also you will be persecuted for saying such things. Compare these words that are separated by thousands of years, and think also about the deadness of consciousness, then and now.

184. Urusvati knows how difficult it is at times to transmit thought to far-off distances. It is especially difficult to penetrate the layers between the spheres, which can prevent even the most clear-cut thought from entering, and cause it to merely glide over the surface. In certain examples one can observe that the thought is unable to penetrate the personal aura of the recipient. This evidence is overlooked by investigators who assume that thought transmission depends upon the power of the sender, ignoring the important factor of the individual quality of emanations of the recipient. One should consider not only the size of the aura, but learn its contents as well. The same thing is true of the pulse. Not only should its rapidity be observed, but also its quality.

One can imagine the intensity of the messages of the Thinker. Besides the usual conditions, these messages are endangered by the possibility of theft, and attract numerous entities, who do not understand the meaning of the message, but try to feed upon particles of mental energy.

We are greatly concerned that the long distance messages from the Thinker should safely reach their destination. A great sacrifice is required of the Thinker in order that all the spheres may be pierced by His thought. He acts for the benefit of humankind, knowing that, in its ignorance, an ungrateful humanity will meet His solicitude with disdain.

185. Urusvati knows that there are many methods of healing. At one time, healing was considered an art that for best results required the inner fusion of the will of the practitioner with the will of the patient. It was believed that intellectual analysis alone would not bring success.

The Thinker taught that just as the artist convinces his audience, the physician influences his patient, and in this way the artist and the healer derive their power from the same Source.

It is also said that man succeeds when he fuses with the Higher Will. People assume that the power of their Teacher is limited, but each Teacher has his own Teacher, and the Higher Will is the harmony of many consciousnesses. When We say, "Let us build the future," We mean that your will should be harmonized with Ours. Even the loftiest structure can fall when the earthly will tries to damage the foundation!

"An arch, properly constructed, can be a beautiful fulfillment. It can stand for a thousand years, but should even one stone be taken away it will collapse." Thus spoke the Thinker.

The Teacher can create a better future, but the disciple must realize and accept it. It is not easy to recognize evolution. Sometimes it comes in silence, but at other times the outcry of the masses can be a sign of the advance of humanity. Why should you limit yourselves to silence or the influence of noisy crowds? Certainly the Higher Will does not restrict itself in this way.

"The builder of a temple is not restricted to the use of only one kind of stone, and will select the best from all of nature. Only then can he be a true artist." Thus spoke the Thinker.

"The grandeur of Cosmos cannot be imagined, and

people are unable to recognize the best gifts sent to them or to harmonize their consciousness with the Higher Will. Each person is responsible for much destruction in space, but the Higher Will is ever ready to help by projecting the new future." Thus spoke the Thinker.

186. Urusvati knows that humanity itself has created and increased its illnesses. The Thinker said, "Nature does not require the suffering that people have brought upon themselves. Even childbirth need not be painful, and some women prove it. But countless generations have brought into life all kinds of illnesses, and it is difficult to say how many generations will be needed to root them out. Not only medical authorities, but everyone should try to eliminate disease.

"It is foolish to assume that the gods have sent diseases as punishment, and it is wrong to think that the High Forces would afflict the innocent as well as the guilty with suffering. People themselves have generated infectious diseases through their intemperance and filth."

And again the Thinker spoke, "Sometimes people will see various images in stones, leaves, trees, or grass. Stones cannot by themselves emulate a human face, therefore the image must be born in the consciousness of the onlooker. But even the imagination has to have some basis for the creation of such images. In fact invisible entities surround people, who are unable to see them but feel their presence. The consciousness grasps certain of these impressions and later seeks to give them form in nature. Many such images, beautiful and frightful, surround man. Some he may call ghosts, but for them he is a ghost! The time will come when people will begin to communicate properly with the Supermundane."

Thus the Thinker prepared His listeners for the perception of the Subtle World.

187. Urusvati knows why it is unwise to speak badly about those who have passed into the Subtle World. The Thinker often warned people about this, and said, "Do not condemn the deceased, for what will you say to them when you meet again? Who knows, you might have to live once more as neighbors! Prepare joy for yourself." This understanding did not originate in Rome or Greece, but in far more remote antiquity, when people already understood the interdependence of the worlds. The Subtle World requires a careful approach, because everything there exists mentally, and earthly criticism can be extremely disturbing to subtle beings, who, in turn, can respond with unkind thoughts. Retaliation reigns, especially in the lower and middle spheres, and one should not provoke it.

It is also possible that by criticism one may retard the evolution of those beings, some of whom may be at the point of overcoming their unrighteousness. It is cruel to surround them with vibrations like the barking of dogs. In addition, people are unable to judge the motives for another's actions, and unjust criticism will only burden his karma. People judge in ignorance, and thus deprive themselves of joy, and loss of joy is a great misfortune. The Thinker took the idea of care for the Subtle World from Anaxagoras, who said that in tearing its fine texture, we also tear our own garment.

The sage descends into the darkest depths in order to raise up those who long for redemption. The wise one will not condemn those who suffer, but will lead them toward the golden ray of the dawn. Amidst the darkness the sage does not examine all those who await him, but cares only to help the needy. Who knows, perhaps he will lead forth even his former enemies? And when the sage brings them into the light he will smile to see whom he has brought out. They will be ashamed, and condemnation is thus extinguished.

Urusvati has led many out of darkness, near ones and far ones, friends and enemies. All that matters is the ascent toward Light. Darkness blinds, but the one who has come from outside can see the glimmer of the Light. There will be better abodes in the Light. These words should be remembered. The Thinker and Anaxagoras repeated them often, and both of them were persecuted and condemned.

The Inner Life of the Brotherhood will be understood when we are able to comprehend the details in the lives of heroes.

188. Urusvati knows that the duration of a human life depends largely upon the will to live. The Thinker said, "Life lasts as long as man himself wants to remain on Earth." Even fatal diseases can be cured by the human will. Everyone, whether a messenger from the higher spheres, or, at the other extreme, an outcast, must preserve the gift of life. We may not wilfully cut the silver cord that binds us to the Masters.

Those who suppose that after a suicide they will return to the place from which they were sent are indeed mistaken, for the whirl of space will carry them far away, like a leaf in autumn. The desire to live must be expressed consciously. Man must realize what he is striving for, and remember that he has good deeds to perform and a mission to fulfill here on Earth.

The Thinker also said, "Learn to revere the Muses, who help you to become heroes. The Muses lead you to achievement, they accompany you in battle and in labor, and greet you with garlands of victory. The Muses transform your sufferings into beauty. The

Muses will find you in the gardens that are adorned with the trees of knowledge. The Muses will not abandon those who revere them. Know how to serve the Muses, the Gate-Keepers of the Beautiful."

Thus the Thinker directed human consciousness to Truth.

189. Urusvati has had much opportunity to observe extreme hypocrisy. The Thinker once said, "Fellow citizens, tell me where you bought such smiling masks. You must tell the comedians, so they too can obtain them. Do not think, citizens, that you have deceived anyone with your benevolent masks, and that no one will dare to look behind them. Are not the city fathers also guilty of hypocrisy? One might almost think that the wrinkles in their brows are from care for the welfare of the people, or that they wear masks only for the amusement of the crowds! But be careful, there may be someone daring enough to unmask your smiles, and reveal your hypocrisy." Thus the Thinker warned the citizens, and they hated Him for it.

Likewise He said, "Is it worthy to build the majestic Acropolis simply as a monument to your weakness?" The Teacher foresaw the decline that was soon to begin, and that falsehood and hypocrisy would accelerate the coming of the end.

The Thinker also said to His disciples, "Betrayal is born in the house of hypocrisy, and history records betrayal as the basest crime. I do not need to tell you this, since you know enough about the supposed nobility of people, and also about their criminality. I am speaking to Space. Let Space shout, let it cry out loudly, let it tell people about their end. Even when I am in the far-off worlds, I shall to try to save humanity.

"Criminality must be understood as the most terrible infection. People speak about the suffering caused by illnesses, but they do not want to admit that criminality ruins not only the body, but also the soul. Do not lose time. Warn friends about the danger of betrayal."

190. Urusvati knows how little people understand the link between cause and effect. The Thinker related the legend of a man who was filled with a desire to search for gold. "He thought that a certain place at the foot of a large, over-hanging rock seemed suitable to begin his search and started to dig excitedly. A passerby saw there was a danger the rock might come down and warned the man. But the glimmer of gold was so attractive that he continued digging until the rock began to fall. The passerby, seeing the danger, cried out a warning in time to save the man from certain death. The man was not grateful, however, and blamed fate for causing him to lose the gold.

"People are not aware of the dangers they create for themselves. Not only did the passerby receive no gratitude, he was even denounced for not having shouted the warning sooner! Gold usually plays an important part in such stories, and in actual life also it is the source of much error." Thus spoke the Thinker, and the disciples asked Him, "Will people ever learn to discern causes?" The Thinker reminded them that a thousand earthly years are but a moment in the cosmic scale.

We always remember how the Thinker was able to unify the consciousness of humanity with the Consciousness of Cosmos.

The Thinker related, "Three men performed great deeds: the first one with full knowledge and consciousness, the second while intoxicated, and the third accidentally, in ignorance. Which one was worthy of the garland?"

The disciples indicated the first man. The Thinker remarked, "Verily, you are right. The first one should be recognized, for in full sobriety and knowledge, amidst dangers, he manifested true courage. Actions performed while intoxicated are unworthy; nor should we accept as heroic an accidental good deed or a good deed performed in ignorance. Such 'achievements' can be displayed even by wild beasts.

"O, knowledge, when wilt thou come to humanity? You can hear the crowd roar, whether for a wedding or for a calamity. In both cases the crowd displays its ignorance. Verily, there should be more schools in which people are taught the meaning of life, and in which teachers act not as sycophants of truth, but as representatives of Truth. People must learn to protect their teachers when they are abused by tyrants. The teachers should renounce riches, but their fellow-citizens should provide them with an environment conducive to knowledge. Do not assume that the significance of the teacher will soon be understood. Thousands of years will pass, and still the teacher will not be fully accepted."

Thus spoke the Thinker, and these words are true in every age.

191. Urusvati knows that before great calamities there may be either dark and threatening manifestations, or light and beautiful ones, when nature becomes especially attractive, as if offering its last smile. The Thinker called this "the magic of nature." He said, "Everything is so beautiful at such a moment, like a consolation for our yearning hearts. Darkness and storms can be signs of coming minor misfortune, but for great calamities nature puts on her best garments, as if to console. This magic of nature is like a balm that soothes the traveler.

"I do not fear the thunderstorm, but I tremble before the beauty of Cosmos. Could it be that I am seeing it for the last time? Must we overcome our trembling before the grandeur of the Universe? But how otherwise shall we perceive the far-off worlds? In the late hours of the night we soar into space, and when we return our earthly sheath seems too tight for us. May we not be fooled by the magic of earthly nature; it is but a drop in the ocean of Infinity. When we are oppressed, we should think of Infinity."

The Thinker said about the chain of lives, "Not only does it exist, but it is of manifold nature. There are complete incarnations, but also partial ones. A strong spirit can give part of his energy. This can be called a sending of the ray or a sending of energy. It provides an intensification of power that broadens the consciousness. It does not depress, but deepens straight-knowledge. In some people a natural keenness can be sensed. They themselves might have accumulated it in their former lives, but it also could have been sent to them as Grace."

If we discuss the far-off worlds we must accept the idea of distant influences. A strong spirit, while in the far-off worlds, may be filled with a desire to increase the work for good, and thus will send a particle of his energy for the inspiration and daring of those on Earth. Formerly, mothers prayed that double strength be granted to the incarnating soul. Some legends record the existence of certain nations that knew about the power of the spirit and about the Subtle World.

192. Urusvati knows the legends that tell us about the fulfillment of desires. The Thinker said, "People rarely discriminate between a desire that comes from within and an influence from without. They assume that all their desires come from within and rejoice when they are fulfilled, not realizing that at times these are not their own desires, but are received from outside. Such desires are already fulfilled in space, and people have only responded to an event destined to happen. They may have thought that their desire had come from within, when, in reality, it had resounded from the outside."

Legend tells us about the tree that fulfills all desires, but the explanation for this lies in the healing power of the leaves, which, when used as a medicine, make people more receptive to higher commands.

When the disciples asked, "What should one do if people do not listen to useful advice?" the Thinker answered, "Then be silent. There is no obstacle more solid than negation. When someone becomes ill with negation, leave him alone, otherwise he can be driven into a rage. You cannot force a change of the mind, which: given time, it may regenerate the afflicted part by itself and heal the one infected by negation."

The disciples asked, "What shall we do if no one will accept the truth?" The Thinker replied, "Remember that you have legs! Your oppressors will drive you away and you will then have an opportunity to speak the words of truth elsewhere. Thanks to the persecutors, the Truth will be proclaimed in many places."

193. Urusvati knows how deplorable is the rubbish-heap of hurt feelings. The Thinker told His disciples, "Be not offended by the malicious and ignorant who oppose your righteous path. Hurt feelings will only weaken your forces, devouring the will and crushing life. When you resist evil, do so not out of offense, but for the reestablishment of good. You cannot be hurt by the opinions of the ignorant. Be sorry for their ignorance, but do not accept them as fellow seekers or their judgments as the truth. It is wise not to answer them at all. Schools should teach that he who follows the right path is immunized against such offenses, and that only the unwise poison themselves by allowing their feelings to be hurt."

The disciples also asked, "Where will we be after death?" The Thinker answered, "Not as far as you think! Each of you during his life visits the future abode in dreams, and has traveled to the destined spheres more than once. Everyone has access to the Supermundane Realm, and therefore should learn to have a wise attitude toward all events during the day and at night.

"It is often said that sleep is similar to death, but people forget what this truly means. Sleep does not resemble actual physical death, but, in the Subtle World, is similar to that experience. Some people, when entering the Supermundane Realms, drag along with them a sleepy, benumbed existence, and therefore fail to learn or improve themselves. But those with a developed mind can immediately begin their next ascent."

These words of the Thinker are similar to those I have spoken. When you study the Inner Life of the Brotherhood, you should compare the Teachings given in different ages.

194. Urusvati has observed that despite their apparent contentment, the inhabitants of Kamchatka, Lapland, and the extreme North deserve better living conditions.

The Thinker told His disciples, "We make a mistake when we categorize nations by what appears to us to be their most important characteristics. We do not sufficiently study their faiths and customs, know little about their origins, and simply judge them by their alien, outer appearance, and our knowledge of a few local details. Satisfied with our ignorance, we are no better than fools!

"The nation's leaders and judges should travel the world and learn to understand people before taking up their responsibilities toward their fellow citizens. They must search for the sources of their happiness and will learn that few live in contentment.

"Judges should be knowledgeable and honest. One can evaluate the level of consciousness of an entire nation by its judges. Where judges allow themselves to be bribed and thought is confined, the soul of the nation is for sale. It would be easier to find brigands that are more honest than two-faced judges!

"Do not be deluded by the bright fires that burn in the hiding-places of corruption. Let him who has eyes see what goes on there. Search for joy, and do not be surprised if you find it in a hut.

"Harken! People will fall into such an abyss of crime that they will crucify the best One."

195. Urusvati knows that an inactive, sleepy earthly life is an obstacle to progress in the Subtle World. The nerve centers, which have their prototypes in the subtle body, cannot become keen in a life without action.

The Thinker said, "How can we trust a military leader who was never in a battle? How can we know the quality of a ship which has never been to sea? Truly, exertion is blessed, for through intense labor we prepare ourselves for higher understanding. One cannot move without bringing the muscles into motion. One cannot rise in spirit without sharpening the consciousness. Only in labor do we experience that ardor which takes us to our highest Guides.

"When we meet Them we must find the strength to ask whether we have fulfilled our tasks. They will tell us where we have succeeded and where we have failed.

In our earthly life we seldom pay attention to the commands of our Guides, whose thunderous commands and warnings resound in our consciousness only as slight vibrations. We tremble only when we sense the Great Presence, and Their words do not often reach us."

The Thinker also said, "In the human organism rhythm and harmony lie dormant, but we must awaken them, for this music must become an important part of our education. Without rhythm and harmony we will not enter the Highest Realms. The Universe exists by motion, which is regulated by rhythm, but people do not realize that the beat of the heart is a symbol of the movement of the Universe." Thus did the Thinker direct attention to the Highest Realms.

196. Urusvati knows how people filled with hate will attempt to destroy even the indestructible! There was a time in Athens when heralds officially proclaimed that those citizens who dared even to utter the names of Pericles, Anaxagoras, Aspasia, Phidias, and their friends would be driven into exile.

The mobs, urged on by officials, demanded the destruction of the statue of Zeus, because it reminded them of the despised Phidias. If the names of these accused were found in manuscripts, the fearful citizens hastened to burn the writings, regardless of their value. Those who were particularly cautious even avoided passing by the houses of the accused citizens. The sycophants rushed to write epigrams describing in insulting terms the downfall of Pericles. Anaxagoras was depicted as an ass braying in the public square. And the circumstances surrounding the death of Socrates are known to everyone.

The Thinker said, "We know the names of Pericles, Anaxagoras, Aspasia, and Phidias, but not the names of the judges who condemned them. We remember the statues by Phidias, but not those who wanted to destroy them. We might hope that this shame of humanity has taken place for the last time in history, but I fear that such a hope is only a dream.

"Man is a social animal, but human herds do not know how to graze in peace, and do not realize that horns should be used only in defense. Even a bull can be an example of decency. May thought direct humanity toward the Infinite."

The Thinker also said, "The Guides are concerned about the preservation of Beauty. Phidias was cast into prison, and by this act humanity cast itself into darkness. People are amazed at their cruel fate, but have they not earned it themselves?

"O, government authorities, O, persecutors of Truth, your names have faded away, but your burden has become heavy. Only recently We met a leper who does not remember what truth he had reviled." Thus warned the Thinker, and each one of Us, at certain times and in Our own way, has uttered the same words.

People do not like to listen to those ideas that they have decided beforehand not to accept. In the cruel hour of fratricidal strife people invoke the name of Christ, and false witnesses take oaths on the most sacred objects. Such irreverence is all the more blasphemous. People are not afraid to utter a false oath or to ridicule the faith of others. They always find time for criticism and slander, but they have no time for labor. They may at times think about community, but do not know how to cooperate, even in their daily life.

Truly, Urusvati knows that it is impossible to destroy the indestructible.

197. Urusvati knows how many genuine, good

deeds have never been recorded. If a person dives into the ocean to save someone who has fallen in, it is considered a great self-sacrifice, but it would be just as great an action to prevent the accident in the first place. Much labor is expended to prevent misfortunes. Many fires are extinguished, but just as many are prevented. No one knows how rescue comes, for sometimes the danger is not even suspected. Man is usually unaware of those to whom he owes his life.

The Thinker said, "How do we know whether, at this very moment, we might need to be saved from something? Do we really know what threatens us? We are content to think that our day has been a peaceful one, but fail to see that the poisonous viper, lurking behind us, has been driven away by an invisible savior! Let us express our gratitude to invisible saviors.

"No one should think that the space around us is empty. On the contrary, we can feel with our hearts the presence of invisible beings. Some call to us, others embrace us with a slight breath, still others fill us with joy or sadness, or whisper advice to us. A fool will say he alone is responsible for all these feelings. Ignorance fills man with self-importance. It would be wiser for him to say that he applies all his effort, yet is grateful for invisible help.

"The time will come when a person who speaks in Athens will immediately receive an answer from Corinth. Man will master space and realize that it is filled."

198. Urusvati knows that he who strives forward must face the storm. But people are afraid, and prefer to remain under shelter. There are few who would stand in a downpour of rain or pelting hail even for the sake of hastening their progress!

The Thinker said, "We must be careful with characterless people, who sometimes should simply be left to their errors. Most people do not understand how fleeting earthly possessions are, and it is impossible to convey to them the true meaning of life. But after experiencing many incarnations they will gradually be liberated from the enchantment of objects. They will learn to admire creativity without attachment to the created things. But we should not force upon people what is beyond their capacity. They should be told about Truth, but one cannot force it upon them. Compulsion will provoke rebellion so strong that there will be retreat instead of progress.

"For example, every schoolteacher can observe how carefully one should treat pupils in their adolescence. The teacher should know how to talk about life in such a way that each listener will think that he has come to the right conclusions by himself. Such a teacher is like a good gardener who understands what kind of wind best carries the fertile seeds."

199. Urusvati knows that the Teachings of the Masters have not been fully recorded in human history. Often only details were stressed, while their underlying principles were omitted. Envy and negligence deprive mankind of many achievements.

The Thinker said, "If you want to find a rare manuscript, do not look for it only in the libraries. It is better to roam about the market places, and even to pay attention to the wrapping paper being used! We sometimes found beautiful fragments of rare manuscripts being used to wrap vegetables. I remember a poet who once advised a writer not to use an ink that was poisonous, for it might harm someone who later buys cherries wrapped in the paper. Indeed, even We cannot be sure that Our writings will reach future generations in their original form."

And again the Thinker said, "The followers of Aesculapius used the most diverse healing remedies. They stressed that in Nature everything has its healthful uses, and that there is a natural remedy for every disease. A physician must also be a naturopath and follow the example of Hygeia in guarding the health of the people.

"If a man becomes ill, it is because his physician is not also his friend. May physicians become friends of humanity, not their gravediggers."

200. Urusvati knows that in the remote past people knew about the far-off worlds. This should not surprise you, for people possessed true knowledge even in ancient times. However, the vast majority had peculiar notions, thinking, for example, that Earth was built on the back of a cow, a turtle, or some monster. Even today, along with true knowledge and a vast range of information one can find similarly ridiculous superstitions. One might ask how knowledge was transmitted in ancient times, or how people of different nations could exchange information without a written language or other means of communication. Those who are aware of clairvoyance and astral flights can answer this question easily, but it would be difficult to explain such things to a narrow-minded person!

Be not surprised that the ancients were better at keeping secrets, for they believed that the sacred dream must not be discussed with the ignorant, and the most precious experiences were kept within a close circle. It is amazing to see how such extremes can coexist! But even today people have not changed in the levels of their consciousness.

The Thinker said, "Each man has within himself a potential force that can bring him into direct contact with the Highest World. This force builds the essence of his consciousness and enables Us to transmit information into its core. He who can establish constant contact with the Highest World is able to help build the future, but if this communion is lost, man is limited to the life of a beast.

"Beautiful symbols have been given to people but they treat them as superstition. They look at depictions of winged creatures and consider them to be fantasies. But does not each one of us soar? It does not matter whether the flights are made in the luminous or the dense body, they do take place, consciously or unconsciously. Sleep is a great gift of the gods, and opens the entrance into the Supermundane. Insomnia was always regarded as a punishment, because it deprived man of a natural communion. Friends, we must be grateful to the Higher Spirits, who allow us to have communion with Them.

"Man usually remembers only dimly his experiences during astral flights, but in the depth of his consciousness he preserves the precious treasures. I cannot claim that I am able to express in words everything that I experience, but, just as a mother feels within her body the first signs of her baby's life, so can all people feel within themselves the accumulation of subtle observations.

"Friends, We fly and easily assimilate the radiance of the far-off realms. Some will oppose this statement, and will argue in their ignorance that these realms do not exist, that they are only mirages, but We who have approached them know their essence.

"Friends, do not repeat in the market place what you have just heard, for people will consider you mad. The time will come when these words will be understood. Even the most innocent questions should not be asked prematurely. Ignorant people can easily become tigers, and it is better not to create such beasts.

"Friends, I wish to relate to you alone how I remember the distant world. The distance that separates us from it is enormous, but the flight is instantaneous. To land on this remote ground is impossible for Us, even in Our luminous bodies. But We can see the outlines of the oceans, rejoice in the beautiful colors, and even see the birds and the fish. People there are not like Us, and, wonderful to see, they can fly! Their speech cannot be heard, perhaps because of the resounding of the spheres. I remember the blue of the water, like sapphire, the green of the meadows, and the mountains, like emeralds. It would seem that man is incapable of stepping upon such pure soil. Even the air is unbearable for Us.

"Nevertheless, after experiencing the flight, We suffer upon the return to Our physical body. It is stifling, as though one were putting on a tight, uncomfortable garment. Thus, every experience is both beautiful and difficult."

201. Urusvati knows that We have many reasons for speaking about unification. We have given the example of the horse that delayed a whole caravan, and spoken about the interdependent forces that hold an arch together. Now We shall add the words of the Thinker.

One day, the disciples asked Him the meaning of unification. At that moment they were passing a gigantic wall, and He pointed to the powerful stonework saying, "Observe how these stones support each other. We cannot say which of them is the most important. They are not joined by anything, yet they have withstood many earthquakes. They are held together only by unification and the natural affinity of their surfaces.

People try to join stone artificially, with clay or different mixtures, but such structures are frequently destroyed by earthquakes.

"If people attempt to strengthen their relationships by artificial measures, they will not be protected against dissolution. It is better and stronger when human hearts unite spontaneously. Such unions need no artificial aids, least of all the bond of gold. Beware especially the bonds of gold.

"I affirm that even the most ardent people may not be able to judge and correlate values; only human hearts build an adamantine wall."

The Thinker also said, "Man will not be able to fly until he finds suitable wings. The symbol of Daedalus will be an eternal warning, but We shall often discuss the far-off worlds. By thinking about them we shall find the wings.

"Let everyone tell us how he imagines the far-off worlds. Each one will be right, no matter how vivid his imagination, for, in truth, there is nothing that does not exist, and our imagination can invent only a small part of the reality.

"Do not feel disappointed that your imagination is limited, for compared with Infinity all is limited. Let us acquire true striving in the midst of Infinity."

202. Urusvati knows how difficult it is for people to discriminate between the essential and the trivial. Moreover, when people sense the approach of an essential event, they avoid it with petty excuses instead of facing it directly. It is interesting to observe how people cling to trivialities as a way of avoiding facing the essential. They do not realize that the essential contains the beautiful. One should learn to distinguish clearly what insignificant details are particularly appealing to the human mind, for only by understanding such insects will one be able to exterminate them.

When the essential comes, it comes in a special silence. But at such intense moments the clowns will produce their clamor, and ring their bells and strike their tambourines. It can be observed that just before a great event the mobs grow agitated, for they can sense its approach.

The Thinker said, "It is amazing how people will rub dust into their eyes and then run in search of a physician. But they will not allow all the dust to be removed, they have become accustomed to it, and it is as if the dust has become a part of their eyes. Let us not blind ourselves with dust.

"Every hero whose heart is pure is a dispeller of evil, and the biographies of such heroes should be studied in schools. Students should also learn what was done to Pericles and how people have treated their heroes. Thus should human history be written.

"How long will it take for the common people to conquer their fear of great men? Perhaps some patient toilers will appear who will gradually remove the dust from their eyes.

"The heart suffers unbearably when the blood is made impure by dust."

203. Urusvati knows how some people insist that life on Earth should be, quite simply, earthly. What, precisely, do they suppose earthly existence to be? Such people have no interest in Supermundane concepts, and care only for the mean and paltry life that they have established by constantly demeaning all higher concepts. They do not realize that there is no such thing as "earthly." Everything belongs to the Cosmos, every stone is part of the Universe.

People are not pigs, deprived of the ability to raise

their heads toward Heaven. One does not survive by earthly rubbish, but by the higher emanations. And yet for thousands of years there have been many who have stubbornly promoted the importance of a purely earthly existence. Not only the atheists, but also the theists have denied the Subtle and Higher Realms. It is hard to understand how such opposing mentalities could agree on the denial of the fundamentals of life. Prompted by fear and ignorance, they do not dare face the most beautiful. Even the gaining of knowledge does not help them to approach the psycho-physical realm, and the theists do not allow their deities to lead them to approach the higher realms.

The Thinker said, "We should not belittle life by limiting ourselves to Earth alone. Three worlds are given to us, but we must earn our right to each one. We become attached to the perishable Earth and forget that we can partake of life everlasting!

"Let us not be deluded into limiting ourselves to the sense of touch. We are given other senses that we should utilize for total perception. But do we know these senses? The Supermundane has its own expressions. Indeed, we are rich in the treasures bestowed upon us."

204. Urusvati knows about the enemies, visible and invisible. Those who conduct research in thought transmission should take note of the hostile conditions that accompany their experiments. Thoughts can be intercepted by spatial entities, and it is known that during experiments some people can hear thoughts.

The investigator should pay attention to the particular nature of an experimenting group, since it has been observed that harmony among those who are present assists the transmittance and prevents interception. Moreover, if nearby friends maintain a mood that is harmonious, they also help to protect the thought transmission. Those who are confused or irritated act unwittingly as collaborators with the spatial thieves. The auras of irritated people act as the strongest destroyers of the currents. They may deny their collaboration with the spatial thieves, but in fact are their accomplices in evil. At some time, when in the Subtle World, they will regret their lack of self-control.

People do not understand that each of their light-minded deeds is observed by invisible entities, and that thought should be cultivated under the most favorable mental conditions.

Fools assume that thought can be strengthened by the use of narcotics, but the mental spasms that result do not contribute to evolution. Even the emanations of drugs attract dangerous entities, which pick up fragments of thought and weave harmful tissue out of them. Everyone can remember how their useful thoughts were sometimes distorted. Look for the cause in your surroundings, and you will surely find it.

The Thinker said, "O, poor thought! You have no protection. No sooner have you taken wing than evil talons are ready to tear you to pieces. Just as a handful of gold disappears when thrown into a crowd, so can a thought in space be easily seized. Thought may be received by a worthy spirit, but there may be thieves among those passing by. We must keep our bodies clean, but we should maintain even more purity around our thoughts."

205. Urusvati knows that the Supermundane should not be understood only as extraterrestrial. Included in the study of life are the higher worlds and the highest concepts. Earthly life is built upon immutable laws, an understanding of which includes the correlation of all the worlds and acceptance of the true importance of the Subtle World.

It is correctly pointed out that people are incarnated for specific purposes. For example, humiliated and tortured people return to Earth to remind others about their unacknowledged rights, but most of these people cannot overcome the desire for revenge and retribution, and few reach the noble heights of all-forgiveness and pure self-perfectment. There are those who return to the very place where they were abused and mistreated and wreak terrible vengeance. They hide themselves among the common people, bringing about sedition and hindering the progress of the country.

If people understood the consequences of this violence, they would be more effective in the building of their country, but few care to understand that blood shed in hatred is in need of purification. Thus, many times have We reminded you about the need for self-perfectment and an understanding of the Subtle World. Each one of Us has called to people in order to provide this knowledge.

The Thinker said, "Behold, the furies are created by you. Gods care not for vengeance; it is people themselves who create these horrible monsters. We all forget that we pave our own way. How can I find words that are simple enough for everyone to understand?"

We must understand the causes of strife and discord. If we remind ourselves about our life among the shadows, we shall be able to understand that it is precisely there that our future existence is prepared.

206. Urusvati knows that the duration of the stay in the Subtle World, depending on conditions, can vary from a few months to thousands of years. It would be difficult to provide all the reasons, but the chief one is the free will. One may ask whether a long stay in the subtle spheres or a short one is more beneficial for the soul; both can be of equal value. Similarly, one may ask if the soul can choose not to return to Earth at all. Truly, all is possible, but the stay in the Subtle World must then be made more useful than that on Earth.

We have mentioned that powerful Beings can transmit a part of their Ray to someone on Earth who then receives illumination. Such a Ray has an effect on the recipient that is the equal of an earthly incarnation. Divisibility of the spirit can be utilized, and the transmissions will then bring spiritual enlightenment to several people simultaneously. This is an even higher service to evolution.

Thus man can truly build his destiny. He can develop his thinking capacity to any degree and can expand his generosity to the point of self-sacrifice. His power of thought will grow as it circulates in a spiral, and the more he gives, the more he receives. This truth should be taught in schools.

Likewise it may be asked whether the free will can lead one to the far-off realms. Certainly it can, if exercised with sincere self-denial. You already know about those Beings who left for other planets. This achievement is extraordinary since it strengthens the mind and creates new horizons of thought. The Thinker pointed out many times that He would one day go to another world and from there establish communication. Centuries would be needed for the fulfillment of this task, but nothing is impossible if one's will is directed toward the goal.

207. Urusvati knows that many do not accept the idea of the energy of thought. Furthermore, there are some who believe that thought transmission is limited, using as evidence the fact that radio waves cannot penetrate certain strata of the atmosphere. That observation is correct, but is not applicable to directed human thought, which has a special energy not comparable to radio waves. The strata of space are subordinate to thought, which has no obstacles. When We discuss transmission of thought over great distances We specifically have in mind directed thought.

The Thinker said, "Learn how to think. Begin with the most simple thoughts. Best of all, learn how to dream about beautiful objects, and learn to dream vividly. Only dreams will develop one's imagination, and where can we go, how can we assimilate the most beautiful observations without imagination? How can we remember in our mundane life the sparks of the Supermundane Radiance if we do not train ourselves to dwell on images? Verily, striving toward the Sublime will train our imagination.

"Nothing remains static. Imagination must grow or it will be extinguished, and who knows when it may be possible to rekindle it? Philosophers must have strong imaginations, just as artists must in order to create. Dreaming is born during the days of childhood. Children must be helped to develop their thinking."

Thus spoke the Thinker when He asked His disciples to become dreamers, for only in this way are born the images of great governments and of general happiness. Happiness lives in dreams.

208. Urusvati knows how instantaneous and unexpected some visions can be. Especially striking to us are the visions in which people appear whom we do not know. There are many reasons for this. These people may not really be strangers, but may have been known to us in the Subtle World. It is also possible that two people will have consonant vibrations that produce simultaneous visions of each other. If people were to write down their visions and share them with people they trust, so much would be clarified. But such observations are neglected, and human consciousness loses an opportunity for practical learning.

For example, someone was playing the piano somewhere and generated the vibrations that resounded in Urusvati's consciousness, forming a vision of the unknown player. Such consonance affects the fiery tissues. People make contact with each other through consonant sounds, and thus create collaborations.

The seeming instantaneousness of many visions can be explained by the laws of the Subtle World, where physical time does not exist. The brevity of the visions is only illusory, for man's perceptions are limited by the physical plane, and for him the subtle images come and go quickly. But in the conditions of the Subtle World we enter into the mental spheres, and the events appear to unfold naturally. Thus one can increase his experience in the Subtle World and learn to understand the earthly illusion of instantaneousness.

The Thinker drew attention to the difference between perceptions in the physical world and in the Subtle World. He said, "Invisible creatures pass by swiftly, and only a slight breeze might indicate their presence. At times they approach us in the form of a blue cloud, but we only rarely discern the presence of such uncommon guests. When we do, we should greet them, 'Welcome, good friends! We open our hearts to you; do send us help from your beautiful realms.' "

209. Urusvati knows that the all-pervading energy can be stimulated by both natural and artificial means. Everyone understands that natural methods are superior, yet much more has been written about artificial ones. It is true that artificial methods have been studied in detail since ancient times, but now, at the transition between two eras, it is time to turn to the natural methods of manifesting the Primal Energy.

Ancient man was much coarser, and mechanical rhythms and rituals were necessary for the awakening of subtle energies. But now that the nervous system is considerably finer, mankind can see that will and thought are natural attributes, and therefore must be utilized in natural ways.

It is wrong to excite the mind with narcotics, for such methods harmfully affect even future generations. Artificial stimulants are as harmful as the most severe diseases, the only difference being that the effects of disease manifest quickly, whereas the effects of narcotics develop over a long time and affect future generations. Man thinks little about the future and cares little about what he contributes to it.

The Thinker said, "We do not seem to know for whom we build the stronghold. If we understand that we are building it for ourselves we will shape the stones more carefully. One should not rejoice when one's earthly life is finished, for no one knows where he will have to labor again. Therefore, wise men should think about where they may have to settle their accounts."

210. Urusvati knows that changes in all realms of nature will take place at the coming of the new race. Most people will not notice these changes, and if they do, will be too hesitant to mention it.

Even clear indications of new types of diseases do not stimulate research. It is essential to observe all one's surroundings. Unusual developments will be observed in the animal kingdom, and the vegetable kingdom will also offer many confirmations. Diseases of animals and plants will remind us of epidemics among people. We have acquired the ability to protect ourselves against the known scourges, however, it is not the plague, cholera, or even cancer or meningitis that will threaten us, but new types of nervous ailments, which may become fully epidemic. These ailments are maladies of psychic energy, and can be contagious. Yet, it will take a long time for physicians to pay attention to these new kinds of disease. They could be called fiery fevers, but whatever we call them, it is important to understand their cause.

Changes of race will not inevitably bring disaster, but it is important that the psychic energy should be kept in a pure condition, since polluted energy produces disastrous spatial manifestations.

Thus the Thinker affirmed, "Let us not forget that everything is in motion. No one has the right to pollute the cosmic current, for he will increase the suffering of many, and primarily his own. But it is fear that keeps people away from the subtle worlds."

211. Urusvati knows how difficult it is to achieve harmony of consciousness. We do not speak here about the leveling of all consciousnesses, because, owing to cosmic multiformity, equality does not exist. Because nothing is repeated, the harmony of all parts is essential. It is difficult to imagine what complicated methods would have to be applied to try to equalize consciousnesses. One person may already be approaching the summit, while another has not even reached the foot of the mountain! Truly, in their thinking they have nothing in common. If you give them equal knowledge, for one it will be insufficient, and for the other too much, confusing him and even causing him to betray.

The Teacher must often ponder what the student can assimilate without harm. It is better to leave things unsaid than to say too much and create circumstances that lead to betrayal. Understanding all the varieties suitable for harmonization embodies the essence of wisdom.

Thus we may observe that at times the Teacher hastens, and at other times holds back, watching over many processions of pilgrims simultaneously and regulating their pace. Much happens that man is unable to see as he marches forward. The Teacher sets the milestones far into the distance. He points out various signs that from the ordinary point of view may have no significance, but in fact are great symbols. It is not surprising that these milestones are given ahead of time, since in the Subtle World the question of time does not exist. Such signs are not evaluated in the earthly sense, but according to their significance.

The Thinker said, "Who can know the measures that are used in space? All we can do is be observant and not apply to giants the measures of dwarfs."

212. Urusvati knows that the signs manifested by nature can be exceedingly varied. But people often tend to notice only gloomy omens, and thus sink into superstition. For example, an intelligent observer will know that even when crops are abundant, if the currents are discordant there can result extremes of good and bad.

A wise person does not necessarily rejoice at unexpected success in his affairs. A farmer knows that a particular tension of currents that is beneficial for his own harvest may provoke harmful repercussions in some distant land. And so it is in everything.

Even in ancient times the wise men knew that certain signs of success or failure could signal dreadful consequences. It is hard to imagine the catastrophes taking place in space that reach us centuries later. One cannot prevent what has already taken place, but one can acquire sufficient spiritual forbearance to accept what comes. When We speak about the need for equilibrium, We foresee many changes which people do not even suspect will come to pass.

The Thinker often warned of the possibility of cosmic catastrophes. People laughed at Him, but how could they be sure that there had not occurred a catastrophe in far-off space which would reach Earth a thousand years later? Yet the harbingers of such an event can reach people and disturb their consciousness.

Teachers must repeat about the coordination of the worlds.

213. Urusvati knows that all that exists is imbued with Primal Energy. Why do people need to be reminded so often of this truth? Human awareness does not seem to have any affinity with the idea of Primal Energy. People discuss energies, but do not dare to acknowledge that fundamentally there is only one.

It should be recognized that the energy of thought is one of the highest manifestations of Primal Energy. It is impossible to isolate thought from the fundamental energy of Cosmos. Precisely, it is thought that eternally moves the fundamental energy. Thought generates certain currents that serve as the awakeners, or, so to speak, the rejuvenators of the Universe. Thus, when I say that thinking beings participate in world-creation, it can be understood literally, not allegorically. It follows then, that man has a great responsibility for the quality of his thought. Each kind and strong thought produces beautiful vibrations, but an evil one strews Earth with deadly dross.

A teacher must educate students to dwell continually on the beautiful. Every aspirant can enrich space. Do not think that soil needs only material fertilization. Although they require much time, experiments should be made on the influence of thought. We often devote ourselves to such prolonged research, for sound understanding cannot be reached through hasty conclusions. If continuous research is carried out, it will be clearly demonstrated that subtle energy requires subtle approaches. I must remind you again that the measures of dwarfs should not be applied to giants.

The Thinker spoke to people about this, constantly reminding them that lofty subjects must be studied when in a lofty state of mind. "Let us always apply goal-fitness."

214. Urusvati knows how much the concept of rhythm is misunderstood by humanity. The ancient teachings about the significance of rhythm have been lost, and today's idea of rhythm is limited to music and crude dancing. Scientists speak about vibratory rhythm, but their conclusions do not go beyond their laboratories. Rhythm should be expressed in all work, in all creativeness, in all of life. Only experienced workers are aware that rhythmic labor is the most productive.

Verily, a true *karma yogin* knows the joy of rhythm without artificial tension. A *karma yogin* works not because someone compels him to, but because he cannot live without labor. This yoga is closely connected with rhythm. Mutual benefit only results when a very powerfully expressed rhythm can blend with similar vibrations everywhere on Earth. In its invisibility such help becomes true harmony. Unfortunately, in daily life such spontaneous and limitless cooperation is very rare.

Every worker also receives help from the Subtle World, and people would be much more successful if they realized that this invisible cooperation exists. Scoffers will say, "Can it be that even carpenters, farmers, and masons receive help from the Subtle World?" This mockery is out of place, for each appreciated labor receives help. People should think more about the inexhaustible store of energy in the Subtle World.

I shall speak of one more truth which is little understood: People are often upset when their ideas are seized and used by others. Actually, the spreading of useful ideas should give joy, but the majority are not magnanimous enough to feel that way.

The Thinker said, "Ideas are borne on fleet wings." It is joyous to liberate a bird from its cage, and it should be equally joyous to set free a salutary idea. Thought must nourish space, otherwise people will be deprived of the opportunity for progress. Let us free ideas from all bondage and chains. Let us not rely on wardens, but speed our own liberation.

215. Urusvati knows the importance of discerning subtle differentiations. Yet, such fine definition, indescribable in words, is rarely understood. How can one explain why one thing is permitted, yet another, differing from it by only a hair's breadth, is an unthinkable violation? Only a broadened consciousness can discern the border between creation and destruction. Many ancient cults combined creation and destruction into one symbol, thus indicating the closeness of these concepts, which are so crudely evaluated by the ordinary mind.

It is just as difficult to judge to what degree one should affect another's karma. Take, for example, a teacher who wishes to help a disciple who is being tested. The teacher might ardently wish to influence his pupil, yet the confused student does not notice the encouraging signs and glances. Of course, the teacher cannot intervene to prevent the pupil's mistakes, and regardless of his desire that the test be successful, must keep silent and try to lead the pupil to the right path in a tactful, indirect way.

Many circumstances should be considered before attempting to interfere with another's karma, since near ones may be involved. People do not understand that good and evil are so subtly interlaced, and many will scoff at such an idea.

The Thinker often pointed it out, using the example of school examinations. But, of course, people did not want to listen.

216. Urusvati has heard explosions in the Subtle World. It may seem strange to you that there are explosions in the Subtle World that can be heard, but everything relating to the Subtle World should be understood in a subtle way. Explosions can occur in any sphere. They cannot be heard by the physical ear, but cause an unusual trembling of the heart, and through clairaudience a precise impression of an explosion can be experienced. One should realize that the subtle spheres resound constantly in the sensitive ear.

Ordinary people are unable to perceive such subtle signs. They are either unwilling to admit the existence of the Supermundane or become upset at the idea of it.

In the literature of various nations one can find puzzling indications. For example, Shambhala is said to be located in the extreme North, and the northern lights would seem to confirm this. But let us not forget that similar electrical discharges can also be observed in the Himalayas.

The Thinker pointed out how careful we must be not to reveal truths for which people are not yet ready, for great confusion would result. Let us follow His wise advice and find means that fit the people's consciousness.

If We could find simpler words, We would use them. Indeed, great simplicity is needed.

217. Urusvati knows that the poisoning of the atmosphere is increasing at this time. The consequences of this are evident in many aspects of life. People suffer from many bodily diseases because of their individual weaknesses, and society suffers from epidemics and social upheavals. We often warn about the need for unity, for harmony is the best prophylactic. Great equilibrium is necessary; if it could be achieved throughout the world, the most dangerous hours would pass without harm.

Equilibrium is maintained by the exercise of one's free will, but people do not want to accept their individual responsibility in this. Infection takes hold not only because of a predisposition to certain ailments, but also because of the loss of balance. A pilgrim without balance will not be able to walk safely through the narrow passage and will be afraid, pursuing his way in great anxiety. Such imbalance will destroy him and infect those close to him with fear.

Indeed, the poisoning of the atmosphere is now increasing. Be vigilant. We are aware of such times, for We Ourselves have gone through them more than once during Our earthly lives. It is best to be aware of this and to gather the power of equilibrium. Thus, we shall withstand and outlive all upheavals.

Whenever the Thinker endured such tension, He said, "Threatening clouds have obscured the sky. Let us stay at home lest we disturb the stillness. Even the most fearful storm cannot continue without end."

218. Urusvati knows the magnetic power of names. Every sound corresponds to a specific cosmic ray, and also is linked to powerful signs of astrological significance. You know that sometimes We do not forbid the utterance of Our Names, while at other times We have advised you not to utter them, even in thought. This is because while sometimes the combinations of sounds do not generate powerful magnetic currents, at other times a Name sounds in space like the blow of a hammer. At such times, for the safeguarding of equilibrium, Our names should not be uttered. But this is also true about personal names, and even the names of places.

In ancient times names were of astrological origin. In many nations several other names were usually given to a child so that his astrological name would not be uttered. It is better not to utter such a name, even during auspicious moments, for it can act like a bolt of lightning.

People generally do not know the difference between magnetism and hypnotism. Hypnotism deals with personal forces, whereas magnetism is a cosmic phenomenon. The Thinker often spoke about the significance of these energies, and used to say, "The moment a man exclaims, 'Oh, how unhappy I am!' he immediately increases his trouble. But he who declares, 'I am happy!' opens the gates to happiness.

"This is not to say that man commands his happiness and unhappiness. It goes much deeper, because man is dealing with powerful energies. As soon as he has expressed a mood it is registered in space, and invokes the Highest Forces. Let us not be ungrateful or imprudent."

The Thinker constantly taught His disciples to watch their words and never to utter them unthinkingly.

219. Urusvati knows that the subtlest combinations are unrepeatable. Once the Thinker noticed that His listeners had not completely understood the concept of uniqueness. He took a large bronze mirror and covered it with an even layer of sand. Then He tapped out different rhythms at the edge of the mirror, causing the sand to fall into different designs. Afterward, the Thinker asked His disciples to repeat precisely the same rhythms and produce the same designs. Of course, no one could do it.

The Thinker said, "Words do not always convince, but the simplest example can illustrate the generosity of nature. Nature is unrepeatable in its splendor. The Law is one, but its expressions are beyond counting. You could not repeat the designs for many reasons, but mainly because the cosmic conditions had already changed.

"Such subtle variations should give you joy, for they indicate that your possibilities are infinite. All is in motion and nothing repeats itself. This Law must be applied throughout all of life.

"I give you this advice now, but it will be of value only if you apply it immediately. There is hardly any benefit in medicine taken a year after it is prescribed. In the secret archives one can find many examples of unapplied counsels. The hunter is advised, 'Quick, do not miss the bird!' But the hand delays, and the arrow is shot in vain, perhaps even causing harm where it was not intended.

"If people realized the law of uniqueness, they would speedily advance in self-perfectment. The dead intellect whispers that each day is a repetition of the previous one. One constantly hears such complaints, but each moment is different. Your consciousness can never return to its previous state; even in cases of a degenerating consciousness, it will regress, but not in the same way. Infinity exists in both macrocosm and microcosm. Even a song cannot be repeated exactly, because the conditions will be different each time. If you return to a city where you have not been for many years, everything will appear different. Your consciousness will never be able to duplicate the previous state. Some people feel distressed when they think about unrepeatability, but a wise man will rejoice, for he senses motion."

Thus did the Thinker bring encouragement. One can see the complete application of these foundations in the Brotherhood. I quote for you the words of the Thinker because you know how He labored for the Brotherhood.

If someone says, "I want only to follow the Teaching of the Great Pilgrim," he will limit his progress. But We appreciate his loving the Great Pilgrim with all his heart, for the heart is inexhaustible. Is it right to suppress such transports of the heart when you know about the labors performed for the good of humanity?

Complete devotion, complete heroism, fill the spirit with adamant self-denial. The wings of self-renunciation will carry us to the Brotherhood.

220. Urusvati knows how much We are in contact with the Subtle World. For complete knowledge it is necessary to be in touch with the various spheres. Much misunderstanding has grown around the concept of the Subtle World, and in particular the concept of uniqueness, which is the same in the Subtle World as on Earth.

There are many descriptions of the Subtle World, but all of them are limited by the individual experience of the observer. Thus one person speaks about the lowest level, of almost monstrous ghosts; another describes sleeping shadows; a third finds an absolute similarity to the physical world; and a fourth talks about luminous bodies. They all describe what they have seen, but their perceptions were limited, causing them to think that one stratum is the entire Subtle World. Because of this error people quarrel and accuse one another of falsehood. If they could understand the manifoldness of the Subtle World, they would realize how beneficial it would be for them to strive to the higher spheres.

According to a certain kind of person, nothing worthwhile exists for him here on Earth and therefore he has no reason to live. However, if he carries such thoughts with him into the Subtle World, he will continue the same idle existence there. If people limit their idea of the Subtle World by their earthly experience, they will prevent themselves from acquiring new experiences. Few think about the higher worlds, and most would be afraid of the radiance of *Materia Lucida*. The possibility that thinking will become keener frightens the limited mind. While still on Earth, people should suggest to themselves where precisely they would like to continue their progress. They must concentrate their free will, so that their thought works as a messenger making provisions in the Subtle World.

The Thinker used to say, "Let your thought fly ahead of you and prepare your next beautiful dwelling."

221. Urusvati knows that on Earth people are constantly surrounded by subtle entities. Usually, they do not notice them, yet at times they feel breaths of air and light touches, and on rare occasions will see so-called ghosts. But We must point out that apart from such external perceptions, every refined person senses inner tremors, and is subject to nervous stimulation or depression caused by the approach of subtle entities.

Animals, and especially dogs, sense the presence of strong subtle manifestations. One may ask whether they recognize subtle entities mainly by sight or by scent. Their sight is not as acute as their scent, which is very precise. One may also ask what type of dog has a stronger sense of the Subtle World—of course, the long-haired ones, because they can accumulate more electricity. Similarly, people who collect more electricity can sense more strongly the presence of subtle entities, either at night or by day.

One should not consider the manifestations of the Subtle World to be extraordinary. Everyone possessing a refined receptivity can under proper conditions sense the presence of the dwellers of the Subtle World. Some of these appearances may be distressing, and although the sendings of the will help to repulse them, it must be tensed without delay, for if momentary fear is allowed, the will cannot be mustered later.

The Thinker knew that the will must be in full readiness. He used to say, "The sword of defense is given to everyone, but know how to use it without delay."

222. Urusvati knows how sometimes a single word can distort the whole theory of cosmogony. The philosopher said to the citizens, "You should feel that Earth is like the center of the Universe, then you will realize the entire duty and responsibility of man." But his followers misconstrued one of his words and an entirely different concept of the world was created.

Many examples can also be cited of how people have distorted the essence of the Teaching, because words have different meanings in different languages. There have always been innumerable dialects, with even neighboring clans using their own idioms. In the past there were also so-called sacred languages, which were used by the priests and hierophants. Certain sacred words infiltrated the popular language and were wrongly used. In that way, the breakdown of languages has taken place in all centuries.

One should not easily excuse unworthy deeds on the basis of misunderstandings due to differences in language. Unfortunately, shameful deeds are the result of evil willfulness and envy. If one examines the reasons for the persecution of the best minds of different nations, and compares the reasons for the persecution and banishment of Pythagoras, Anaxagoras, Socrates, Plato, and others, one can observe that in each case the accusations and reasons for banishment were almost identical and unfounded. But in the following centuries full exoneration came, as if there had never been any defamation. It would be correct to conclude that such workers were too exalted for the consciousness of their contemporaries, and the sword of the executioner was ever ready to cut off a head held high. Pericles was recognized in his time only after people had reduced him to a sorry state. Only in that state could his fellow citizens accept him as an equal!

A book should be written about the causes of the persecution of great individuals. By comparing the causes is it possible to trace the evil will. I advise you to write such a book. Let someone do it! Through research it will be possible to discover the inner similarities between the persecutions of Confucius and Seneca. Our Brothers and Sisters suffered persecution, and Our memory preserves many such events. Joan of Arc, Aspasia, and a whole list of gloriously heroic women of various centuries can be named. We do not regret experiencing such trials, but there is a need for reflecting on them, because each persecution retards an urgent plan. However, even this We turn to Good.

The Thinker used to say, "I wonder, do you persecute me or drive me onward?"

223. Urusvati knows that the human consciousness is formed from subtle accumulations. It will seem almost too simple if We tell you that each incarnation, like a medicine, is intended to cure a particular unhealthy feature of the individual. The color white may seem equally simple, yet it contains in itself all colors. It may astonish you to observe succeeding incarnations that are extreme opposites, yet without sufficient polishing a precious stone has no luster. Thus, everyone should remember how difficult it is to deepen the consciousness.

It is especially lamentable to see how some light-minded people in their conceit imagine that they have achieved the goal. One can read many books, but mere reading is not assimilation. We advise you to observe the manifestations of nature, in which is revealed the complexity of existence in its entirety.

Man seldom utilizes the accumulations from past lives. Often a small danger takes on the aspect of a frightful monster, and a person is transformed from an experienced witness into a hounded fugitive. He forgets that the monster he created himself will continue to grow, and that sooner or later he will have to face it and destroy it. The Guides whom man meets in the Subtle World advise him to free himself as soon as possible from his own creations, but if he is full of earthly limitations, he will reject the advice. Therefore, it is of paramount importance during one's earthly life to cognize this subtle existence.

The mind can function clearly in the Subtle World only if it was sufficiently exercised in the physical world. You remember how someone who had just entered the Subtle World was helpless, and could not even fashion a garment for himself because he had lost the clarity of his thinking, which can be preserved only through free will. If one understands precisely what he has to achieve, then the advice of the Guide will be assimilated. The Guide approaches those whose ears are open.

You know by now how often Our Sisters and Brothers visit the Subtle World. They do this first of all to help those who are under observation, and second, to constantly exercise their individual subtle energies in various spheres, for this helps one to feel at home everywhere.

It can be observed that a man who speaks with feeling can overcome natural impediments, but the moment inspiration is gone, his defects return. In the same way, one's mental ardor can become continuous, and like wings will carry one to the Guide. We can work best where there is flame, and therefore warn against fear, depression, and despair, which, like damp coals, cannot produce the needed fire. This comparison came from the Thinker, who possessed a remarkable gift for dispelling depression. The Brotherhood needs such abilities, for both the physical and Subtle Worlds. What We say now has an intimate connection with the life of the Brotherhood.

224. Urusvati knows that thought-transmission over great distances requires self-abnegation. No human thought can disappear in space, but there is a great difference between a thought that flies out without purpose and one sent with a specific aim. The latter message will pass through various spheres and be subjected to many influences. Imagine the path of such a thought as if it were a radio message—many circumstances can expose it to danger, and there may even be contacts that will bring about disaster. There can even occur a short circuiting of currents that will cause suffering to the sender. The purpose of Our remarks is to remind you that though the mission of the Thinker was indeed not an easy one, the results were great.

It is said that thought resounds in space. This should be understood literally. You heard the resounding strings and the silver bells. The tension of thought produces sounds throughout space. There are many legends about events that were preceded by manifestations of sound. This is quite correct—precisely before great events, such a manifestation of thought may be heard.

It is not the events that resound, but the intensified thoughts accompanying them, which may issue from an earthly source, or be projected from the Subtle World. The substance of thought is the same everywhere, and acts as a linking bond between the worlds. One should pay attention to manifestations of sound, and compare them with events.

The Thinker said, "After much thought I am convinced that I live in two worlds. One can observe the dual nature of things, gross and subtle. Let your ears learn to distinguish spatial sounds. Trumpets can deafen one, but resounding space thrills the heart."

225. Urusvati knows that sometimes the vibrations of space attain such tension that they become like physical tremors. Although it is difficult for most people to distinguish such quiverings, in Our Abode they are particularly felt, and all who are attuned to Us feel these intensified vibrations.

People often speak about the synthesis of science and spirituality, but the understanding of these two concepts remains vague. They must be connected by a special flame which We call exaltation. Without this ardor not only knowledge but even spirituality remains dead and unconnected.

Do not be surprised that there can be such a thing

as "dead spirituality." Truly there is such a condition. We often come across people who have all the qualifications of spirituality, yet in life are cold and inert. What benefit is there in spirituality earned once upon a time? Like soured milk, many products can be made from it, but it is impossible to return it to its original state.

The same also applies to knowledge, which should not be mechanical or limited. I repeat that the fire of exaltation is the best connecting bridge, which also serves as a balancing force amidst the storms of space.

When the Thinker used to repeat, "Be not afraid, do not escape from earthly disturbances," He knew the significance of exaltation.

226. Urusvati knows that even in earthly life one can transcend the sense of time. When one is deep in thought it ceases to exist. We have always reminded you that thought devours time.

Through control of thought one can easily realize the conditions in the higher spheres of the Subtle World and overcome time. Intensified thought is the best purifier of the human organism. If you encounter scientists who are in bad health, you would be right to conclude that their thinking is confused, and that their ability to think in the abstract is not equal to other sides of their life. If they could achieve a strong mental life, they would not only enjoy excellent health, but could also overcome the sense of time.

There is nothing new in this. "New" does not really exist—there is either forgotten truth or still unrealized truth. No one can claim that he has brought something new to the world, because only the moment before someone may have projected that very thought into space. People should not compete to be innovative, but should train themselves to think about the useful and the Beautiful. It would be better to think about essentials and how one can contribute the utmost good to the world. The most useful thoughts are those dedicated to Beauty. Ugliness is not fitting for evolution.

The Thinker proclaimed that Beauty is the most essential, and His power to convince many of this was great.

227. Urusvati knows that goalfitness and appreciation are among the most essential foundations of the Brotherhood. It is unreasonable to think that the Brotherhood would accept someone's services and later discard him as one would a worn-out garment. If the co-worker proves to be helpful and never commits betrayal, he certainly will not be rejected. Such a co-worker is appreciated and will be recognized. However, recognition can take different forms and is not always noticed. Look into the consciousness of those who expect signs of appreciation and you will be amazed to see that, like the child who prefers a shiny toy to a valuable object, false gems are preferred. Many cherish a secret desire to be admitted into the Brotherhood with the sole idea of obtaining an abundance of gold from the Abode! Such people make no distinction between the Brotherhood and a bazaar.

Extremes often dwell in the same personality. On the one hand, a man may be ready for higher perceptions, yet on the other he pictures Us as moneychangers and waits expectantly to be given a small coin. Such a man forgets that only goalfitness can secure the higher perceptions. Like fireflies, he gives only fleeting light, then merges again into darkness, and is indeed far from goalfitness.

So many blasphemies are uttered in the world, yet people think that their slanders can go unpunished.

Every one of you can remember times when the highest concepts were slandered in your presence. Not only verbally, but also mentally, the salutary bonds are severed, and each explosion results in the destruction of good emanations.

You can see that this truth must be repeated. You have witnessed how people approached you motivated by self-interest, yet dared to pronounce the word "Brotherhood." Witnessing such behavior, one may rightly conclude that the life of the Brotherhood should be described only with reverence.

Cunning people will pry, "Tell us, what do they eat? How do they spend their time? With whom do they meet? Is it possible that they regulate prices in the market? Tell us everything about the Brotherhood in detail and we will amuse ourselves by broadcasting it."

Indeed, We appreciate those few who remain silent rather than broadcast unwisely.

The Thinker was particularly concerned about wise dissemination of the Teaching, and practiced strict discipline to prevent the word from reaching those who were not ready to receive it. A foolish broadcaster was looked upon as if he were obsessed, and often he was.

The Thinker was also very concerned about clarifying the significance of appreciation, and compared it to the watering of a garden.

He said, "Every tree can be cheerful or sad. We might assume that this is just a reflection of our own moods, but how much do we really understand about the sensitivity of Nature?"

228. Urusvati knows that many remarkable events pass unnoticed because the consciousness is unable to register them. The same thing happens during scientific experiments. Observations of the transmission of thought to a distance will be limited and superficial if the nervous state of those who are present is not taken into consideration. It is not enough for people to come together in a certain place at the same time; it is also essential to maintain harmony and avoid irritability.

Nor is it enough to assure each other that everyone is absolutely calm. How can one hope to achieve beneficial results in an experiment when one is boiling within with distracting irritability? When intensified energy is needed one must understand the danger of irritability and anxiety, which function like barriers preventing the flow of water in a stream. Experimenters pay no attention to irritability nor do they realize that such a state of mind affects the entire group. Few understand that squandering another's energy is a crime against that individual. Does man have a right to claim another's property in this way?

In many cases people overlook the required conditions during experiments and then complain that the most important was not revealed to them; when We sent mass manifestations they were attributed to coincidence!

The Thinker said, "Man cannot see or hear unless he is free from prejudice."

229. Urusvati knows about the action of the Law of Karma. One can observe that karma overtakes not only the one who commits a crime, but also those who participate in it indirectly. There is truth in the saying that for one person's crime a whole nation suffers. It is not only the motive that unites participants in crime, but aspects of their nature also bring them together. Who can tell the degree of affinity of blood relationships, or judge the degree of participation? Some may have encouraged the criminal verbally, others mentally. Who can define this, or determine the main cause?

Few care to think about how broadly karma moves, or to search within their own Chalice of Accumulations to discover how and when they have participated in crime. We can only remind you about the law, but free will must choose its way.

Urusvati often hears about the fears of Sister O., who grieves when she sees the cruel karma being created by those who do not think about the essence of their deeds.

People have become very fond of the word "karma." It is now repeated in various parts of the world, but few have learned its meaning. They speak casually about the Law of Karma, but, alas, do nothing to liberate themselves. They firmly believe that somewhere there exist the Lords of Karma, who will be kind enough to free them from even the most grievous fate!

Few understand that the effect of the Law cannot be changed without mutual effort. Man is ever ready to create a painful karma by thought and deed, yet he hopes that by some miracle from beyond the mountains he will be liberated from its grievous consequences.

People sound like children when discussing karma, and expect someone else to take responsibility for their behavior. They blindly accumulate karma, then later are full of complaints and indignation, and only intensify the current of effects. Among Our labors an important place is given to the observation of people's karma while accompanying them on their path. We cannot change the Law, but within the limits of possibility We are ready to hint at a better path.

During His many lives the Thinker never tired of warning people. Many listened to His careful warnings, but few understood His advice. The Thinker smiled sadly when He listened to people discussing karma. Sometimes He would say, "It would be better for you to mention this Law less and live more purely."

230. Urusvati knows the various degrees of reaction. The Thinker said, "You may pour a poisonous solution from the smoothest glass, yet some traces of the poison will be left on the sides of the container." He also said, "One scratch can cause profuse bleeding, whereas another can remain almost unnoticeable. Yet, no one can say which scratch will become the source of infection."

In the same way We watch the non-bleeding wounds, which are more dangerous than the profusely bleeding ones. People know how to wound without a knife; such wounds are difficult to heal. There are poetic works dedicated to bloodless wounds. We know such wounds and are ready to send Our healing vibration. An experienced physician pays particular attention to the wound that does not bleed, and carefully observes how various individual conditions can affect the use of medicines.

Thus, life itself gives us examples of the diversity of influences and reactions. Little attention is paid to the role of receptivity in the process of mental suggestion. A short word may have great effect, whereas a torrent of speech may leave no impression.

The Thinker used to say, "When you want to clean your house do not clean just a few articles, but scrub the whole place." In communal life one should particularly heed such advice. Many drops of poison remain at the bottom of the human Chalice while people think that all the poison has been drained. We often remove such poisonous drops. Some will smile and say, "Only drops?" But even a drop of certain poisons can be deadly.

231. Urusvati knows that even during difficult days joy generates power. Long ago We said that joy is a special wisdom. Truly, joy must be recognized, and realized. Gloomy people are clouded over by troubles and sorrows and they cannot see joy. Through the net of sadness people become blind and lose their strength, and cannot help themselves. Nor are they able to receive Our help, because depression and irritability block the way. It is as if no one had ever told them about the harm of depression.

Depressed people are considered unfortunate. Think about this last word. Did anyone deprive these people of their fortune? They missed all good possibilities by themselves and initiated their own misfortune long ago. Discontent, malice, and irritability cut off the path to joy, and their dark thoughts robbed them of the source of strength. Egoism prevented them from recognizing joy and whispered, "Joy lies only in personal gain." Thus, the most fruitful joy can be hidden under an ugly cover of despondency. Those blinded by despondency are indeed the most pitiful people.

Man possesses the great gift of cognizing joy. The high forehead that was given to him is a sign of lofty aspirations. From the far-off worlds down to the smallest flower joy offers herself to people. A new supply of strength comes to you every time you allow yourself to be joyous, for there is an intensity in joy that opens the next gate.

Who gave people the right to assume that they will be forever unfortunate? Ignorance was the source of this lie. But a wise hero knows that even at the hour of persecution the path to joy is not closed. People forget the simple truth that everything is in unending motion. Sadness will be forgotten, but sparks of joy shine forever.

Our life is long and We can confirm that joy is never forgotten and is an unending source of power. Blessed are those who are able to take their joy into the Subtle World. When We say, "Joy hastens," it really is approaching. But often people are unable to notice joy, for they have bound themselves by deliberate suggestion. Thus joy loses its power. Look everywhere, and gather all the sparks of joy.

The Thinker taught, "Know how to recognize joy. Among the Muses there is the Muse of Joy, but you can invite this Protectress only by beautiful words and thoughts. Do not attempt to threaten and demand, for She comes only by the path of Beauty."

232. Urusvati knows what initiation is. There is much confusion about this concept. Some think that initiation is the acquisition of knowledge, but it is only a path. Others think that the act of devotion in itself is initiation, but that, too, is only a path. Still others state that to be initiated is to guard a secret: even that is but a path.

Initiation is daring to approach the Image of Light and not fearing to look at It. Uniting with Light requires courage and a high degree of self-denial; this fearlessness is in itself a beautiful initiation.

The Teacher imparts many wise truths, but finally He will say, "Now walk alone, without fear." A particular tension of consciousness is required toward the end of the path. Intellectual knowledge breaks up and vanishes, and the pilgrim remains alone on the cliffs of ascent. Only the flame of the heart can warm when the accumulated coverings have been rent by the storm. Voices are heard, but they do not resemble the Call of the Beloved. Be prepared beforehand to face the Light and to accept It without fear.

It is impermissible to speak in the marketplace about the awareness of Light. An initiate will not disclose his precious experience. No one can compel him to utter the unutterable. This is the difference between an initiate, and a deceiver, who knows how to roll his eyes and sing sweetly about visions that only he can perceive. True messengers are not talkative.

The Thinker expected His disciples to carry carefully what had been entrusted, up to the end. He understood as Socrates did the significance of Truth. He said, "Truth requires a strong repository. Make of yourself a treasure chest!"

233. Urusvati knows the variety of conditions that may relate to one's incarnations. The Thinker said, "Once upon a time a great leader delivered a brilliant speech, and when he had finished he began to look for something on the ground. A simple silver ring had fallen from his finger. People smiled and suggested that he cease looking for an object of such insignificance and little value, but the leader said, 'You do not know the origin of this ring. Perhaps the whole speech was delivered on its account.'"

And so it may happen with incarnations. People may have to return just to find a little ring that is of great importance to them, but of no value to others. People cannot understand why some great incarnations are followed by seemingly insignificant ones, but who can tell what valuable object must be found during the difficult journey? Often, in the course of general self-perfectment, a small, precious stone is required that seems insignificant, but is of great value. Various incarnations indicate that an important task must be performed for the sake of general evolution.

There are many reasons why we rarely reveal incarnations. Most people are unable to bear such knowledge, and would not be convinced by many things. For instance, they do not understand why some individuals meet frequently over the span of their lives, and others only after thousands of years, yet their closeness remains at full strength. People have not learned that besides direct closeness there may be relationships based on other feelings. Although there may be no intimate nearness, the bonds of great respect, friendship and appreciation remain in full force.

You must remember that vibrations can attract or repel people, and you should observe such attractions and repulsions with great attention. Much has been written about this, but not enough is applied in actual life. Mainly, we should not judge the great and the small by earthly measures. Often one small seed is of more value than a whole haystack.

Let us learn to rejoice at every high degree of excellence; it brings us closer to Brotherhood.

234. Urusvati knows how much We encourage scientific experiments. When you are asked how one should regard the experiment of a rocket to the moon, answer, "With respect."

True, We know that researchers will not obtain the results they are hoping for, nevertheless, there will be useful observations. One might hope that their minds would be turned toward the Subtle World and that scientists would then have to come to many new conclusions. They would realize that only by the flight of the subtle body can they obtain the information they seek.

Let us point out that people come to truth by many different ways. Some may use the shortest way, but others have to build a Tower of Babel and create complicated formulas in order to arrive at a simple conclusion.

We do not oppose even the most complicated experiments. Everyone has his own nature and finds his own path, and it would be a mistake to direct people to only one method. There are cases when the soul brings remote recollections into a new life and attempts to apply them. Let people experiment as they wish! Even by firing a rocket toward the stars, one's thoughts will be directed to those worlds. It is not wise to interfere with the current of thought.

Time and again man has attempted to revive the ancient scriptures. In all ages his efforts have been steadily directed toward this task, even though using different languages and living in different places.

The Thinker used to say, "Sometimes you gaze at me through the eyes of many centuries!"

235. Urusvati knows that astronomy is meaningless without knowledge of psychic energy and the subtle body. In discussing the far-off worlds, one should abandon earthly measurements.

One can be drowning in astronomical calculations, yet be no nearer to the far-off worlds. Even spectrum analysis depends for accuracy on many conditions, and mechanical apparatuses are useless in communication with the far-off worlds. Of the billions of heavenly bodies, only thousands can be located, and even the most powerful telescope will be as naught when confronted with Infinity.

Nevertheless, let us treat each scientific task with respect, but we must add psychic power to our knowledge. Observatories should retain reliable clairvoyants. Mechanical and psychic processes should be united, and we should not be annoyed if the indicated cooperation requires thorough coordination and supervision to guarantee accuracy. Every experiment requires confirmation and brings new ideas, which in itself is useful. Such experiments were already being conducted in Babylon and Egypt; however, in those days true coordination could not be achieved since mechanical sciences were not advanced and could not be of much help to psychic research.

The work in Our Tower is based on the conformity of two principles, the physical and the psychic. Only thus is it possible to come to correct conclusions. It is hard to imagine the complexity of interplanetary conditions. Aviation in its early stages was confronted with inexplicable obstacles. If we continue our careful observations along these lines we will come upon the most striking evidence. Thus, clairvoyants could be wisely utilized for certain experiments.

A rarified atmosphere is conducive to the production of certain phenomena, and the invisible forces produce a strong chemical reaction. The planetary rays, acting upon these chemicals, in turn create endless combinations. What a vast field exists for research, if only the research workers would rid themselves of their prejudices!

The Thinker pointed out many times that the mind should be combined with the heart. The student cannot be heartless. The cruel scientist is far from Truth, the obstinate one not worthy of knowledge, and the depressed one blind to the treasures of nature. If the scientist cannot overcome yesterday's limitations, it would be better for him to give up science.

I dedicate many discourses to the Thinker because we must remember His tireless work. He devoted centuries of labor to the deepening of thought, for without such self-sacrifice it would be impossible to achieve the transmission of thought to such vast distances. Therefore, it is ridiculous to think that one can learn and achieve within a few years! Finally, it is not time that matters, but the degree of aspiration.

236. Urusvati knows that astrology is used in medicine and by some government leaders who consult the astrological signs. One might think that these practices would strengthen the importance of astrology as a science, but in reality this is not so. These statesmen do not admit that they consult horoscopes, nor do the physicians and judges reveal how they arrive at some of their conclusions. They obtain the information secretly, and outwardly ridicule it. Thus, astrology is tainted by people's ugly approach to it, and a hypocritical approach to this science is reinforced. How much wiser it would be to accept this ancient science and affirm it, just as one accepts the newest scientific discoveries!

So much could be achieved if our eyes were not blinded by prejudice. Who would then deny that astrology is a science, and that there is a correlation between the planets? Even primitive man in the remote past could sense these special atmospheric influences. Science seems to confirm this chemical interdependence, but scientists fear being suspected of sorcery. Certainly, there are plenty of charlatans who endanger the reputation of astrology, but there are frauds in all sciences, yet no one rejects science as a whole because of this. One must speak plainly in order to remove prejudice from human consciousness. Many physicians, statesmen, and judges secretly consult astrologers. Let them find the courage to acknowledge it openly, at least as an experiment. This will introduce the subject to the general public. People long for knowledge, but they must be encouraged and helped in their approach to it.

The Thinker taught His disciples how to overcome prohibitions that were dictated by ignorance. Let learning flourish now!

237. Urusvati knows that all facets of human life should be harmonized. And though it is well known that people of great talent often indulge in vice, and some even excuse such behavior on the grounds that genius includes a bit of insanity, no one asks how much greater their creativity might be without such indulgences.

One can cite examples of alcoholics who were highly creative, but perhaps their work would have been much greater without intoxicants. No one can prove that creativeness is dependent upon artificial stimulation. One should think of those great creative workers whose lives are known to have been harmonious and without excess.

In ancient days excesses were called "the chains of hell." A great truth underlies this saying. Artificial stimulation is degrading and limiting, whereas inspiration arrived at naturally is limitless, for it follows the laws of Infinity.

Thus We remind people that any disharmony is ruinous. Lack of understanding of harmony makes life ugly and such ignorance is criminal. One cannot think about evolution when people themselves destroy the very foundations of life.

Especially at present, at the threshold of the New Era, one must think about the health of the nations. It may seem that today, when people have lost trust in one another, it is out of place to speak about health, but every teacher must speak about the ways to the future.

The example of the Thinker will be instructive.

Even when He was sold into slavery, He spoke about freedom and harmony in life.

238. Urusvati knows what extraordinary self-control is needed when one dedicates oneself to perpetual vigilance. If you ask people whether they are prepared to be on guard all the time, their answer will probably be, "All the time! But when will it end?" And if you tell them that there is no end and that their responsibilities will increase forever, it will be hard to find among them a worthy watchman.

Yet We are perpetually vigilant. We have adapted Our entire existence to a state of vigilance. We can rejoice and We can grieve, We can perform tests and deepen knowledge, all without losing Our vigilance. There cannot be, nor is there, any end to such a state of consciousness. We acquire such awareness in the earthly world as well as in the Subtle World, and We can assure everyone who strives toward such awareness that it can indeed be achieved, but the task must be accepted voluntarily.

We can mention individuals who achieved such vigilance, who accepted the required state of mind, applied it joyously, and were ready to take the cup of poison. We can mention the philosopher Seneca, who suffered greatly during Nero's reign, but whose consciousness remained undisturbed. Seneca inherited the mentality of the Thinker and endured the most trying times of ancient Rome, yet was able to remain the solace of many. His discourses about ethics were indispensable during those confusing days of little faith. Perhaps Seneca is less well known than the Thinker, but his work has great significance. He wanted to create a Leader, but received a terrible blow from his own disciple. The cup of poison did not confuse the clarity of his mind, and many learned from him how to cross the border of earthly life. We respect such examples amidst the confusion of ignorance and pride.

239. Urusvati knows that the effectiveness of energy is increased by an intensified feeling of love. Some may think that under certain circumstances this would be impossible. For instance, can love co-exist with indignation? Yes, for indignation is only possible with love. If a person does not love, he cannot be indignant. He will never be distressed by anything, and thus will be unable to intensify his energy.

There are two types of people, the flaming and the flameless. They are like opposite poles and will never understand each other. These two extremes also exist in the Subtle World. People leave Earth with their characters formed and in the Subtle World follow their habitual ways. It is very difficult to kindle the flameless ones; a special shock is needed to light the precious ruby of the heart and awaken the slumbering hearts. Of course, much energy is wasted in this process. People do not understand what extreme measures are needed to awaken and kindle their hearts so that they may learn how to increase energy by an intensified feeling of love.

We revere the words of the Thinker. He said, "The sleeping heart is like a tomb. Decomposition is its lot, and its decomposition spreads degeneration. May we be spared degeneration."

240. Urusvati knows that every aspirant is attacked by the dark forces. One such good man exclaimed, "I feel as if I have become the center of a whirlpool!" His words were close to the truth, since his condition was analogous to certain chemical experiments in which one drop of a very strong essence is added to a mass that is not of equal quality. Acting as a center for the mass, it produces the effect of a whirlpool. Such a state does not last, and soon the precious drop will spread its influence and improve the entire substance.

In human relations, when the crowds attack a lofty individual they form a similar kind of whirlpool around him. But in time the power of the individual overcomes the chaos, and a benevolent influence is gradually exerted upon the broad masses. Often human relations can be compared to chemical reactions, and the conclusions will be most instructive.

People often feel desperate because they have been severely wronged, but they should understand that it may have been their very presence that provoked chaos. A strong individual will recognize that it is preferable to arouse chaos than to allow himself to become part of the unmanifested substance. There are many examples from centuries past when chaos clashed with great individualities, and it can be observed that those great workers influenced the masses in the loftiest ways.

The Thinker constantly repeated that the fury of chaos is the highest recognition of the leader.

241. Urusvati knows that each deviation from the original plan creates complications. Again We shall use an example from chemistry. If we add one drop of a foreign substance to a complex combination, the entire compound will be weakened. The substance can be strengthened, and much energy can be used to change it, but the compound will never be the same as the original one.

If one is not convinced by the example of a single horse stopping a caravan, perhaps this example from chemistry will be more convincing. A drop, one small drop, can change the nature of an entire beneficial substance.

People may believe themselves to be the followers of the highest teachings, yet at the same time irresponsibly distort the destiny of entire nations. Again they will complain that We threaten, but is a warning about danger a threat? He who calls himself a scientist should not violate the laws of nature.

When We speak about unity and harmony people regard it as an abstraction. They expect real messages, but only according to their own understanding of reality. They do not realize that in the Tower exact programs are planned that can be brought to fruition only if the co-workers are fully united. Some day I will tell you how certain historic events were impeded by seemingly insignificant obstacles created by co-workers who were not aware of what they had done. Let the co-workers try to imagine how complex and difficult Our Work is! Let them think about the kind of currents that must be mastered!

You know how the free will of humanity is directed. There can be warnings of many kinds, even earthquakes, but free will prefers destruction of its own choosing. People know that explosions cause rain, yet they will continue to disturb the atmosphere even if threatened with the fate of Atlantis. There are some responsible scientists who try to remind humanity that the harmony of physical laws should not be broken. But people are indifferent, and do not realize what harmful forces are evoked from space by disharmony. A great effort should be made to restrain such free will.

The Thinker said, "How can We foresee all obstacles? What a sad sight to see man in chains, especially when he does not even suspect that he is imprisoned. Yet the chains can be broken!"

242. Urusvati knows that he who sows the wind

will reap the whirlwind. But no one cares when this storm will take place and whom it will destroy. People speak about karma and limit it by their own criteria, but karma acts progressively. This storm will, indeed, affect many, and the punishment will fall upon the sower of the wind.

When, then, will the fierce effect of the storm be manifested fully? Of course, time is relative, and the gradual development of the storm cannot be measured by earthly hours. However, one thing is certain—the one who sows shall also reap.

The progress of karma can be observed in historic events. We advise the study of biographies and histories, wherein one can observe how karma develops and falls upon people in order to restore balance. People generally regard karma as punishment, but the great law should not be limited in that way. The law acts in the name of equilibrium, and the damage done by the violation of balance cannot be judged by earthly measures. Only from higher planes can it be seen how a crime expands in its effect, once committed.

We speak of a drop of poison, but one small word can be equally poisonous. It is lamentable indeed that people do not consider the words they utter. The process of evolution is long, but it does not seem to improve the quality of human thoughts and words. Let us recall the high standard of Hindu and Greek philosophers. Can the twentieth century take pride in an equal refinement of thought?

The Thinker said, "There were probably better thinkers before our time. Let us not hope that we have succeeded; rather let us hope that our mistakes will ease the path of others and lead them to perfection."

243. Urusvati knows that We advocate the conservation of vital energy, yet We also advocate maximum tension even to the point of self-sacrifice. This sounds contradictory, but in Our concept of truth both ideas should be harmonized. It is necessary to conserve strength, otherwise you can harm not only yourself but also your higher Guides. But vital energy must be available for use in moments of extreme emergency.

In this way We are greatly concerned about the health of Our students. Every leader cares about the welfare of his co-workers, but We also ask Our co-workers to help Us to help them. We can foresee approaching danger, but without the cooperation of Our co-workers We are unable to prevent the entire process from occurring. Indeed, all illnesses have a psychic origin. Thus one must gradually learn how to preserve one's forces, and if the forces are dedicated to the service of Good, such concern is not selfish.

Remember that energy may be urgently needed for some selfless endeavor, and forces that have been dissipated cannot be speedily gathered. The dark enemies will not miss the opportunity to strike a weak spot, and the moment may come when all one's forces will be urgently needed. You should maintain a sacred store of strength, and the enemy will surely sense that in you there is a reservoir dedicated to Service. Great wisdom is needed in order to maintain true equilibrium.

The Thinker used to teach, "Learn not to dissipate the strength that was entrusted to you. Safeguard, but do not become misers."

244. Urusvati knows that hypocrisy is based on heartlessness. Indeed, the bond with the higher spheres is formed through the heart, a heart generous in all its expressions. But the violent rage of heartlessness is fierce and spreads widely. People may intend to harm only one, but then injure many. Terrible is the karma of these heartless fools who mumble lofty utterances about truth, while actually defaming it.

Heartless thinking is the plague of humanity. Ancient philosophers did not include heartless people in their concepts of government. Plato in his *Republic* and Aristotle in his *Politics* had in mind organized societies of intelligent co-workers, and did not tolerate tyrants, hypocrites, or swindlers. It is impossible to imagine a strong state consisting of hypocrites and swindlers. Hypocrisy is incompatible with the highest beliefs and knowledge, and a false foundation will serve only a false structure. We do not approve of the slightest manifestation of hypocrisy, and believe that this vice begets all other corrupt feelings.

The Thinker opposed instantly the slightest trace of hypocrisy in his disciples. He would say, "In this case, go to the priests and pay them with gold for their prayers. They assume that the gods will accept hired prayers."

245. Urusvati knows what harm is done by a little knowledge in the wrong hands. Imagine an ignorant person who takes certain statements from the Teaching at random and begins to fill space with words he does not understand, because he never cared to undertake the preliminary purification necessary for the broadening of his consciousness. Unfortunately, even a fool can strike a certain rhythm whose resonance can create disharmony, and destruction may follow. But people usually do not think about the possibility of such consequences, nor do they realize that the first priority of the student should be to emphasize the betterment of his consciousness.

Only if there is inner striving can one achieve the harmony that enables him to apply many formulas of the Teaching. But some fools demand immediate delivery of the philosopher's stone, and do not even take the trouble to seek out the literature on this subject. They expect the Teacher to send them a talisman with which to find hidden treasures, and assume that, without taking the level of their consciousness into consideration, He should immediately reveal to them the secrets of Nature!

You have received numerous letters which confirm My words. Such people are ever ready to threaten and abuse the Teacher for failing to enrich them with gold! As much as I regret it I must mention these ignorant ones, because they fill the ranks of harmful betrayers. Let everyone understand the simple truth that knowledge is fruitful only when it can be accepted.

The Thinker compared knowledge to a fruit tree. He used to say, "A dried-up trunk certainly will not feed the pilgrim."

246. Urusvati knows that We do not approve of artificial or mechanical methods of achievement. All the best things come naturally. In ancient days, when man's nature was coarser, certain artificial methods were sometimes needed to discipline the free will and to create and support the bond with the Higher World. But it is certainly very clear that man may know all numbers, memorize all sacred names, and learn all the secret meanings of the alphabet, yet by doing so he will contribute very little to the evolution of mankind.

The gifts of nature are more precious when they are received naturally and as the result of previous accumulations. Science will approach Higher Knowledge through such observations. It is essential to acknowledge to what extent nature assists evolution. To force is to act fanatically, or in other words, against nature, and only the consciousness can reveal when one learns and works for all humanity.

Let us take as an example a person who writes many letters. If he writes with only himself in mind, he will not achieve the right results. And he is mistaken if he thinks that he is writing to only one person in particular. A letter full of lofty thoughts does not belong only to the author, or to the one to whom it is addressed, but to all of humanity. We should not be concerned with who will benefit from our thoughts. In addition to our personal intent, the letter is being sent into space, and it is not for us to worry where the thought it contains will find shelter. The only concern we ought to have is that our thought should serve for good. Perhaps it will be received somewhere in an entirely unexpected language, or enter the consciousness of a child and be expressed by him in later years. Perhaps the thought will reach a person who is leaving the earthly state and will be applied in the Subtle World, or it may be of help to that person during the crossing. Perhaps workers will be inspired by the thought, spiritualizing their monotonous work. The thought will help a sick person by giving him faith in his physician, or elevate a woman far beyond the boundaries of her domestic duties. The thought will whisper to the warrior opportunities for heroism. The thought will point out to the farmer the planetary significance of his labor, for the farmer is responsible for the crust of the planet, and a letter to him will be essential. You must write to the architect, to the judge, and to the artist. It does not matter if some letters do not arrive at the intended time. Let him who writes letters remember that he has many readers; so much the worse if the contents of the letter are base or insignificant. Harmful thoughts should not be recorded.

We hear many letters. Each recorded amity gives

Us joy. Let all letters carry the great message about the evolution of humanity.

The Thinker said, "It is of no importance whether I speak or write, the recorded thoughts will follow me. If the thoughts are of help to someone, they will become my wings."

247. Urusvati knows that indignation is sometimes appropriate. It would seem that people should know this, but it must be emphasized often, or goodness and benevolence will be misinterpreted. How can man remain silent when terrible crimes are committed before his very eyes? No one has ever advocated remaining indifferent to the debasement of human dignity, for by such indifference one allows oneself to become an accomplice of the crime.

Even earthly leaders expect people to learn to live in danger. We also advise such tension, because constant tension disciplines vibrations. It is a mistake to think that tension harms the body. On the contrary, such a conscious awareness creates the necessary metabolism that helps to renew it. Tension is not the cause of fatigue. Only depression reduces vitality, but exaltation creates a beautiful renewal. Thus, we should not fear tension; only ignorant people will regard it as a fatiguing misfortune. They will be able to relax in the grave! But a man who is ever ready to ascend will welcome the growing tension as festive gates to renewal, and will flame with indignation when the Highest concepts are degraded in his presence.

We love to see the radiance of righteous indignation. During the waning of the old world such tension is especially needed, and one should know how to direct this quality most effectively.

The Thinker pointed out that indignation as a reaction to injustice can be a wonderful healing of the blind.

248. Urusvati knows how diverse are Our messages, which sometimes come as short commands, and at others times as faint reminders. Sometimes they are stored in the Chalice, to be applied at the appointed hour. In such cases, people begin to recall something heard somewhere, and the recollection becomes more and more persistent as the indicated date approaches. These recollections from the very bottom of the Chalice must be treated with great care. In them are many events which by karmic law can only be revealed through the consciousness.

It is of paramount importance to observe children when they receive such guidance. They often declare that other children visit and play with them, and that during their games they have conversations on interesting topics. They sometimes invite adults to join them in the games, but the grown-ups do not see their little friends and regard their statements as fabrications. Such accounts originate in all nations, however, and should not be treated as childish inventions. One should pay great attention to the statements of children.

One should also heed the visions experienced by seriously ill people, who often see images of individuals, unknown to them, who try to ease their sufferings. Sometimes these images remind them of dear ones who have passed away. Such approaches from the higher spheres are varied, and we should appreciate the care and concern that is so exquisitely revealed. Unfortunately, people prefer to attribute everything to frightful ghosts, forgetting that there are also higher manifestations.

The Thinker, having heard about a vision of relatives, remarked, "Perhaps High Spirits materialized through those forms."

249. Urusvati knows that even an accelerated evolution must go through lawful stages, or chaos will inundate it, and under such conditions it is particularly difficult for a person to cope with his own free will. Even intelligent people cannot always reconcile the personal with the evolutionary. They cannot grasp the idea that there are dates destined for the world that they cannot separate themselves from. Such lack of understanding would be harmless if it were not for the rebellious action of the free will, causing harmful conflict. Man stubbornly persists in his own perceptions and does not admit other solutions. Much energy is required to tame such a free will, therefore, when We speak about alertness and flexibility of mind, We want to prevent the harm that comes from such stubbornness.

When We speak about unification, We have in mind an important achievement. It is correctly noted that the so-called "complex of immortality" is an equal tension of all energies. It is precisely this unity of energies that creates the highest state. But people do not want to discipline themselves to be freely unified. They consider unity an abstract idea and would prefer that the Teacher give them specific instructions, little understanding that preparation for the unification of energies is a vital necessity that must take place in one's everyday life. The Living Ethics consists of disciplines that enable you to become more conscious in any sphere, but alas, people avoid such daily disciplines. They will often invent an utterly impractical meditation in their attempt to conquer the higher planes, yet neglect their immediate obligations. The Greek philosopher said, "He who knows how to rule his household will also be able to rule his nation." Of course, household duties are not meant in the sense of cooking and cleaning, but rather in the sense of a conscious awareness of general perfectment, or unification.

Urusvati is rightly interested in preserving Our letters about unification. There are many of these. If you only knew how often We keep repeating the same thing! These letters should be sent as reminders to various countries. People should hear about unification as they do about their daily bread. And if someone insists that he has heard enough about unity, know that it is a sign of his irresponsibility. In time, every word about unity will be applied literally, and the great, voluntary unification will come as a stage of evolution.

The Thinker said, "It is not in my power to reach the far-off heavenly bodies, but indeed I am privileged! For it has been entrusted to me to observe them, and to meditate upon their greatness."

250. Urusvati knows that often a short thought, quick as lightning, is of more value than lengthy contemplation. But this is not readily understood. People think that artificial profundity is stronger than a swift thought, not realizing that lightning thought can be evidence of the highest influence. Long ponderous thoughts can usually be traced to some earthly origin, but it is far more difficult to determine the source of a fleeting thought, which is of such speed that one cannot fully comprehend it and put it into words.

Such messages can deal with the loftiest concepts. But they are often misinterpreted, the subtlety of their meaning is distorted, and they usually vanish without a trace. We are often the source of these messages, which We send out for the general good of humanity without knowing who the recipients will be. Thus thoughts are engendered in various parts of the world. But it is lamentable that so many of these glorious guests are rejected by the human mind.

Long ago, the Thinker taught His disciples to pay attention to short, swift thoughts. "The sparks of the Highest Intelligence pierce us like lightning. Blessed is he who knows how to keep them in his heart. Indeed, you should perceive them with your heart, which cannot be burnt by their flame, whereas the brain could be seared."

251. Urusvati knows about the diversity of cosmic events. The subtle quality of manifestations of the fundamental energies should be especially emphasized. People expect only the grossest phenomena, and will accept nothing less than complete darkness at midday, or the entire earth in flames. But sudden, spectacular events such as these do not occur, because the harmony of Cosmic Law does not permit such shocks.

However, Nature's book is full of subtle omens, and people should be able to read them. Only the blind will fail to see the fiery signs, and only imperceptive physicians will not distinguish the fiery diseases. People say, "The sun rises, the moon shines, and everything is in order; yet for some mysterious reason we feel threatened." Those who can see will point out unusual events that are influencing human nature, while other events will pass unnoticed. Many things happen in unpredictable places, and if you were to record the whereabouts of earthquakes, floods, epidemics, unusual atmospheric events, and unexplained tensions, you would have a book about the sickness of the planet.

We greatly value the ability to observe objectively the omens of nature. Learn the symptoms of disease. Physicians must not cease observing; if they do, they are not physicians. We pay attention to many cosmic signs. The planet is very sick, and man cannot remain indifferent when his whole being is filled with the influences of the subtlest energies.

The Thinker said, "Who can determine the measure of Nature's forces?"

252. Urusvati knows how ignorant most people are about the origins of events. They cannot perceive even the culminating points, and are satisfied with effects alone. But a sensitive heart will tremble at the very inception of an event. Perhaps no proper words can be found to describe this feeling, but its unspoken meaning will at once resound in the depths of the heart.

When We say, "Affirm the success," it will be asked, "But where is the proof that it has taken place?" People do not understand that something beyond mere words is happening, and this "something" determines the combination of energies. An inexperienced eye cannot catch the first vibrations of atmospheric tension. An untrained ear cannot hear the developing accumulation of forces. To a casual observer nothing is happening, and everything remains as it always was, covered with dust!

When then did something meaningful happen? The reaction of the worldly one will be that nothing has taken place, and he will become indignant, asking, "Where is that affirmed success?"

Therefore, care should be taken when you speak about the inception of events. Only a well-tested consciousness will embrace this idea. One should not expect people to rejoice about something that is not evident to them. And if We add that many events originate on days when signs are favorable, most people will not understand it. Superstitions are readily accepted, while scientific conclusions are ridiculed. Thus, today We shall say, "Affirm success."

The Thinker said, "Every man can accelerate a cosmic event by the smile of his heart."

253. Urusvati knows how important is the relationship between microcosm and macrocosm. Science traces fluctuations in the motion of the Earth, but no one considers their cause. And when We say, as We have already said, that their cause lies in the accumulation of gas spread by humanity itself, no one will believe it or admit that there are also such abnormalities in the functioning of other planets. But if one planet is sick, other parts of the Universe will respond. People are familiar only with epidemics on Earth, but similar manifestations also occur on a macrocosmic scale.

The dangers that We repeatedly point out, caused by unbalanced, purposeless ways of living, are part of the supermundane existence—hence, the title of these particular notes of the Brotherhood. But instead of being actively concerned about their negative effect on the macrocosm, people ask how beings of other planets clothe themselves! If a house is on fire, however, and someone were to ask the owner about his clothes, the question would be considered inappropriate, or insane. How then can We impress upon the human mind that right now we are experiencing a fiery Armageddon in which much can be destroyed? We want to draw special attention to this so that people will understand how much depends upon them. Let us not be afraid to repeat "how much." Let these words make it clear that each microcosm is responsible for the macrocosm. Do not assume that such a comparison is out of order. The bond between the microcosm and the macrocosm is the foundation of the world.

Pointing to an ant, the Thinker said, "He has come from afar; do not disturb his labor."

254. Urusvati knows how much people confuse peace of mind with the inner peace that is the source of peace for all else. Seeking for inner peace should be encouraged, for only this equilibrium makes higher communion possible and opens the doors for the best decisions.

However, there are those seeking inner peace who are filled with selfishness and false modesty, and believe that they will acquire inner peace by doing nothing. These are not bad people, they do no evil, but their "good" is of little value. What kind of peace can come from inertia? True inner peace can be likened to Nirvana, in which all the energies are so intensified that they are unified in their ascent.

People should strive for inner peace while participating in life. In the best teachings it is clearly indicated that one can be at peace even on the battlefield. There is much beautiful imagery that teaches us how one can transmit truth and be spiritually uplifted even in the noise of battle! We must remind those who are lost to inaction that by their way of life they may create an illusion of peace, but their spirit will not be strengthened, nor will it succeed.

The Thinker said, "The ocean is stormy and agitated because the elements are ignorant of the higher laws, but the human spirit is enlightened and can be at peace even in the midst of a storm. Inner peace is an imitation of the Divine."

255. Urusvati knows that people love to immerse themselves in the past. Everything about it fascinates them, and they are ready to forget the ugliest events in their past in order to cling to those things so dear to them. They detest the tempo of today and cherish the hope that life will return to the slow-flowing current of yesterday. If you tell them that this is impossible, and inform them of the coming of the New World, you will be labeled a destroyer of traditions and a dangerous revolutionary!

But who is strong enough to bring back the former weak currents when the river is already overflowing its banks? Indeed, the new rhythm is tiring for those who are unable to accept it. An unassimilated rhythm can even become destructive. Uncontrolled gases can be deadly. A technique wrongly applied can cause calamities, and many dangers have arisen because of ignorance. Nevertheless, the new rhythm has already entered life, and people cannot ignore the new conditions that are flooding it. Returning to the past is impossible, and one must harmonize oneself with the new conditions. For that purpose, people should pay attention to the humanities, and the art of thinking must be revived.

Scientists are discovering new characteristics of the human brain, and such research is useful for establishing the equilibrium of rhythm. The brain and nervous system will provide unusual discoveries that will create possibilities for adjustment to the new rhythm.

The speed of life will seem frightening until people develop a speed of thought sufficient to outstrip it. People must accept cosmic conditions or there will be dangerous discord. The motion of Earth will slow down, but at the same time the influx of energies will be accelerated. Each disharmony is destructive in itself, and each disunity brings disruption. When it was declared that ideas rule the world, the power of thought was affirmed.

Intelligent thinking must help humanity to accept the new rhythm and cognize the New World that has already drawn near. Truly, the New World pours forth its influence, and has manifested its power in the radiance of scientific achievements. May we overcome all the suffocating dangers through concentration upon the New World!

Mankind must realize that life now takes on supermundane meaning. People may still ridicule astrology, but they have accepted the idea of the influence of cosmic chemistry. Instead of the limited formulas of the past, humanity will now see unlimited supermundane achievements. In these new achievements there will be place for both the intellect and the heart. One can affirm that the gates to the New World are wide open, and in this realization there will be no place for remorse or depression.

The Thinker said, "Soon people will learn how to fly. New spheres of Light will become accessible. May people be worthy of such gifts!"

256. Urusvati knows that decisions are made in the Subtle World concerning the tasks in one's future earthly life. Most people in the earthly state do not accept this, but those in the Subtle World know that their incarnations will take place with their knowledge, and, more importantly, with their consent. When they are about to incarnate, people understand the karmic load that will compel them to undergo certain trials, but once in the earthly state they lose the memory of how their destiny was determined. Similarly, dwellers of the Subtle World are fully aware of life on the far-off worlds, but once they are in their physical bodies they usually lose this knowledge completely.

There is a story about the mother of a great leader who dreamed that her son would become a great benefactor of humanity. However, the son could see no reason why he should immerse himself in the problems of human affairs simply because of his mother's dream, and he turned toward a life of meditation.

The true cause for this was deeply rooted in his own past when, over many lives, he had developed a love for and dedication to meditation, while neglecting self-sacrificing work for the good of others.

In spite of his refined consciousness, this man did not realize that it was not his mother's dream that was urging him on toward this work, but that while in the Subtle World he had realized to what extent he was unable to harmonize the abilities given to him, and decided that in his new incarnation he would dedicate his entire life to the service of humanity.

Thus we have a living example of a highly refined individual who blamed his mother's dream for motivating him toward what should have been the true purpose of his life. It often happens that people who fulfill the tasks that they themselves have chosen become discontent with their own decisions.

The Thinker often used to say, "Let us search the past; perhaps we shall find the lost keys!"

257. Urusvati knows the tension that is needed for supermundane tasks to be accomplished on Earth. Some will call this state inspiration, others exaltation, and still others, effort, but all those who must fulfill such missions experience it. The nervous system will react strongly to this particular tension, which can even cause a raising of the body temperature.

If one watches the temperature of healthy people it can be observed that sometimes there are unusual fluctuations of both temperature and pulse. During work these fluctuations are particularly noticeable. Many think that this is due to normal exertion, but careful research will show that the nerve centers are being influenced by external factors.

Indeed, the Subtle World continuously influences the physical world. Subtle messages will cause unusual vibrations of prolonged duration, because the messages are not realized as mere passing thoughts, but must be transformed into decisions and physical readiness.

Do not assume that people easily recognize such subtle influences. In most cases, they will even protest and try to avoid cooperation, fearing that it will diminish their own self-absorption, which for them is a great treasure.

We only want to remind you that supermundane messages are not rare; they come often and are most varied. People should not avoid collaboration with the supermundane spheres, but should rejoice when cooperation with Us is entrusted to them.

The Thinker often said, "Can I be so fortunate as to have the privilege of helping my Teachers?"

258. Urusvati knows that many complex obstacles must be overcome before We can help people. Imagine a narrow mountain path filled with galloping riders, or a street crammed with a crowd running in panic. Then imagine trying to save from the stampede an individual who is not prepared for the help that is offered to him. We cannot hold back the crowd because great confusion would result, and if We stopped him, for even one moment, he would be crushed. However, it is quite different when the one who is to be saved can sense that help awaits him. As if by a magnet he can be drawn to a safe place that has been prepared for him. But for this to happen he must be ready to accept the rescue.

We should also note the difficult cases, such as the person who imagines that he is ready to accept help, but in fact resists it with his entire being. Such contradictions are not unusual. On the contrary, it is full cooperation, when help can be rendered, that is exceptional. It is deplorable when man assures himself that he is ready, but his own nature makes cooperation impossible.

We can affirm that the most energy is spent not in giving help, but in overcoming the obstacles to its acceptance. It is impossible to imagine the diversity of these obstacles! Among them are many varieties of karmic conditions—atavism, ignorance, and dull-witted skepticism. These obstructions must be overcome not only in the person who is to be saved, but also in those around him. These difficulties are among the labors of the Brotherhood.

We must tell people about their free will, and not leave them with the idea that it is worthless. Free will is the highest gift, and the time has come for people to learn how to use it.

The Thinker taught about free will, which can make man divine.

259. Urusvati has heard it said that the forces of darkness are more powerful than the Forces of Light. This is a harmful delusion. One should acknowledge that the forces of darkness are united and fierce in their attacks. But there is nothing surprising about this, for they know their finite nature and must defend their very existence. Even the methods of fighting are different, for while We are ready to receive many blows to Our shield, We can end the combat by a single arrow.

Remember that although the jinn often participated in building the temples, there never was a case when a Brother of Ours was of service to the dark forces. In all nations and all ages, there exist legends about the servants of darkness who were compelled to serve the Forces of Light. There is great significance in such legends.

You can observe the rapid advance of evolution. Not only by generations, but even by decades, one can measure the considerable progress of life. Experienced observers should carefully and objectively collect facts about the progress of evolution through the decades. Truly, one can declare that the New Era is approaching! Even if many things are misunderstood and distorted, new possibilities are entering life, and will in time influence humanity's level of consciousness.

Indeed, the jinn also labor in the hope that new discoveries will enable them to fulfill their dark endeavors, but their hopes are in vain. With each new generation, there are more conscious aspirants, who are born to do good.

Let us not be shortsighted when speaking about the destruction of the world. It is true that Armageddon is raging and incredible crimes have been committed, but it is also true that against the background of these terrors a speedy evolution rushes onward. Is it possible that people do not see how much of the new is entering life? We should not permit the doubting worldlings to proclaim that the dark forces are victorious. That which belongs to Infinity cannot be conquered.

The Thinker wisely encouraged His disciples, and prophesied the victory of the Forces of Light.

260. Urusvati knows that free will can overcome even karma, and cases can be cited in which the will was able to alter karma. It is commonly believed that repentance has great power, but it would be more correct to call this state of consciousness complete realization. First of all man must know why he should seek new achievements. One should strive for full realization because only a one-pointed will can indicate the right path. There are many wavering and weak attempts of the mind, but these will not turn the key of fate.

Some religions prescribe the confession of sins. There is no doubt that such confessions help to form a clear understanding of one's actions, but this is only a first step. People should train themselves so that their self-appraisal will be precise and correct. When man faces his Guide, he himself should understand both the positive and the negative aspects of his personality. Only man himself can know the true source of his deeds.

By observing the course of one's actions one can determine their causes and effects, and thus independently prepare oneself for future tests. There are some who require periods of sleep and long reminiscence in the Subtle World, but others will immediately begin their preparations for the further journey.

The Thinker loved to say, "May we not waste our time."

261. Urusvati knows how much more oppressive the lower astral strata are than even the basest earthly state. The lower layers of the Subtle World influence all of Earth, and its inhabitants should learn to protect themselves against these poisonous influences.

What should people do to protect themselves from such invisible corrupters? First of all, they should accept the constant proximity of these malicious neighbors. Do not think that this suggestion is unimportant. On the lower astral strata good feelings are rare, there is a prevailing envy toward everything that lives on Earth, and every breath of earthly life is pleasing and attractive to these dark, dissatisfied spirits. It is almost impossible to convince them that they should focus their attention not on Earth, but on how to free themselves from their prison.

People can struggle with base astral entities only when they are firm in their understanding of their own future path. Their passing into the higher spheres will then be easier, and they will not feel the arrows of the dwellers of the lower astral plane. Unfortunately, most people do not choose the higher path and therefore remain unprotected.

Those few who do understand this bear a heavy burden. The Brotherhood itself suffers greatly from the light-mindedness of the inhabitants of Earth, who, instead of defending themselves against these harmful entities, attract them.

The Thinker taught, "Do not allow demons to approach you."

262. Urusvati knows how difficult it is to find room for great tasks in the midst of earthly life. There is a saying, "To find a place for good is as difficult as packing a trunk." This saying alludes to the problem one faces, when packing a trunk, of finding room for the many small objects that have accumulated. Similarly, in earthly life the human consciousness is so full of petty concerns that there is no room for great tasks. This situation is not perceived by those who do not carefully observe their own lives. Their trunks are often so full that there is no space left for even the smallest object, and the most harmful details go unnoticed.

In a crowded life there is often no place for even minimal trust. There are many instances of developing events that were disrupted because of the lack of trust. One can well imagine how these failures affected those whose trunks were all in order! People refuse to understand how their thoughts and deeds are reflected in distant events. In addition to earthly matters there are supermundane ones to be considered, and even with the best intentions, reasonably good people can cause disruptions.

Sometimes it seems as if there is no way out, but feelings of hopelessness are impermissible. At times of particular tension, a feeling similar to despair may arise. This is not a hopeless condition, for it carries within it the seed of resolute decisiveness. At each turn of the path, one feels this tension. There may be a decrease in strength, but this is only a reflection of the inner tension that is felt most strongly when an important decision, not yet realized, is ripening within. In such a case We advise great caution. Care should be taken of one's health, for the centers can become inflamed and vulnerable.

We always stress work, but advise rest during such times of tension. This kind of relaxation has nothing to do with idleness; it is a sharpening of forces. However, understand that We are now talking about great tasks that require complete sacrifice.

The Thinker loved to say, "Can we not find even more that we can sacrifice?"

263. Urusvati knows that most people avoid looking into the essence of events and are satisfied with superficial observations. How differently history would be written if real causes and motives, and the true Leaders, whose existence humanity does not even suspect, were revealed! Instead of kings and rulers, there would emerge individuals who had remained in the background, unknown because of prevailing ignorance, or required to go unnoticed because of the law of the Brotherhood.

People would then see that many events that take shape without apparent reason are in reality well-planned. At times an entire country or group of people may be condemned by the world, but then, it is precisely that country or those people that give birth to the most brilliant achievements. Few realize that there exists a power beyond earthly considerations that can affect the flow of events.

Ages ago it was said, "Look among the condemned for the righteous," for the world often attacks those who carry the message of truth. If people made an effort to carefully investigate the essence of events, they would discern signs of Our influence.

People should study the figures central to events. They would then understand that these individuals often are mere figureheads, around whom swirl events that lie beyond their comprehension.

Observe that Our warnings regarding certain countries have come true. Some people may call these warnings threats, but We do not intimidate. We warn out of compassion, but if Our warnings are rejected the flow of events will follow its course.

People imagine that cataclysms come only in crude and violent forms, but there are other cataclysms, even worse than war. The most painful example is the corruption of a nation. Truly, this sickness is worse than destruction by flood or other catastrophes of nature.

It may be recalled that We repeatedly warned certain countries, and they rejected Our advice. Their free will preferred to choose destruction through slow decay. Compare the character of a nation before and after Our warning. Great deeds become rare, and people lose the ability to preserve their values, degenerating into criers in the bazaar. Corruption creeps into all spheres of life, and though people can easily choose to follow the Advice, they prefer to bring on their own doom.

Whole volumes could be written about the sickness

of such nations. If people excuse themselves by claiming that they cannot see the essence of events, one can only pity them for their blindness. People should study and be vigilant in life in order to recognize their true leaders. If the nightingales are killed, how can one hope to hear their song? We record all the consequences of ignorance, and this chronicle of humanity is deplorable.

The Thinker always warned against mistakes that cannot be corrected.

264. Urusvati knows that prayer is often hypocritical. We have already spoken about the significance of prayer, but it is necessary to mention the harm of hypocritical or hired prayer. People do not realize the extreme harm in any kind of falsehood, but hypocrisy and bribery are its grossest expressions. One should realize how pervasively each false thought spreads. It is indeed blasphemous to hire someone for prayer. It is criminal to try to deceive Him who is considered by people as the Most High. Monstrous examples can be cited of people who mumbled prayers and at the same time plotted murder.

People should be taught not only to esteem truth, but also to develop the ability to contemplate the Universe. Of course, We do not mean that everyone should become an astronomer, but We do advocate thought about Infinity. How can people continue to lie while learning about the grandeur of Cosmos?

People should be taught that it is as shameful to deceive themselves as to deceive each other. Unfortunately, there can be no law that forbids inner lies, but a state of consciousness can be reached in which it becomes shameful to lie. Let people think about the beauty of the world, and let them know that every thought is immediately known to Someone.

It is strange that some people attach themselves to the Teaching, yet continue to commit shameful deeds and to utter lies.

The time has come when the fundamental principles of life must be renewed. Urusvati correctly feels that humanity needs simple words. It is absurd to learn to recognize the higher energies without knowing their purpose!

The Thinker was concerned about every thought, knowing that the purpose of each thought is to serve the Common Good. He said, "When people understand the meaning of the Common Good, happiness will be theirs."

265. Urusvati knows that in the depths of one's consciousness there is an indelible awareness of the coming detachment from one's old state. Man knows the turning points of his life from within his consciousness, and though their outer manifestations come much later, the consciousness is aware of them, leading the way.

One must learn to detect the signs of change in the depths of one's consciousness. These signs may be expressed either psychically or physically. Many mistake such signs for a disease, whereas others attribute them simply to a bad mood. But few realize that they are experiencing a departure from their former level of consciousness, and are starting a new step. Few will welcome such signs, because, as a rule, people fear the new or unknown. But there will be some who are prepared, and these few will rejoice, for they know that each new step is a reason for joy.

It is impossible to remain forever in even the best subtle spheres. Some sorrow, not wanting new tests, but others, like good warriors, aspire to new victories.

One must listen to the call of consciousness. The

Master first of all considers the level of consciousness of the disciple, and then transmits knowledge accordingly. Man's great advantage lies in his ability to realize his progress, and it is so much more joyous when this progress is also for the Common Good. Let us not be fearful. Courage and striving are the wings that will help us to soar toward the goal.

The Thinker often spoke about the wings of man, and pointed out that physical wings are not sufficient. "Know how to become detached, then you will be able to soar into the Higher World."

266. Urusvati knows how vehemently every intelligent achievement is opposed by the fury of ignorance. Truly, the brighter the light, the denser the darkness. It would be wrong to assume that the dark opposition is an illusion. On the contrary, it is a real fury that intensifies progressively and knows no constraint in its tactics.

It can often be observed that as one member of a family strives for enlightenment, the other members will aggressively mock his aspirations. Indeed, this one member needs all his courage to oppose the rude attacks of the others. It rarely happens that an entire family strives toward the Light in a united effort against darkness. Certainly, opposition to darkness develops strength, but to have to oppose one's own family is an uphill task. There is no greater tragedy than darkness in a family. This is a most urgent problem, which must be resolved, for such families breed the calamities of the next generation.

We deplore the fact that there are so many disagreements within families. Even the best warriors lose their strength due to such disharmony. Instead of goodness, blasphemy and evil talk defeat aspiration and cause waste of the precious panacea of psychic energy! People do not appreciate this gift, and it can be spilled as from a broken vessel. Wherever possible one must help families to maintain their balance.

We watch the most difficult situations and project Our help, but sometimes the discord is so great that the organism struggles against Our influence and its health is affected. In such cases, We must temporarily withdraw, for the remedy would be too strong.

The Thinker believed that all physicians should understand the Law of Equilibrium.

268. Urusvati knows the many different ways in which Service is interpreted. For some it is a life preserver, for others a millstone around the neck. Some understand the practical value of Service, but for others it is just a vague abstraction. Between these two extremes there exist many different approaches, among which people aimlessly grope.

Very few accept the fullness of Service in its vitality and its achievements. These few know how the steps of Service have been formed and are ready to carry the living word wherever it will serve the General Good. Such heroes are ready to renounce the comforts of life in order to be able to offer inspiration to others. These few realize that, in addition to making scientific discoveries, it is necessary to unearth the spiritual treasures. Now, when multitudes of people are hurriedly shifting and seeking, it is especially difficult for mankind to reconcile material progress with higher spiritual values. The present age resembles a certain period of Atlantis, when the Atlanteans, too, could not find the necessary balance. But today people are aware of this discord, and this gives Us hope that the most vital nations will find the needed equilibrium.

We see where the idea of synthesis can be assimilated. It will be found not where the pendulum of life is dead, but only where it swings fully. There the significance of the General Good is well understood, and it is known that Good can come only from Good. Although this formula is not yet uttered, it nevertheless is ripening in the depths of the consciousness, and this is very important.

Urusvati is justifiably amazed to see that people enjoy the comfort of the General Good, yet do not strive to work for it. These walking corpses only prepare a grave for themselves! Where and when will they see the usefulness of the Common Good? It is service, first of all, that opens the path to realization of the Common Good. Neither garb nor ritual, but only service to humanity, is required.

Words about cooperation have been uttered for many centuries, and the ideals usually outran the material possibilities. But now people have found many useful applications, and the time has come when it is necessary to think about the General Good.

The Thinker liked to say in jest, "I would like to know for whom we have just finished our dinner, for whom we have replenished our strength. If it was only for ourselves, it would not have been worth eating!"

268. Urusvati knows that people have fantastic ideas about the past lives of great spiritual individuals. They imagine that these evolved spirits were surrounded by the most favorable conditions in all their past incarnations, as if they never suffered, were never in need, and never endured the persecutions that they in fact so often experienced.

People do not believe that great thinkers, such as Plato, Pythagoras, or Anaxagoras, lived the lives of ordinary beings. It is essential to understand that even the most lofty personalities cannot avoid the fullness of their earthly emotions, which are kindled in proportion to the scope of their mission.

Indeed, you should not assume that Plato, when he was sold into slavery, did not react to all the turmoil of such a situation. Of course, he went courageously through all trials, but in his heart felt great bitterness because of the injustice, and it was because of this that he was able to speak so brilliantly about the best forms of government. Pythagoras too was persecuted, endured great poverty, and suffered all kinds of physical humiliation, but these tests did not diminish his ardor. Likewise, Anaxagoras was deprived of everything, yet even on his difficult path he knew how to prepare for himself a majestic crown of thorns.

Many lives must be compared in order to understand how the light that shines so brightly is kindled by the blows of destiny. Chaos can be seen as the hammer that strikes the sparks. Only the unwise think that the Teacher hovers above everything and feels nothing. On the contrary, the Teacher feels not only his own burdens, but also the burdens of those who are connected with Him. Such near and dear ones can be either in their physical or in their subtle bodies. They may be close physically, or physically separated, yet close in spirit.

Do not imagine that the Teacher remains isolated. Every one of you can sense mental messages, but the Teacher feels them more strongly. We call these perceptions supermundane, yet they include all earthly feelings. We do not separate Existence by conventional divisions.

May all people learn to love supermundane thoughts. In time man will realize that in Infinity there is neither mundane nor supermundane, but only Existence.

269. Urusvati knows how varied are the sendings of psychic energy. In addition to sensing the psychic currents, one may also feel some physical effects, such as burning sensations in the different centers, or tension resulting in nausea.

The most unusual symptom is the sudden swelling of various parts of the body, especially the extremities. No one can explain the cause of these swellings and an ordinary physician will probably not believe the existence of such an ailment without seeing it for himself. However, this is not so easy, because, though the size of the swellings can be very great, they come and go quickly. Urusvati experienced this, but before the physicians could confirm it, the swelling passed without the slightest trace.

We call these manifestations "the knocking of psychic energy," and although the nerve centers are the channels for this, it cannot be called a sickness. It can be observed that such swellings may occur during the transmission of thought over great distances.

There can also be bleeding from the various openings of the body. This should not be thought of as ordinary ruptures of blood vessels. The cause is the pressure of the psychic energy struggling within the organism; this can affect any organ. Therefore, We strongly advise paying attention to all inexplicable symptoms.

It should not be assumed that such neural abnormalities must always accompany the awakening of psychic energy. If the planet were in a normal condition, one could also expect the manifestations of psychic energy to be normal, but as long as people are poisoning life in every possible way, psychic energy will be manifested in most unexpected ways. People should study the interrelation of psychic and physical phenomena, because such manifestations of energy are frequently mistaken for physical ailments. The Thinker predicted long ago that humanity would experience the various conditions that He called supermundane.

270. Urusvati knows how much one's free will contends with the more profound Primal Energy. Sometimes it may seem that the free will acts without higher control, but greater than the most powerful will there is a certain force that can completely transform the sendings produced by will power. In spite of the mind's desire, the pendulum of life points out a different, unchangeable solution. Any honest observer can testify that often it is not his own reason that determines his actions. In addition to the reasoning will that is based upon the experience of everyday life, there is another, profound wisdom, which abides in the depths of the consciousness.

Contact with the higher worlds is not achieved by an increase of will power, but through the deeper consciousness, the repository of pure Primal Energy. Unfortunately, people do not distinguish between free will and the action of Primal Energy. They assume that the physical action of the will is the most tangible and thus the most effective.

People's dependence on free will is reinforced by their passion for technology, and We have already spoken about the danger of this attraction. The free will must not contend with the Primal Energy, for this would bring great pain and even ruin. And so we arrive once again at the idea of the golden mean.

How beautiful can be the role of a flexible free will, which, through discrimination, can recognize higher wisdom and subordinate itself to it. By knowing this wisdom, man will also know the profundity of his own soul, and will learn to respect that force within himself which leads to the best achievements. Man's good fortune is his access to Primal Energy, and his misfortune that he does not accept this blessed power, but usually condemns it. What a dreadful thing it is that man refuses to accept his best treasure!

If a black-haired man insists that his hair is blond, he will be thought mad. Likewise, one who distorts his innate qualities is, in a sense, also mad. People are careful about their physical heart, for they have learned that the heart is the center of the physical life. But they have not yet sufficient information about the correlation of the free will with the Primal Energy, and regrettable disharmony is the result. Instead of the harmonious coexistence of the two forces, conflict and competition exist between them. One of the causes of the planet's sickness lies in the uncoordinated forces of man. People should think about this.

The Thinker spoke about two essential forces within man, his intellect and his wisdom.

271. Urusvati knows the unique characteristics of this Armageddon. Similar battles have taken place in the past, but what is unique about the present? As always the Greatest Forces are involved, but humanity is also involved as never before! The entire planet is participating in this battle, each one in his own way, and everywhere the tension is unprecedented.

Now let us try to imagine how all who are involved in this battle are connected with the Subtle World. The invisible hordes of that world are far more numerous than the earthly ones, and they are connected to even higher spheres. Therefore Armageddon must be thought of as a supermundane manifestation. One must have a clear idea of the character and size of the present battle to appreciate its full significance. Only then can one begin to comprehend the battles here on Earth.

Even without experiencing the grandeur of the Great Battle, one can clearly see that the world has gone quite mad. Even logic cannot explain the conflicts of nations, which can bring no good. For the average person the reasons are entirely obscure. The truth is that nations are subject to invisible promptings to ruin the planet. As above, so below. At Our Abode, it is terrible to see how all the spheres of the Subtle World are involved in this battle, and that, like great dark clouds, they press upon the earthly planes.

Let us not assume that when the supermundane battle expands it does not affect us here on Earth. On the contrary, it is reflected upon the entire earthly space, and involves not only the warriors, but also all ordinarily neutral beings. It not only brings illness, but also poisons the mind, and this, of course, is the most perilous. It is no wonder that sensitive organisms prefer to leave! But it is better to be in the thick of battle than to receive passively a rain of splinters and poisoned arrows. I strongly affirm that the events are approaching a climax.

Long ago the Thinker indicated that the time will come when all living things will find themselves in great confusion.

272. Urusvati knows that it is the heroes and martyrs who build nations. Pythagoras and even earlier thinkers knew this truth, but ancient truths should be reexamined in the light of science. So say the scientists, and they are right.

Who, then, are the heroes and the martyrs and how can they be described? From the scientific point of view, like living volcanoes, they throw out the intense energies needed for evolution. In this we can see an example of how subtly ethics and biology are entwined. The Teachings of the New Life show that exaltation is a blessed intensifier, and people cannot exist without these explosions that open the way. If cosmic explosions can be creative impulses, then human explosions are likewise needed for evolution.

Many people call the heroes and martyrs fanatics, but We do not approve of this label, for it belittles the better side of heroism. On the contrary, a real hero knows the truth of self-renunciation. He does not attempt to destroy anything, but tries to apply his powers in the best possible way.

They are foolish who assert that martyrs belong only to the remote past and do not exist today! Heroism and martyrdom are increasingly in evidence, and are presently characteristic of entire nations. These examples are not as clearly discerned, but it can be said that certain nations are creating a completely new rhythm of life.

The Thinker knew that the many would be formed into nations, and that the self-sacrificing work of nations would be of great value, and understood as heroism.

273. Urusvati knows that egoism is like a smudge on a glass, and that there are different kinds of egoism. In addition to personal egoism, we can see examples of family egoism and even racial egoism. It is easy to imagine how many distortions of truth issue from these accumulations of poisoned feelings! Moreover, there is even egoism on a planetary scale. You often hear scientists declare that life exists only on Earth. They claim that Earth has exclusive and uniquely favorable conditions, and have no idea about the existence of the Subtle World.

There are scientists who boldly insist that in all

Infinity there is no life except on Earth! It is not enough to call such a claim impertinence: only the crudest egoism can bring forth such an ignorant concept. These scientists make no effort to examine the conditions that exist in Cosmos, and base their judgments upon their own very limited observations!

True science does not prescribe limitations. It is especially distressing that in an age of the expansion of thought there can be such stagnant and stupid pride. What other words can we use to describe the attitude of those who affirm that even Infinity is subject to their judgment? Such people cause great harm because they impede the potential for broadened thinking.

Many so-called phenomena are being observed on Earth. Unusual human abilities are manifesting themselves and are beginning to be studied. However, as soon as negation and prohibitions appear, obstacles to evolution are created. Truly, free will can cause disasters.

The Thinker taught about the harm of limitation.

274. Urusvati knows of the harm that is created by caste systems. We should not have in mind only the castes of India, because, unfortunately, castes exist under different names in all countries. They are just as harmful everywhere and should be eliminated.

There is a story about a physician in ancient times who treated people of different castes with equal attention, and because of this noble attitude the people wanted to stone him. When asked if he would also apply the same care to people of other nations, he answered that everyone should be treated alike, and he was forbidden to practice medicine at all.

Such examples belong to past centuries, but even today one can see similar acts of ignorance. The right remedy should be sought for such superstition and savagery. Such divisions once had a practical purpose, but it was outlived long ago, and today cannot be considered rational.

Only science can help by proving that caste systems are unscientific. But science can help only if it is combined with a right understanding of the Subtle World. It can be proved that the spheres of the Subtle World are governed by principles for which earthly systems are inadequate. Contact with the Subtle World is more intense than it appears. The supermundane consciousness prompts man to observe the Subtle World, though he may call it by various names. The work of all scientific fields should be directed to an understanding of it, but instead of seeking knowledge, people attempt to obstruct every new possibility.

Do not be surprised that even the most material science will inevitably lead to the gates of unlimited knowledge. Many earthly systems will have to be transformed.

The Thinker was concerned about the spiritual welfare of His disciples, and took care that they should not stumble over illusory obstacles.

275. Urusvati knows the many manifestations of psychic energy. But numerous misunderstandings develop about this concept. Some deny its existence altogether; others think of it as some kind of miracle; still others accept it, but claim that psychic energy is a privilege meant only for the few. The truth is that psychic energy permeates all that exists, and because it is an energy, it has all the characteristics of energy. For example, it can stimulate and intensify the centers, but at the same time it can aggravate any disease that may be in the organism.

To a certain degree, the propelling force of psychic energy can be directed. In healing, an uplifting or highly concentrated thought can be directed toward an ailing organ. Any kind of blasphemy or destructive thinking, however, will intensify the flow of the energy toward an affected organ and aggravate the sickness. Wise is the physician who tells his patient not to blaspheme or hate. We have often pointed out that a pure thought is benevolent and has healing powers; it opens the gate to the healing power of Primal Energy.

Nowadays people attribute many illnesses to neuropathy, thus coming closer to the idea of Primal Energy. It can be said with certainty that the course of every illness depends upon the condition of the psychic energy, but people refuse to understand that free will is a strong factor in their dealings with it. The better one understands this, the better one can help oneself.

In ancient times, the force of energy was attributed to the Power of the Mother. People even prayed insistently to Her for help, and thus were able to intensify the energy. It does not matter whether a prayer is stormy or unshakably calm; the one essential feature is that it be a conscious call.

The Thinker said, "I can imagine how the call will reach the Majestic Mother! With one gesture of Her Hand she will direct our sorrow into a channel of joy. There is a temple of laughter in Sparta, and many diseases are cured there. Fortunately, there are no temples of mockery. Avoid blasphemy!"

276. Urusvati knows My advice to write down unusual and rare manifestations. There are many reasons for this. You have read about radiesthesia, but you should know that there are several kinds, which differ greatly. Radiesthesia can be of sound, smell, or taste. People may at times feel as if they are permeated by a particular sound. If such a phenomenon occurs repeatedly it has a certain purpose, either to indicate something, or as a reminder. The same happens with the senses of taste and smell, or when, for some reason, a person may begin to feel an attraction or aversion to certain sensations. Thus, by means of their senses, people receive signs of warning and protection from the depths of their own consciousness.

Seldom do people pay attention to such promptings, which can be studied only through lengthy observation. But who cares for such drawn-out processes? People read about instantaneous enlightenment and imagine that they can succeed without spiritual practice and protracted experiments. They do not want to hear that certain experiments require a time equal to the span of several generations; they desire immediate enlightenment, even if such an accelerated process could destroy their neighbors.

Special caution should be taken during periods of disturbed cosmic currents. You have read about cosmic dangers, but there are many more of them than scientists can detect, and the important point is to know what currents can counteract them. One should not only consider the dangers, but also be ready to resist them by all possible means.

Long ago, the Thinker noticed that the smoke of campfires is harmful, and urged people to use a kind of wood whose smoke does not obscure the consciousness. He knew then that at some time mankind would poison itself and all that exists.

277. Urusvati knows how carefully one should treat one's psychic energy. Many do not understand that even the inexhaustible Primal Energy needs care. All who strive can testify that sometimes the energy is so intensified that it seems to become exhausted. We advise particular caution at such times. There are many causes for such apparent exhaustion, ranging from the state of one's personal health to cosmic conditions.

We have mentioned how My Friend became ill when it was necessary for him to fulfill several missions at once. The cause of his illness was an excessive tension of psychic energy. Let us not forget that My Friend sallied forth with an increased store of energy, yet suffered a lengthy illness. We oppose the excessive use of psychic energy. One can imagine how difficult it is to restore one's equilibrium after such exhaustion, and much time is needed for the restoration of all one's forces. If the cosmic currents are favorable, equilibrium can be established more easily, but this does not always happen. My Friend was afflicted during a relatively calm time, but nowadays such an illness would last much longer.

We watch the useful workers and warn them if We see that the strings are too taut. Especially now, the planet is experiencing a period of unprecedented tension. Fatigue, drowsiness, inflammations, and excessive activity of the heart, all these precede a decrease of psychic energy.

We know that under present earthly conditions perfect equilibrium is unattainable. This is a danger that should be noted. When conditions on the planet become even more complicated, many will recall Our advice about treating psychic energy with care. During inharmonious times even a simple transmission of thought can be exhausting. This should be taken into consideration.

The Thinker used to say, "Why is it sometimes easier for Me to lift a log than to concentrate my thought? I am not ashamed to admit it, for I know that this happens not because of my laziness, but because of something beyond my control."

278. Urusvati knows about the fatigue We have described that was experienced by My Friend. There are three methods of combatting it. One can deliberately increase the tension to such a degree that the original fatigue is lost in the whirl of the new stimulation, or relax completely without thoughts or tensions, or change one's location, so that the spatial and ground currents are completely different.

We always warn against such excessive fatigue. But, although many earthly illnesses are the result of such excessive tension of psychic energy, it is impossible to free a thinking being from the tension that accompanies the battle with the dark forces.

You may be sure that We are aware of this struggle, because, just as a galloping horse raises a cloud of dust, the magnet of psychic energy stirs up a whirlpool of chaos. Many examples from daily life can be cited that would illustrate the progressive assaults of chaos from century to century. These will continue to increase, and all the power of equilibrium will be needed to withstand them. Now is such a time, and every sensitive person should be prepared to guard himself against chaos.

The preservation of psychic energy is necessary for the Great Service. People forget that the Great Service has many characteristics, the first of which is commensurability. Study the earthly lives of the Great Teachers and note their special kind of commensurability. I have in mind particularly Their earthly lives, when They were unaware of Their former lives.

Also, They toiled in many eras. Each had His private life, amidst the customs of the particular time and place. Their inner wisdom often rebelled against ludicrous remnants of the past, but in order to fulfill Their task They had to apply the utmost commensurability. It was also necessary to oppose blasphemy and obscenity. The Teacher knows that these vices pollute space.

People are not at all inclined to admit that their thoughts and speech may cause irreparable harm. It is impossible to convince people that they are destroying psychic energy. They nourish those harmful entities which we call devourers of psychic energy. Apart from during fits of anger and irritability, obscenities are uttered through ignorance, but the resulting harm is the same.

Only commensurability can save man from such self-poisoning. Imagine how the Teacher feels amid such a poisonous atmosphere, not only in the earthly life, but also in the Supermundane. Obscenity goes against the idea of the General Good and should be sternly opposed.

One can enumerate the dangers created by man himself, which manifest especially when the cosmic currents are intensified. What We say now should also be applied in the coming years, because the sunspots and storms of space are fierce.

The Thinker used to say, "Beauty will save us from obscenity."

279. Urusvati knows how difficult it is for people to accept the diversity of evolution. Each one insists that there is but one law, and cherishes a different notion about cosmos. When they find contradictions in the various scriptures, they accuse them of inaccuracy. These disputes and misunderstandings arise because of the inability of the ordinary intellect to imagine a scheme with infinite possibilities, and a universal law with many aspects.

Nevertheless, one should become accustomed to cosmic diversity. Our planet, with its subtle spheres, can be influenced in the most unexpected ways by the far-off worlds. It is wrong to think that our solar system is entirely isolated. On the contrary, all the worlds are subtly interrelated. The fundamental law is immutable, but each planet creates and projects its individual characteristics.

Individuals of much older stages of evolution coexist on Earth with the people of the sixth race. One can observe that the outlook of people varies from the most primitive to the enlightened. We meet with contrasts not only in the earthly realm but in the Subtle World also. It is important to know about these intrusive influences of distant systems. They act like explosions and storms, and can bring a form of revolution. Therefore, do not assume that the Subtle World is strictly and forever ordered. One must become accustomed to the idea that even in the higher spheres there can be collisions of psychic forces.

Only an awareness of the great manifoldness can save one from the perils of limitation. One must feel oneself living in the Infinite, and then gain strength by directing one's consciousness to the far-off worlds. In this way, the idea of the manifoldness of evolution will become clearer.

The Thinker was able to embrace the whole Cosmos with His mind. People used to say, "It is better to err with Plato than to join the intellectual negators." Thus were the best concepts realized in ancient days.

280. Urusvati has heard the many sounds of Nature. Truly, Nature is never silent. Our Ashram has a reputation for stillness, but this should be understood relatively. It is quiet in comparison with earthly, human noise, but Nature continues to send forth Her sounds. The whispers of the mountains and the noises of the waterfalls and streams near the Ashram, merge into one intensified choir. But all these voices of Nature cannot prevent one from hearing the calls of the Supermundane.

People mistakenly assume that the music of the spheres can be forcibly evoked. One can hear these sounds, but their sources are too distant and cannot be evoked within the Earth's vibrations. One must imagine all the stormy, violent cosmic turbulence in order to understand the humble position of our Earth.

Some still believe that Earth is stationary, that it is the center of the Universe, and that human life exists only here. But if people continue to believe that Earth is the center of the Universe, and that they are the only crown of creation, there will be a new convulsion of ignorance. Such misconceptions are absurd and harmful for evolution, and even without them, people are hopelessly unaware of Infinity.

Scientists should understand their responsibility and point out the danger of such conclusions. They must have sufficient integrity not to insist on unproven theories, however spectacular they may be.

There are certain attitudes that should be assumed with the utmost caution. For example, self-confidence is an excellent concept, but conceit is the grave of evolution. The planet Earth should not be belittled, but her true place amidst the grandeur of the Infinite should be realized.

The Thinker often directed people's attention to the far-off worlds. Though He fully realized the small place occupied by Earth, He would never belittle the beauty of His birthplace.

281. Urusvati knows how essential is the joy of being. It is not only a healing remedy but also the best helper for communion with Us. Where does this stimulating feeling, called the joy of being, arise? It does not come from wealth or self-satisfaction, but is often experienced amidst the most grievous difficulties and persecutions. In times of stress, joy is especially valuable and healing. We call it the joy of being, for it does not depend on personal circumstances, success, or profit. This joy has no earthly reasons; it comes as a forerunner of the highest currents, which spiritualize the entire surrounding atmosphere.

Can there be feelings of joy when one is afflicted with disease or when one is the victim of injustice and insult? Indeed, for even in such circumstances the eyes may sometimes fill with fire, the bowed head may rise, and new strength may be experienced. Then one will begin to rejoice at life, perhaps not at one's earthly life, but at real being.

What strong thoughts will come to those who perceive the joy of being! The atmosphere around them will be purified, those near them will feel relief, and We will smile from afar and approve the better currents. We shall even be grateful, for each preservation of energy is benevolent.

Everyone who wants to succeed should remember the joy of being. Each person who wants to contact the better currents should know the path that will bring him to Us. One need not fabricate special scientific reasons for such joy; it comes through the heart, and is absolutely real. This joy will enable one to better hear Our calls.

Sometimes the Thinker gathered His disciples for a discourse, which He called a Festival of Joy. Only spring water and bread were served. On such occasions the Thinker said, "Let us not besmirch the joy with wine and rich food. Joy is above everything."

282. Urusvati knows how harmful it is to pollute space. We have already offered many indications about how to avoid causing harm, but now We advise you not to dwell on mistakes or remain in places where there is blasphemy or irritation. Gossiping about mistakes pollutes the atmosphere around you, and attracts the fluids that will intensify the original errors. In the same way, it is harmful to stay in a place that is polluted by blasphemy or irritability. I speak as a physician.

Both blasphemy and irritability are especially harmful when the cosmic currents are tensed. They cause an inflammation of the mucous membranes that cannot be attributed to a sickness of the stomach, intestines, nose, or throat. There may be pain in one specific area, yet all the mucous membranes are inflamed, and diagnoses fail because they do not deal with all the symptoms. This illness may be considered Armageddonal. Eyes and intestines, stomach and teeth, throat and heart all collectively produce an unexpected combination of symptoms. This condition requires serious attention since it destroys the mucous membrane, and can be transferred to the nervous system.

Understand that this is a general inflammation and should be treated accordingly. Very light food should be eaten, nothing raw or irritating. Avoid catching cold, tiring the eyes, and succumbing to irritation. Medicines will be of little help, and alcohol should not be taken. Nothing should be taken too hot or too cold, and laxatives should be used only in small doses and preferably not every day.

I warned long ago about fiery illnesses to which refined organisms are most sensitive. But people ignore these new aggregate diseases. They can be quite exhausting; frequently inadequate treatments are prescribed and the harm is increased. It is true that every illness is based on inflammation, and inflamma-

tions are related to fiery disease, but some diseases are caused by an external fiery tension.

Many people perish from these unknown ailments, and even the highest organisms will suffer if they are overworked or exposed to irritation. The illness of My Friend is an example. He went out with a great store of psychic energy, but the ignorance of the people around him, and their irritability and stubbornness, created a poisonous atmosphere. When in Our Tower We can use a special ozone, but I cannot deny that even there We suffer from the poisoned atmosphere.

The Thinker warned that one should fear the poison in a cup less than the poison in space, for poisoned space has even more deadly currents.

283. Urusvati knows how much We value readiness for action. Activity can be of two kinds, external and internal. A person may not yet have the opportunity to begin external activity, although his inner resolve is already fixed upon seeking truth and a desire for self-perfectment. But his striving creates within him a sort of magnet, which attracts the outer possibilities.

We are continuously in motion. Even when We remain in the Ashram We are at the same time moving into the far-off realms through the power of Our striving.

One should know that activity is beneficial; however, amorphous particles of one's organism can seriously impede activity. There is a type of person who resists the idea of being active. These lazy specimens are especially harmful, and there are many of them.

A readiness to move purifies one's thinking, and We rejoice to see this transformation of outlook. Possessions lose their hypnotic power and cease to burden the consciousness. People can then understand the balance between owning things and renouncing them. What remains is a respect for human labor, and selfish greed is dissolved in the whirl of movement.

How beautiful are thoughts about motion! They are a source of inspiration for Us. We overcome the idea of time when We are in motion. We can solve problems when We adhere to the concept of motion. Be not surprised that in many people there is an intuitive desire to fly, for this is a sign of our epoch. But people should move even more in thought, and thus forge ahead of even the speediest flights. I know a valiant country that is ready for such high flights.

The Thinker indicated a certain nation that will conquer the North and said, "Observe the seven signs in the sky; they point to the country of the conquerors."

284. Urusvati knows that at times the human consciousness expresses itself abnormally in a dual way, as a kind of split consciousness. This can be a sign of obsession, but there are cases in which the duality is the result of the promptings of past incarnations. There are also times when the future is glimpsed, and as if hypnotized, the individual is drawn away from the present reality.

A split consciousness occurs more often than people suspect, and cannot simply be attributed to bad character or bad habits. It often occurs during a temporary blacking out of consciousness, when, as some researchers believe, the consciousness comes in contact with waves of chaos and the abnormality results. This observation is undoubtedly sound.

People usually do not study the normal state of consciousness, and therefore do not learn about its abnormalities. We advise the study of human consciousness, so that the many kinds of abnormality will be more easily recognized. Nor is it correct to assume that a disease of the organism always influences the consciousness adversely. Indeed, sometimes it is a sickness that elevates the consciousness. We will not now enumerate the varied circumstances that influence human consciousness, but simply wish to point out that duality of consciousness is a common, though undesirable, condition.

It is very difficult to help people so afflicted since each state of mind requires a particular technique of suggestion. Sometimes the duality is of such a contradictory nature, and the fluctuations occur so frequently, that it is impossible to apply suggestion, which can be quite useless or even harmful.

Truly, man needs to learn about his psychic energy. Many experiments are taking place, but so far the results are not satisfactory since the researchers work without any system and overlook many facts.

The Thinker pointed out that such research should be continuous, and conducted objectively, without personal bias.

285. Urusvati knows that the danger of psychic epidemics is increasing. In the Puranas it was predicted that toward the end of *Kali Yuga* humanity would be driven to acts of madness. It is very dangerous that people do not recognize this state, for while it is possible to cure a patient who does not resist treatment, if he struggles against it the beneficial effects of the medicine will be diminished.

But how do you explain to people that their leaders and their teachers are insane? How can you convince a nation that immediate measures must be taken for the restoration of its health? Indeed, Our prescriptions would be quite different from the measures offered by the medical authorities! This will be especially obvious in the psychic sphere. People do not yet acknowledge obsession, and though many books about the subject are available, a cowardly consciousness will deny the facts. Many materializations can be demonstrated, but those who want to deny will somehow justify their disbelief.

Indeed, such mental confusion fully corresponds with the end of *Kali Yuga*, but it was said that if the confusion reaches its climax, the only way to correct the situation will be through fiery purification. The examples from the past are eloquent. People have already begun to speak about Armageddon. A few years ago they would not have thought about the closeness of decisive events, but the Teachings are serving their purpose, and even the skeptics are now aware of the terrors of Armageddon. Thus, the information spreads in its own way.

We do not insist upon identifying the source. Let each one understand in his own heart whence the information has come. Most people hate the messenger who brings knowledge. They may not accept that it is We who warn, but let them at least remember the warning that humanity is acting insanely.

The Thinker warned, "Do not fall into madness."

286. Urusvati knows that certain conditions can be worse than the state of war. You certainly know that We consider war to be the shame of mankind, but one situation that can be considered as worse is the decay of humanity.

Armageddon should not be understood as only a physical battle. It is full of incalculable dangers, among which will be epidemics, but the most ruinous consequence will be psychic perversions. People will lose trust in one another, and will compete in doing evil. They will develop a persistent hatred of all except their own kind, and will sink into irresponsibility and depravity.

To all these insanities will be added the most shameful—the intensified competition between male and female. We insist upon equal and full rights for women, but the servants of darkness will expel them from many fields of activity, even where they bring the most benefit. We have spoken about the many maladies in the world, but the renewed struggle between the male and female principles will be the most tragic. It is hard to imagine how disastrous this will be, for it is a struggle against evolution itself! What a high price humanity pays for every such opposition to evolution! In these convulsions the young generations are corrupted.

Plato spoke about beautiful thinking, but what kind of beauty is possible when there is hostility between man and woman? Now is the time to think about equal and full rights, but darkness invades the tensed realms. However, all the dark attacks will serve a certain good purpose, for those who have been humiliated in *Kali Yuga* will be glorified in *Satya Yuga*.

Let us remember that these years of Armageddon are the most intense, and one's health should be especially guarded because the cosmic currents will increase many diseases. You must understand that this time is unique.

It is near-sighted to think that if war is prevented all problems will be solved! There are those who think so and imagine that they can cheat evolution, not realizing that the worst war is in their own homes. However, there do exist places on Earth where evolution develops normally, and We are always there.

The Thinker warned that the gifts of all the Muses

must be treasured. Only such accumulations will help to conquer darkness.

287. Urusvati knows that the fundamental fiery energy can make objects not only luminous but transparent. During powerful phenomena the transparency is almost enough to contradict the usual notion of a solid body. But such manifestations can seldom be observed by the naked eye. One cannot expect the fiery element to be manifested in a routine way, since such fiery tension can become as destructive as a strong electrical explosion.

How then can the transparency of solid bodies be explained? Each body carries the fiery energy within itself, and during extraordinary intensification this energy is kindled and the density seems to disappear. There are two reasons why such a phenomenon occurs so rarely—the quality of the intensification, and the qualifications of the observer. It is difficult to observe such phenomena while in the physical body because the heart can be overstrained, and only one or two observations at long intervals may be permitted. Therefore, contacts with certain spheres must be maintained with caution.

Most people miss this point, and do not appreciate the need for such precautions. Even erudite people can fail to understand the immutability of the law, but every violation is punished accordingly and without exception.

Nevertheless, the phenomenon of fiery energy can be observed, and Urusvati can confirm the transparency of the bodies that are aflame with it. Such manifestations can also be observed in Our laboratories, but, especially during these times, even there We must act with caution.

The Thinker warned His fellow citizens, "You can also be ignited by hatred. Fire flows in your veins."

288. Urusvati knows that many small stings can be more dangerous than one strong bite. Considering the present state of the world, this truth should be recognized. People expect great events, at the very least a collision with a comet, yet do not notice the many small daily dangers. They must be reminded that they cause these dangers themselves by their constant quarrelling. This warning is not given in the name of a higher philosophy, but simply for the sake of physical safety!

There were no periods in antiquity that compare to the present era of total global confusion. While in ancient times perhaps thousands were involved, today there are hundreds of millions! Try to imagine the difference in the power of the emanations, and the myriad invisible participants that everybody is surrounded by. Let us not attempt to calculate the multitudes causing disorder in the earthly sphere, but rather consider the innumerable invisible stings.

Especially disgusting are the emotions evoked by small stings. During great calamities feelings of self-sacrifice or heroism may be aroused, but in time of decay there is only wasted energy. I affirm that the worst part of Armageddon is in the decay of organisms. During strong disturbances the Guidance can be increased, but what can be done about gangrenous aggravation?

One should realize that the warriors for Good are not always able to defeat the dark legions quickly. Many conditions, both mundane and supermundane, must be observed. Remember that human cooperative action has cosmic significance, and the image of man is created by man himself. But if all of mankind were just to assume the same grimace, what kind of image of man would then be produced?

Thus people themselves ruin the planet. They prefer half-measures, even quarter-measures, wishing only to remain undisturbed. But let them be assured that the result is nothing but decomposition.

Not everything should be blamed on the dark forces. Why make giants of them? Is it not better to analyze the tastes of humanity? What do people enjoy, and what do they reject? Let us analyze the sciences, philosophy, art, and physical culture along these lines and we shall see precisely where the sickness of humanity lies. If we examine every negation and learn precisely what has caused it, it will become obvious that disgusting causes bring disgusting results. How can one struggle for Light while still surrendering to darkness?

The Thinker understood ages ago that Beauty is also Goodness.

289. Urusvati knows that the understanding of the fundamental principles and agreement about them among co-workers is the main guarantee of success. What can be worse than a mob of people who understand the rhythmic power of words and numbers, but cannot agree about life's fundamental principles? We put particular stress upon the understanding of these foundations, for without it knowledge itself is not only useless, but even harmful.

We are alarmed when We hear someone intoning a well-memorized ritual, for if one repeats the words continuously, an unexpectedly powerful rhythm may be established that could actually destroy him! We condemn such irresponsibility. Imagine what would happen if a group of guards were to start firing their weapons indiscriminately in all directions. They could kill each other! The same thing could happen if a group of people were to repeat a memorized ritual without a harmonious understanding of the fundamental truth that underlies it.

We have spoken before about unification, which means first of all the harmonious, mutual understanding of the fundamental truth. People may raise their hands together in solemn oath, but that does not mean that they are all in agreement. Actions taken simultaneously do not necessarily signify unity, and without inner harmony such actions will only cause disturbances of the atmosphere.

The Thinker constantly reminded others about harmony in music. He hoped that this awareness might help establish harmony in life.

AGNI YOGA SERIES

Leaves of Morya's Garden I (The Call)	1924
Leaves of Morya's Garden II (Illumination)	1925
New Era Community	1926

Signs of Agni Yoga

Agni Yoga	1929
Infinity I	1930
Infinity II	1930
Hierarchy	1931
Heart	1932
Fiery World I	1933
Fiery World II	1934
Fiery World III	1935
Aum	1936
Brotherhood	1937
Supermundane (in 3 volumes)	1938

Agni Yoga Society
www.agniyoga.org

www.ingramcontent.com/pod-product-compliance
Lightning Source LLC
Chambersburg PA
CBHW071557080526
44588CB00010B/937